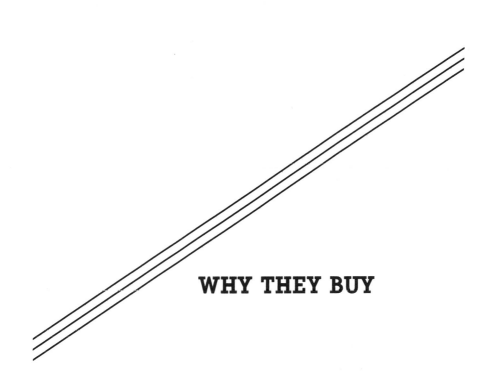

WHY THEY BUY

WHY THEY BUY

American Consumers
Inside and Out

ROBERT B. SETTLE

PAMELA L. ALRECK

JOHN WILEY & SONS

New York · Chichester · Brisbane
Toronto · Singapore

Library of Congress Cataloging in Publication Data:

Settle, Robert B.
    Why they buy.

     1. Consumers—United States. 2. Consumers'
preferences—United States. 3. Brand choice—United
States. I. Alreck, Pamela L. II. Title.

HC110.C6S48   1986   658.8'343'0973   86-13303
ISBN 0-471-84457-8

Printed in the United States of America

10 9 8 7 6 5 4 3 2 1

To the millions of marketers, here and elsewhere in the world, who strive to make the lives of their consumers richer and better—to our readers.

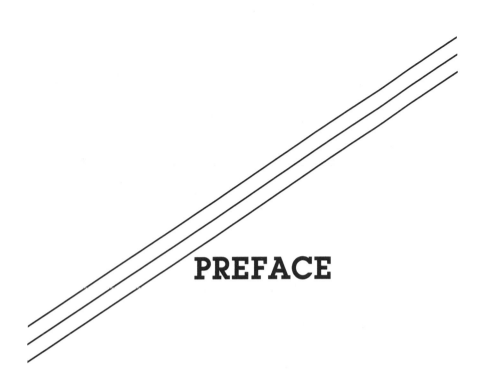

PREFACE

The American marketing system is a marvelous thing! Amidst reams of criticism and derision from its detractors, it has delivered everything from pump toothpaste containers for the medicine chest to low fuel-consumption cars for the family garage—housing, clothing, food, entertainment, recreation, education, political ideas, even religious concepts. It's not just the quantity and quality of consumer goods our marketing system delivers that are awesome, but the absolutely astounding *variety:* You can grab a hamburger, fries, and a cola on your way home without even leaving your car. You don't like that idea? Maybe a low-calorie, gourmet frozen entree from the supermarket, then? There are a dozen or so from which to choose. Well, if that's not right for you, how about exotic fruits and vegetables from anywhere and everywhere in the world? They're all fresh, plump, and tasty. A few passes with the juicer, blender, mixer, and food processor, then into the microwave oven and you'll have your own delightful dinner in no time!

As consumers, we take America's cornucopian marketing system pretty much for granted. When consumers do recognize how good they have it, it's usually the *productive* system that receives the lion's share of the credit. Even among the millions of us engaged in marketing, few of us pause to realize how much time, energy, thought, and care we pour into our efforts to market the right thing to the right people at the right time, place, and price. With persistent vigilance, marketers monitor their consumers, watching to see what they need and want, then pull fresh new consumer goods through the productive machine and put them promptly into the hands of consumers. It's marketing that has the initiative today, and this is a market-driven business world in which we live and work.

Despite the tremendous diversity in the vast array of consumer products and services marketed today, there's still a never-ending demand for more specialized consumer goods. Among the consuming public, commonality is shrinking while diversity of taste, preference, and lifestyle grows by leaps and bounds. You can see it all around you. While general-readership magazines languish or disappear, the range and diversity of special-interest magazines on the newsstand proliferate weekly. As broadcast network audience ratings decline, the sales and rentals of videotapes increase. Mass distribution is going the same way as mass media: Specialty stores continue to specialize even more while department stores departmentalize even further to meet the unique needs and desires of American shoppers. Products go the same way. Once a Coke was a Coke. Today's consumers have more than brand preferences. Some want regular cola, some decaffeinated, some sugar-free, and some both decaffeinated and sugar-free. And there's still more: New formula and Classic; cherry-flavored, too. What's next? Just wait!

As the diversity in demand reaches near mind-boggling proportions, you'd think that marketers would be at the point of desperation to keep up. Hardly! With more flexibility than any other social institution that comes to mind, business and marketing have not only kept abreast, but sometimes exceeded the consuming public's demand for variation and specialization.

The microcomputer industry recently experienced a slump in sales while buyers paused to reflect on the complexity of the many different systems available. It seems the industry actually got a little ahead of the buying public. But better that than far behind.

Our purpose in writing this book is to help marketing professionals and technicians understand and appreciate their consuming publics, even beyond the remarkable level they've already achieved. Today's marketing is a challenging job. It's not easy to understand why some people buy and others don't. Nor is it a simple matter to discover the trends and predict where things are going in the next few years. The majority of business executives and managers are superbly educated and trained in their field, but few are also completely familiar with the behavioral sciences. The academic and technical literature in consumer behavior, psychology, and sociology (to which we've contributed our share) reports the latest research, but usually in terms too abstract and obscure to have much meaning to marketing practitioners. Yet the substance is there—good, sound concepts and ideas that can really shed light on *why they buy.*

We've translated the most potent, meaningful models and concepts of consumer behavior from the obscure technical vocabulary of behavioral scientists to a more practical language that business people will readily understand. With every translation, something is always lost. We know there will be those who decry what they perceive as oversimplification. But we'll not defend this demystification of consumer psychology and sociology—the time has come for it. Our principal concerns are with the accuracy and effectiveness of the ideas and concepts about consumers that we've presented here. We alone are responsible for any errors, omissions, or misinterpretations.

ROBERT B. SETTLE
PAMELA L. ALRECK

San Diego, California
July 1986

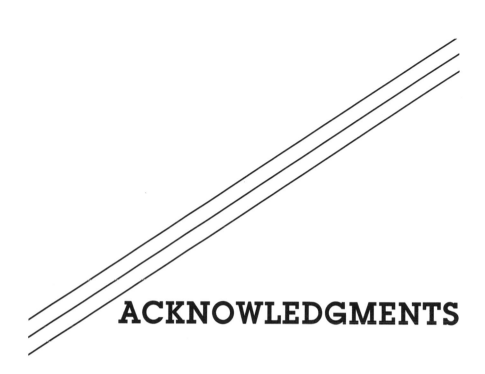

ACKNOWLEDGMENTS

We gratefully acknowledge the help of the many marketing and advertising executives, professionals, and technicians whose often brilliant work provided many of the examples and illustrations included here. In the course of their daily work, they unknowingly gave us all an exemplary picture of expertise and effective performance, and they deserve our recognition and appreciation. Thanks, too, to the several business journals and publications and to their journalists and reporters, for providing additional background information and insight. We are, perhaps, most indebted to our colleagues, the academic behavioral science researchers, whose tireless efforts continually advance the frontiers of our knowledge and understanding. Finally we deeply appreciate the effort, expertise, and enthusiasm of our editor, John B. Mahaney, and the entire crew at John Wiley & Sons.

R.B.S.
P.L.A.

xi

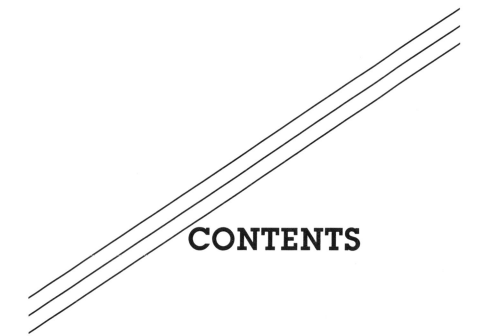

CONTENTS

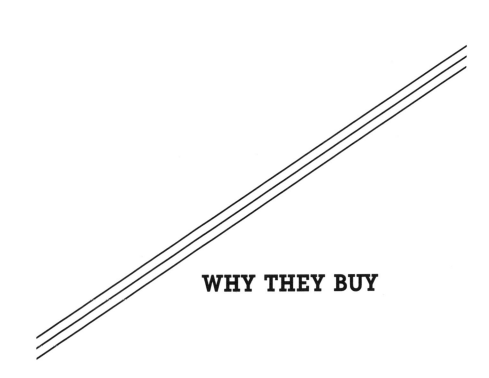

WHY THEY BUY

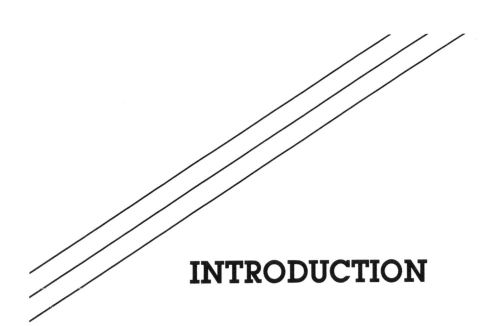

INTRODUCTION

Marketing is one of the most challenging activities in the world of business because it requires making choices that will please others. Most people find it hard enough to decide what's best for themselves. How much more difficult to anticipate and choose what others will want, enjoy, and appreciate! Successful, effective marketing certainly takes special talents and skills. More than that, it demands exceptional sensitivity and familiarity with consumers.

Suppose you were asked to buy a gift for someone who was a total stranger to you. A person you knew absolutely nothing about. How difficult would it be, if you knew nothing about the recipient's tastes, preferences, or lifestyle? If you knew nothing at all about this individual, you certainly couldn't be sure the recipient of the gift would enjoy it. There's a good chance that what you'd pick would be completely inappropriate to this mysterious person.

YOU'VE GOT TO KNOW THEM TO WIN THEM

The marketing executive or business manager who's unfamiliar with the ultimate consumer of the goods is in the same position as you were when you tried to think of an appropriate gift for a mystery recipient. Under those circumstances, your options are limited. About the only thing you can do is *guess* and *hope*. Of course, there are a couple of easy solutions: One is to cut the price—the equivalent of sending money, instead of looking for a specific gift. Another is to look around, see what other people are doing, and then follow along—not an especially creative or effective way to choose a gift or to win customers, either.

Let's try an easier task: How difficult is it to select a perfectly appropriate gift for a close friend? One that you're sure your friend will be thrilled to receive? You can probably think of dozens of things you could buy for this person. More than likely your only problem would be to narrow it down to a single choice from among the many possibilities. And of course you'd have to think up a little message to send with it and decide how to wrap it and deliver it to the recipient—not very difficult things to do, compared to picking out something for someone you've never met and don't know.

When you're as familiar with the customers for your goods as you are with your old friends and long-time associates, you'll be far more likely to make the right marketing choices and decisions—to provide products and services they'll welcome and appreciate. Then, too, the better you understand consumers, the more effectively you'll be able to tell them about the goods, to get them to the people who want them, and to choose prices they'll be willing and able to pay.

Let's Meet the Consumer

We'd like to introduce you to the American consumer in the pages that follow. Undoubtedly you've already met, from time to time, but your contact may have been fairly limited; you may have only a casual acquaintance. We'd like you to really get to know these interesting people. We'll take you to visit them in their homes, see them on the job, and watch them at play. But let's not just be observers from afar. We're more than welcome, after all, because we respect and admire these people and we're not afraid to say so. We need them very much, but it's a two-way street—they need us and they want us to understand them and how they live.

Rather than just standing back and watching, let's get into a conversation with consumers and learn as much as we can about what these people think and believe, what they like and don't like, what they do and what they don't do. We want to know about their needs, desires, and aspirations so that as marketers, we can help them be what they want to be and achieve what they're striving for. Let's step into their shoes, see how they view themselves and their world, how they learn about things, and why they have the opinions and preferences they do.

We won't really know these people until we get to know their families, friends, and associates, as well. We want to see them in action in their social world, to understand some of the pressures they're under, and to appreciate the many satisfactions they find in their affiliations with others. We want to see the whole picture—to see the lives of these new friends of ours as a whole, working, developing system. And we'd like to understand the basic beliefs and assumptions that underpin their lives. Then we'll be able to understand how they make choices, and *why they buy*.

Coming up with "The Right Stuff"

It's vastly easier and far more profitable to create, produce, and market goods that consumers want and need than to try to sell them what they don't want or what they already have. So why do so many marketers find themselves with an inventory of goods they have to force onto prospective buyers? Often it's because they decided to take the easy route initially, only to find rough going, down the road. Lacking an understanding of the ultimate consumer, they produced what was familiar, conventional, or easy to produce, rather than what those in the market needed and sought. At that point, about the only alternative is the "hard sell"—forcing the goods onto the market any way they can.

The better way is obviously to market *the right stuff*, the products and services consumers want and need. So what does it take to make those kinds of marketing choices? Perhaps the most essential ingredient is a thorough understanding of the consumer.

Consumers don't just take a *random walk* through the marketplace; consumer choice isn't really a stochastic process and marketing to them isn't merely a "crap shoot." Purchase decisions aren't always that intelligent or rational, but they are always *meaningful*. Consumer choices may not be reasoned, but consumers are nonetheless reasonable—they can be understood. Occasionally a marketer just stumbles into success, more by luck than anything else. But that's the exception, not the rule. Such flukes can rarely, if ever be repeated. The marketers who do well over time do so because they know the consumers in their market. That awareness might not be sufficient, but it's certainly the *necessary* starting point for success in the consumer marketplace.

THE NONADVERSARIOUS POSTURE

There's a tendency in marketing and business to take an adversarious position; to focus on competitors, rivals, or adversaries. Sometimes the language even takes on a military vocabulary—targets, campaigns, guerrilla tactics, taking your best shot. Usually other firms in the industry are viewed as the adversary, but at it's very worst, this perspective sees the *customer* as the enemy.. The objective is ostensibly to separate the fool from his money! That's about as perverse as marketing can get.

The battlefield is an inappropriate and inadequate metaphor for the business of marketing. The objective of the military is to vanquish the enemy. The objective of marketing is to make a profit. The two are irrelevant to one another. If a competitive firm thrives, it doesn't matter to you as a marketer, so long as you're thriving, too. Nor would it profit you much if they were ruined and you went down the tubes with them. Yet some industries are plagued by destructive price wars and other adversarious manipulations that harm everyone involved, merely because they've misdirected their attention from consumers to competitors.

The Fallacy of Competitive Position

If we assume that consumers have only so much spending power and no more, then our competition includes *anyone* who wants what we regard as our share of those consumer dollars. If you're marketing cars, the other automakers aren't your only competitors, and they may not even be your main competitors. For every consumer who religiously sets aside x dollars or x percentage of income for an automobile and then chooses only among the various cars available, there's got to be a hundred or a thousand who do it much differently. "Honey, should we go ahead and get this beautiful new car, or should we take that vacation trip we've been talking about for so long?" So who's your competition? Not the dealer down the street, that's for sure! Maybe the airline or resort, or perhaps the clothiers who designed the vacation clothes consumers might buy with "your" sales dollars or the restaurants where they'll dine on their vacation trip. But even that view is too confined. After all, they could take the vacation *and* buy a car from you, and decide to send Junior to a public school. Perhaps that private school their son was going to attend is your competition.

Heavy involvement with competitive strategy can mean trouble. The marketplace is the *track*, revenue is the *clock*, the bottom line is your *record time*, and the only valid role those running with you have is to spur you on a little. Run your own race! Learn what consumers are all about and do what you have to do to provide them with what they want and need—what they'll readily buy. But if you watch your competitors, the other runners, too closely, you're likely to lose your stride. If they're ahead of you, it's discouraging. If they're abreast of you, you can't watch them and see ahead. If they're close on your heels, you feel pressured. And if they're well behind you, don't turn around to gloat. It is better to get in your own lane, pick your own pace, take your best stride, and run your own race—from start to finish.

If you know your consumers well, if you really understand them, then there's not much chance the competition will do you in while you're not looking. If there's one thing that's more important than maintaining a good, strong consumer franchise, it's the ability to create them again and again.

TODAY, EVERYBODY'S SPECIAL

We sometimes decry the prevalence of all the different "special interest groups" involved in politics. But this condemnation of special interests assumes that there's a big, homogeneous mass of "common" voters somewhere. But where? We sure don't think our interests are common—they're *special*. What about you? Have you any special interests? Or are yours just common interests? If our interests are special and yours are too, one wonders who has all those common interests. Although even if we found those who did, they probably wouldn't admit it!

Uncommon Man—Uncommon Woman

The common man and woman are myths—nothing more. If they ever did exist, they certainly don't today. This is an afflu-ent population, with a tremendous amount of discretionary spending power. The vast majority of consumers have enough to indulge their *individual* tastes, preferences, and desires. And they have plenty of choices in the consumer marketplace to do it on. So there's very little commonality and plenty of variety. As marketers, we're concerned with two kinds of variation: over *people* and over *time.* Various individuals and groups pursue different interests, adopt different lifestyles, and purchase dif-ferent consumer goods. But they don't stay in one rut very long. So things change very quickly, and what was popular only yes-terday won't necessarily be in vogue tomorrow.

There are only a couple things we can do about this situation: Sit around and complain about it, mourning the demise of the *mass* market, or get busy and sort it out, make sense of it, and make it work for us.

There Are Reasons Why They Buy

Things move so quickly today and there's so much variation among consumers it can get bewildering to even the most so-phisticated marketers. Fortunately the behavior of consumers in the marketplace becomes much more understandable if we recognize what's going on *inside* their minds and identify the physical and social influences that impinge on them from the *outside.* What each of us does when we make a purchase deci-sion depends a lot on both our personal mentality and on our social situation. We use this framework in the chapters that follow to shed some light on *why they buy.*

A close look at consumer needs, motives, and personalities provides a good starting point. So we look inside the minds of consumers first, then turn our attention to the way they perceive the world around them, learn about their options in the marketplace, and develop attitudes toward products and brands, stores and services. After that, we consider the social roles and influences that help shape consumer choices, and look at their family situations. Much depends on the consumer's status on the social hierarchy, and we'll see how social class affects consumption. At the broadest level, it's worth considering the cultural forces that mold us all and how those dictates are changing. As marketers, we can't deal with consumers one-at-a-time. We have to identify some factors that will let us sort them into similar segments. Life stages, family cycles, lifestyles, and the basic demographic characteristics do just that. Then we can hone in on what buyers are doing when they make a choice in the marketplace.

There are few things in life more fascinating or challenging to study than *people*. Here's a chance to take a microscopic and a telescopic view. We do hope that you'll find it not only enjoyable, but profitable, too.

1

NEEDS
The Constant
Quest for
Satisfaction

Ask anyone in the field of finance how to make money by investing and they'll almost invariably give you the same answer: "Buy low and sell high." In the field of marketing, there's a similar axiom for earning profits: "Find a need and fill it." Both of these simple rules are valid— they'll work if you can do it. Unfortunately, the trick isn't so much in knowing *what* to do as in knowing *how* to do it. That's what this book is all about.

Just about everything consumers do in the marketplace is related to satisfying their needs. But ask them about their need for some product and you're likely to get a very incomplete answer. "Why do you need a new car?" The typical car buyer is likely to talk about *transportation* needs. Well, that's probably true, but it's certainly not "the whole truth and nothing but the truth!" Scratch the surface and you'll find that a new car meets many more consumer needs than just that one, utilitarian purpose.

SORTING OUT NEEDS AND GOODS

To sell consumer goods successfully, the product or service has to be designed to meet some human needs. But sorting out consumer needs can be difficult. There isn't a one-to-one match between a specific need and any one, particular purchase: Many different kinds of goods may meet a particular need, and many different needs might be satisfied by a single product or service. Marketers need a way to sort out consumer needs, a way to understand consumer needs and pick the right ones for making a sales appeal.

A VERTICAL APPROACH TO NEEDS

Over four decades ago, psychologist Abraham Maslow noted that people typically try to fulfill some kinds of needs only after other, more primary needs have been satisfied. He identified five different need categories that can be arranged into a vertical hierarchy, with the most primary at the bottom step and those of the highest order at the top:

Self-Fulfillment needs
Prestige and esteem needs
Love and affiliation needs
Safety and security needs
Physical or biological needs

People seek satisfaction for higher needs only after lower needs are satisfied. In addition, they'll abandon higher needs and go back to fulfill a more primary need if it suddenly cries out for satisfaction.

The Basic Physical Needs

The vast majority of consumers in economically well-documented countries find it relatively easy to fulfill their most primary needs—the needs for such things as food, clothing, and shelter. So relatively affluent buyers can find a huge variety of different products and brands that will fulfill their most basic needs very adequately. As a result, they often choose the particular goods that promise the most satisfaction for other, higher needs, as well as the more primary needs. Recognizing this fact, marketers are sometimes misled into ignoring appeals based on strictly physical needs. But that might mean they're neglecting potential opportunities.

> Perhaps as many as one out of five or six adults in this country can't drink whole milk. They've lost their tolerance for lactose, a natural sugar component found in cow's milk. All normal children produce enough *lactase*, an enzyme that breaks down the milk sugar and makes it digestible. But many adults' bodies simply don't produce enough of this enzyme. So they must avoid ordinary milk in their diet. Yet many such adults could benefit from the nutrition milk provides and would really enjoy drinking milk, if they only could.
>
> Lactaid, Inc. recognized the potential market for a milk that would be digestible to adults who can't drink ordinary milk. They developed *LactAid*, a specially digestible, lactose-reduced lowfat milk containing the lactase enzyme, obtained from a type of yeast. This allowed them to license the product to local dairies, extending the market for milk to many adults who couldn't tolerate it previously.

Many companies could benefit by searching out unmet needs that are strictly physical or biological, even within highly developed economies. Of course there are many obvious physical needs that go unsatisfied simply because we lack the technology to invent or create products or services to fulfill them. Medication and treatment for an incurable disease is an example of such an easily recognized, unsatisfied need. But the real opportunities in this area for existing firms and some yet to be created lie in areas that others have ignored. These openings are sometimes called "sleeper" opportunities because they lie dormant for a long time before they're recognized. Then some energetic marketer discovers the unmet need and identifies or develops a product or service to satisfy it. While the ingenious firm reaps the benefits from discovering the sleeper, others who originally missed the boat strive to catch up or catch on, kicking themselves all the while because they failed to recognize the opportunity earlier.

SOMETIMES TOO LITTLE, OFTEN TOO MUCH

Marketers should examine physical needs from two points of view: What's lacking and what's *surplus*. Consumers in affluent societies very often have a glut, rather than a shortage of things to meet primary needs—too many calories, too many "labor-saving" devices, too many food additives, and the like. This results in such things as obesity, sedentary immobility, physical ailments, and many other problems. The negative conditions that result from "too much" create a new set of consumer needs and both new marketing problems and new opportunities for those who recognize that less is often better.

> **The highly publicized relationship between cholesterol and heart disease created serious problems for the beef industry, since red meat is relatively rich in both cholesterol and calories. At the same time, changing dietary trends have greatly expanded the market for poultry, low in both by comparison. While per capita consumption of beef fell by over 20 percent from 1976 to 1985, poultry consumption rose by over 60 percent during the same period—a sorry state for the beef industry, but a fantastic opportunity for poultry growers.**

The poultry industry has enhanced its growth not only by promoting the product as providing *less* of the unwanted ingredients, but also by adjusting unit sizes and repackaging the products. For instance, turkey was once seen as appropriate only for holiday feasting by most families, given the size of the whole bird. Today, turkey is available in a host of sizes and forms, including bone-in and boneless roasts, light or dark only or both, and ranging from the traditional whole bird to pound packages of ground turkey.

Although poultry has been flying ever higher in the marketplace, beef hasn't taken it sitting down. The Beef Industry Council introduced a $10 million promotional program to allay public fears, clear up misconceptions, and tout beef's benefits. But the media campaign, both broadcast and print, is backed by long- and short-term product improvement programs. Improved livestock breeding over a quarter century has resulted in a leaner product. Other, more recent developments include precooked and prepared beef products promoted as quick and easy, good and good for you. But only time will tell whether the beef industry will again get back on its—hooves?

The Need for Safety

Once consumers have satisfied their basic physical needs, they turn their attention to making sure they are safe and secure; that those needs will *stay* satisfied. A limited but substantial range of products and services are sold especially to fulfill people's needs for safety and security. They include many obvious examples: insurance, smoke detectors, home and car security systems, and the like. These kinds of things are designed specifically to provide safety and security, and often very little else. So the marketers of such products focus intensely on this category of needs. But those who sell other kinds of goods, things to meet other needs, often ignore safety and security needs. They don't pay much attention to such needs because they don't feel their goods are directly or immediately related to them.

It's easy to forget that consumer goods are related to needs in two very different ways: positively and negatively. What people buy can either provide or deprive consumers of need satisfaction. Many things we market to consumers will satisfy the needs at one level of the hierarchy and at the same time create a jeopardy at another level. For instance, a high-performance sports car might fulfill the owner's need for prestige and esteem very nicely. But if it tempts him to drive like a demon, it might also jeopardize his safety needs. If that's the way a prospective buyer sees it, would he be likely to purchase the car? The answer lies in the hierarchy of needs. Which type of need is more primary, safety and security or prestige and esteem? Since the more primary needs almost always come first in people's minds, very few consumers would be willing to sacrifice their bodily safety for any amount of prestige.

ALWAYS LOOK DOWN!

When the goods we market are focused at a need category that's above the first step in the hierarchy, we have to take a good, close look at how our product or service will affect more primary needs at lower levels. Rarely will the satisfaction people get for higher needs outweigh significant deprivation that's created at a lower level. More than one marketer has found that out the hard way.

> Cigarettes, liquor, beer, carbonated beverages, and even coffee have traditionally been promoted with appeals to people's need for either affiliation or prestige. In the ads, these products were described as enhancing the consumer's social status or social acceptance, rather than purely for the personal satisfaction obtained from them. What's more, this strategy has been extremely successful—until rather recently. As the health risks associated with tobacco tar, nicotine, alcohol, caffeine, and excess calories were documented and publicized, consumption of the traditional forms of these products began to decline. Many consumers were apparently willing to forgo the social need satisfaction they received from such products in order to meet their more primary physical and safety needs.
>
> Sagging sales directed marketers' attention toward the lower end of the need hierarchy. Many have modified their products to

decrease the physiological risks of consumption. As a result, low-tar and low-nicotine cigarettes, light beer, lower proof spirits, diet soft drinks, and decaffeinated beverages were all introduced. Despite initial resistance, such special brands account for a substantial proportion of many companies' sales today, and their future looks promising. These firms saved their markets and preserved their positions by "looking down" the need hierarchy. Their products still provide social need fulfillment, but they do it without jeopardizing more primary needs.

The Need for Belonging

Few people realize how desperately we all need the company of others. In this society we take great pride in our individualism and try hard to deny any dependency on others. Yet the need to belong is part of our very nature. For most people, "alone" is synonymous with "lonely." Usually even the most antisocial, hardened criminal becomes docile with the threat of solitary confinement. About the only things we hate more than rejection are embarrassment or outright humiliation. If you doubt it, look around! You'll find the same theme everywhere: In books (*The Lonely Crowd*), songs ("Lookin' for Love"), movies (*One Is a Lonely Number*), TV shows ("Love Boat"), and magazines (*Family Circle*).

While the need for belonging is part of human nature, people in our society are more sensitive to separation and alienation because they are very often deprived of intimate affiliations. When you think of it, the vast majority of people who have trod this Earth were born, lived, died, and were buried, all within only a few blocks or miles. They lived in families and clans within tiny villages. They knew every other person with whom they came into contact, and knew them well. In fact, the ability to cooperate and work together was one important reason why our species was able to survive and to thrive on the planet. But how different contemporary American life is! With both geographic and social mobility, we're torn apart from our families and childhood playmates—scattered horizontally and vertically about the social milieu, and cast into huge crowds of total strangers. No small wonder our hearts cry out for companionship and jump for joy at the sight of a familiar face, a friendly handshake, a warm hug.

THIS IS WHERE IT'S AT!

In this society probably more consumer goods are sold with appeals to this kind of need than on the basis of any other single category—in fact, maybe more than on the basis of all the others combined. It sometimes seems that almost everyone who can find any connection whatsoever between their product and love or belonging uses an appeal to affiliation to promote their goods. Some do it brilliantly!

> **"Reach Out and Touch Someone"**
> **"Weekends Are for Michelob"**
> **"Don't You Wish Everybody Did"**
> **"When You Care Enough to Send the Very Best"**
> **"Fly the Friendly Skies"**
> **"Nuthin' Says Lovin' Like Doughboy"**
> **"Gentlemen Prefer Hanes"**
> **"Never Let Them See You Sweat"**

AN INSATIABLE DESIRE

Another reason advertisers focus heavily on the need for love, affiliation, and belonging is insatiability. It's pretty easy for consumers to obtain a glut of physical need satisfaction. All too easy, in fact, as the bathroom scale so often indicates. Safety and security are also oversatisfied beyond a certain point. Beyond the threshold of satiation, people are willing to sacrifice some security in favor of the stimulation and excitement associated with minor risk-taking. Higher on the vertical ladder of needs, only the rare megalomaniac can't get enough power, fame, respect, or prestige. Beyond some point, prestige is alienating and deprives the celebrity of friendships and affiliations, so needs for esteem are also finite. But who has too many good and loyal friends? Who in the world has too much love? Most of us couldn't even imagine it.

Today's consumers have (1) ample resources for goods that promise affiliation; (2) an insatiable need for friendship; and (3) few traditional sources for affiliation and friendship. Is it any wonder that they try to buy it?

Consumer goods can't really provide those who buy them with affiliation or belonging; only *people* can actually fulfill such needs. But consumer products or services are related, either directly or indirectly, to the attainment of love and belonging. Things that permit, promote, or enhance interaction among people; services such as restaurants or cocktail lounges and products such as playing cards or board games, for instance, are directly related to affiliation need fulfillment. Other products and services are only indirectly related to affiliation because they make people more attractive and welcome to others. Clothing, personal care products and services, sports equipment, and a variety of personal possessions with social significance or symbolic value identify people as similar to those whose company they seek. Such goods make their buyers more attractive companions to others with whom they want to interact. All kinds of consumer goods that are directly or indirectly related to social belonging can be marketed primarily to help people achieve the affiliation or belonging they so badly need.

The Need for Status

Like affiliation needs, status needs aren't really satisfied by consumer goods. Prestige, status, esteem, respect, fame, and recognition are all things bestowed by others; they're "people" needs and not "product" needs. Yet as in the previous cases, the products and services consumers buy and use may either enhance or detract from their chances for fulfilling status needs. So people are willing to pay and pay dearly for goods they feel will enhance their prestige in the eyes of others, ranging from the largest single purchase most people will ever make, their home, to the smallest trinkets with which they adorn themselves.

Only *socially visible* goods help consumers win respect and prestige from others. To be socially visible, the product or service has to meet two criteria: (1) others must be able to perceive the product or service or the results of using the goods; and (2) the goods can't be so common or routine that virtually everyone owns or uses them. An expensive, well-tailored suit of clothes has prestige value because it's visible to others and only those with the means and taste can acquire such elegant garments. That doesn't include everybody. By contrast, elegant, expensive lingerie doesn't have prestige value because it can't normally be seen by others. Nor does an ordinary pair of slacks have prestige value. Even though others can see the garment, there's nothing special about it; it isn't distinctive because most people have many such clothing items.

The products themselves don't really have to be visible, provided that the *results* of using them can be perceived. Those who need strong corrective lenses to enjoy normal vision might be convinced to replace their eyeglasses with contact lenses if they feel the purchase will enhance their prestige by improving their appearance. Even though the lenses are invisible when worn, their effect, the absence of glasses, is very discernible. Nor must products that symbolize status necessarily be seen by others. Fine perfume or the feel of plush carpet under foot are both perceptible by other senses. They also symbolize status, though they aren't visually noticeable.

Status need satisfaction isn't confined to consumer products; many services also lend prestige to their consumers. For instance, status seekers may attend entertainments such as opera or ballet, frequent the currently popular night clubs, visit the "in" resorts, or join a prestigious country or racket club—not so much because they enjoy the services themselves, but simply to be seen in the act of consumption! They just want to be seen in the "right" places doing the "right" things with the "right" people. Recognizing this tendency, those who market such services often promote them to social strivers as typical of those who have already "arrived."

> **During years past, when domestic car makers virtually owned the American market, General Motors maintained a fairly rigid progression in price, quality, and prestige among their five divisions: Chevrolet, Pontiac, Oldsmobile, Buick, and Cadillac. At the pinnacle, a "Caddy" became the quintessential luxury, the utter epitome of status, to the point where marketers of other luxury products sometimes referred to their brand as the "Cadillac of whatever." Dealers didn't even sell *used* Cadillacs; they sold Cadillac *resale* cars.**

> **With the encroachment of foreign auto makers on the American market during recent years, Mercedes-Benz and, to a lesser degree, BMW and Volvo began to make inroads on the luxury car market. GM has begun to fight back and fight hard. Calling on the residual image of a status machine in the minds of mature car buyers, they refer to Cadillac as "The new essence of elegance." What they invested in the creation of the Cadillac image in years past now constitutes a substantial *asset* in the marketplace. To tap into their image resources, they tag their ads with a simple phrase: "Best of all . . . it's a Cadillac."**

THE "WRONG-WAY" DEMAND CURVE

Everyone with an elementary understanding of economics knows that the demand curve for consumer goods slopes downward from left to right. The lower the price, the greater the volume of sales; that's always the way it goes—well, *almost* always. High-status products are exceptions to the rule. So ever since Thorstein Veblen coined the term "conspicuous consumption" in his book *The Theory of the Leisure Class* just before the turn of the century, astute marketers of luxury goods have recognized that price, alone, connotes status. They tout high rather than low prices of goods with an upward-sloping demand curve:

"Opulent. Uninhibited luxury." (Decadence perfume)
"The best the world has to offer." (White Shoulders perfume)
"The instinct for the exquisite." (Raffinee perfume)
"The perfume for days of gold and sapphire nights." (Lutece)
"Promise her anything but give her Arpege." (Lanvin)
"The costliest perfume in the world." (Joy de Jean Patou)

The Need for Self-Fulfillment

What is the ultimate motivation in life? If you ask people that question, not one in a thousand will have the right answer. Our minds are filled with Darwinian notions of survival, but survival needs are *primary* needs; they're *basic* needs, but they aren't the ultimate needs in life. The *ultimate* need, the most far-reaching, comprehensive motive in life is *self-fulfillment* or *self-actualization*. But like most profound ideas, self-fulfillment is much easier to recognize when it's described than it is to define in precise terms.

Philosophers and theologians have argued about the meaning of life for centuries, and we surely don't want to join that argument. But there's still an important, unanswered question: What do people do when they have enough satisfaction for their physical, safety, belonging, and status needs? What do they pursue then? The answer is self-actualization, the complete fulfillment of all of their human capacities. This means enlarging and enhancing themselves. It means extending their personal identities, their individuality, their uniqueness.

It's easy to see that most of us are busy trying to fulfill more basic needs than self-fulfillment most of the time. We all spend most of our lives trying to stay alive and healthy, to be secure, to maintain our relationships with our family and friends, and to get some respect and recognition for who we are as people. Most consumers' minds are occupied with their efforts to stay well, get along with people, make a buck, and look good while doing it. It takes a lot of time, experience, and maybe even some wisdom just to meet those basic needs. So most people don't really get to the point where they can pursue self-actualization until they have a few decades behind them. Pursuing this kind of need satisfaction is much more typical of the mature consumer than of younger people who are still striving for the more basic things in life.

A VERY INACCURATE STEREOTYPE

Reference to elderly people usually conjures up images in people's minds of poverty and destitution, loneliness and ill health. In fact, nothing could be further from the truth. Only a very small fraction of elderly consumers in this society fit that stereotype. Yet most people think that way because elderly people in such unfortunate circumstances get most of the media attention. They certainly deserve our concern, but marketers shouldn't generalize that image to the entire group.

In Chapter 12, we take a good, long look at the different age groups in our society and what kinds of markets each one constitutes. But for now, we can point out one rather surprising statistic that may help dispel some of the misconceptions about mature consumers: By the end of this decade, about half of all the disposable personal income in this country will be in the hands of people over fifty years of age! These are precisely the people most likely to have reached a place in life where they can and do pursue fulfillment of their self-actualization needs.

The economic, technical, social, and cultural developments in our society encourage greater and greater multiplicity of lifestyles and personal pursuits. The consumer activities associated with self-actualization are often devoted to *individuation* of personal identity. These people try to *differentiate* themselves from others, to establish their own uniqueness in both their own eyes and in the eyes of others. So they choose products and brands, stores and services according to their distinctiveness. They judge how well the goods fit their own lifestyle and idealized self-image. Marketing appeals devoted to the "common man" or "common woman" don't work well here. Promoting the goods as "not for everyone" or "for the select few who . . ." is more effective for those pursuing self-fulfill-ment.

Both baby boomers and their seniors have embraced a wide variety of activities devoted to the nebulous concept of "self-development." The term means different things to different people, so the consumer goods associated with self-develop-ment encompass a wide range of dissimilar things. They range from running shoes to charity marathons, mantra yoga lessons to self-identity seminars, self-improvement books to biofeedback devices, fitness equipment to tanning salons. Among the move-ment's adherents, services such as cosmetic surgery, hair re-placement, and medical weight reduction aren't merely seen as acceptable, they're often viewed as symbols of self-respect and self-caring. In the past, most people wouldn't think of using such services and those who did tried desperately to conceal the fact; today's and tomorrow's consumers may openly publi-cize it among their friends.

To obtain prestige and esteem from products or services, con-sumers are concerned with *ownership* and *recognition* of the goods among their peers. To obtain self-actualization with con-sumer goods, buyers are concerned with *involvement* and *indi-vidualization*. Owning something and letting everybody know about it isn't enough any more. The goods have to be marketed as unique, special, and distinctive. They have to be promoted to highlight the personal involvement and the effects on the indi-vidual. This means using target marketing rather than mass marketing, selective media, specialty outlets, product position-ing, and pricing related closely to intrinsic value.

> **Consumers' fascination with "plastic" money made credit cards an extremely lucrative financial service business over the past several years. American Express once dominated the market, but banks entered the fray with MasterCard and Visa. That both increased generic demand for universal credit cards and also soaked up a substantial part of that demand. American Express ended up with a greater volume of business but a smaller share of the enlarged market.**

By the mid-1980s the consumer credit card market began to approach saturation, with the average cardholder carrying seven different cards. American Express had introduced the Gold Card back in 1966. Looking for even more growth at the high end of today's market, they also offer the Platinum Card, once a year, by invitation only, to Gold Card holders with a previous year's billing of $10,000 and over.

Ads promoting the Gold Card, targeted to today's big spenders, professionals with $40,000 plus incomes, make references to "fiscal maturity," to "earning" the card, and to those "whose finances are among the top 5 percent of the nation." Rather than appealing merely to convenience and security, American Express clearly moved up the hierarchy of needs to prestige, and even beyond, to self-fulfillment. Ad headlines for the Gold Card declare that "It merely reaffirms what you already know about yourself," and "It says more about you than anything you can buy with it." The earmark of self-actualization appeals is the reference to self-individuation, and credit card services are ideal for such appeals, because they fit multiple lifestyles.

AN HORIZONTAL VIEW OF NEEDS

While it's very useful, if not absolutely necessary, to examine the hierarchy of needs, we aren't confined only to a vertical view. We can also look at consumer needs from a cross-sectional point of view as well. From this horizontal perspective, no one category of needs consistently takes precedence over the others. What's more, this approach permits us to identify more categories and specify them more precisely. These needs aren't classified according to the sequence in which consumers approach them. Instead they're based on the kinds of concerns and activities that consumers associate with them. So these categories of needs are more often closely associated with particular types of consumer products, services, brands, and outlets.

In Table 1, 15 fairly distinct categories of consumer needs are listed on the left, followed by a brief description of each. To the right of each need category, several kinds of related consumer

Table 1. Consumer Needs and Goods

Consumer Needs	Related Goods
Achievement The need to accomplish difficult feats; to perform arduous tasks; to exercise one's skills, abilities, or talents.	Goods that improve consumers' ability or skill; tools and do-it-yourself materials; "how-to" books and practical courses; goods and services related to occupations or professions; some self-improvement programs.
Independence The need to be autonomous, to be free from the direction or influence of others; to have options and alternatives; to make one's own choices and decisions; to be different.	Products and promotions that emphasize the distinctiveness or independence of the individual; wearing apparel and accessories; personal care services such as hair stylists; customized cars and vans; individualized home furnishings; novel appliances and "gadgets"; exotic food and drink.
Exhibition The need to display one's self, to be visible to others; to reveal personal identity; to show off or win the attention and interest of others; to gain notice.	Obviously distinctive or unusual products and designs; unique or highly uncommon clothing and jewelry; bright colors or "flashy" garments, cars, and so on; bizarre hair styles; strange or excessive cosmetic products or applications.
Recognition The need for *positive* notice by others; to show one's superiority or excellence; to be acclaimed or held up as exemplary; to receive social rewards or notoriety.	Products or visible services that show superiority or identify the consumer with famous figures or institutions; plaques, awards, trophies, and so on; sports fan pennants, badges, jackets and the like; home and office "memorabilia" showing gratitude or acclaim by others; fraternity, sorority, or "old school" pins and emblems.
Dominance The need to have power or to exert one's will on others; to hold a position of authority or influence; to direct or supervise the efforts of others; to show strength or prowess by winning over adversaries.	Products that symbolize, enable, or enhance authority; badges of authority or office; things associated with authority figures; firearms and other weapons; equipment identified with war or law enforcement; "power" rather than "manual" equipment; detergents, pesticides, and so on promoted for their strength.

24

Table 1. (*Continued*)

Consumer Needs	Related Goods
Affiliation	
The need for association with others; to belong or win acceptance; to enjoy satisfying and mutually helpful relationships.	Goods that *permit, promote,* or *enhance* interaction among people and goods that make the individual more attractive to others, as described in the previous section.
Nurturance	
The need to give care, comfort, and support to others; to see living things grow and thrive; to help the progress and development of others; to protect one's charges from harm or injury.	Products and services associated with parenthood; child care products; cooking, sewing and "family" laundry goods; all pets and pet supplies; house plants, yard and garden products; charitable service appeals for contribution or volunteers.
Succorance	
The need to *receive* help, support, comfort, encouragement, or reassurance, from others; to be the *recipient* of nurturant efforts.	Consumer products and especially consumer services that serve as surrogate (substitute) care givers; personal services, and especially those that involve touching or contact with the body; facial and body massage; hair styling and manicure; a shoe shine; most counseling and advising services; products promoted to "pamper" the user.
Sexuality	
The need to establish one's sexual identity and attractiveness; to enjoy sexual contact; to *receive* and to *provide* sexual satisfaction; to maintain sexual alternatives without exercising them; to avoid condemnation for sexual appetites.	"Gendered" products that identify a person with others of their sex; clothing and accessories identified with one sex or that enhance sex appeal; products such as perfume or cologne; personal care services such as hair styling; goods directly associated with sexual activity; books, records, films, audio and video tapes of explicit or suggestive sexual activity; entertainments and establishments associated with "dating and mating."

Table 1. (*Continued*)

Consumer Needs	Related Goods

Stimulation

The need to experience events and activities that stimulate the senses or exercise perception; to move and act freely and vigorously; to engage in rapid or forceful activity; to saturate the palate with flavor; to engage the environment in new or unusual modes of interaction.

Products and services with strong sensory characteristics or dramatic perceptibility; goods with intense or unusual sights, sounds, scents, flavors, and textures; things that require, allow, or facilitate body movement or exercise; physical fitness products and services; spas and sports equipment; fabric softeners or satin sheets; flavorful food and drink; incense and bubble bath.

Diversion

The need to play; to have fun; to be entertained; to break from the routine; to relax and abandon one's cares; to be amused.

Goods and services that provide entertainment or distraction; toys and games; cinema, television, plays or concerts; live or recorded music; books and periodicals of fiction or poetry; hobby and avocational materials; sports cars or recreational vehicles; hunting and camping items; boats and sports equipment; recreational travel.

Novelty

The need for change and diversity; to experience the unusual; to do new tasks or activities; to learn new skills; to be in a new setting or environment; to find unique objects of interest; to be amazed or mystified.

Goods that break the routine; new or different products and services; things from other cultures or distant places; ethnic foods or foreign films; curiosities and oddities; unusual designs and arrangements; unique clothes or unusual jewelry; colorful or exciting entertainments; travel to unfamiliar places.

Understanding

The need to learn and comprehend; to recognize connections; to assign causality; to make ideas fit the circumstances; to teach, instruct, or impress others with one's expertise; to follow intellectual pursuits.

Products and services associated with learning or acquisition of knowledge; books and courses of instruction; hobbies requiring study or specialization; reading material that explains or instructs; periodicals containing news or nonfiction; occupationally related goods; adult education programs.

Table 1. (*Continued*)

Consumer Needs	Related Goods
Consistency The need for order, cleanliness, or logical connection; to control the environment; to avoid ambiguity and uncertainty; to predict accurately; to have things happen as one expects.	Cleaning products and services of all types; soap, shampoo, detergents; cleaning appliances; things that match or come in pairs or sets; coordinated clothing; stores with well-ordered merchandise displayed; services provided with regularity; multiple items of the same brand.
Security The need to be free from threat of harm; to be safe; to protect self, family, and property; to have a supply of what one needs; to save and acquire assets; to be invulnerable from attack; to avoid accidents or mishaps.	Products and services that provide protection; insurance; financial services for saving and investment; alarm and protection products and services for the home and car; lighting and safety equipment; goods low in risk or that reduce risk; vitamins and preventive medication.

goods are identified. The lists of related goods certainly aren't all-inclusive or exhaustive, but the products and services identified there are *typical* of goods that serve each kind of need. There isn't a one-to-one association between different needs and various consumer goods. Obviously there's some overlapping. Yet this list of collateral needs is more fine grained than only the five categories in the need hierarchy. So we can legitimately draw some generalizations about what goes with what, about the most common products and services associated with each type of need. It's easy to recognize the utility in doing so: By examining the different needs and the kinds of consumer goods most often used to meet them, we can identify the most appropriate needs for basing an appeal strategy for a particular product or service.

Marketing to Consumer Needs

Marketers often see relationships between needs and promotional decisions more easily than the association between needs and product or service design, pricing policy, or distribution channels. In fact, all aspects of the marketing program should be geared primarily to the satisfaction of only one or two kinds of needs.

Consumers aren't usually aware of the specific needs they are trying to fulfill when they make a purchase decision. Unfortunately marketers are often even less aware of the needs to be satisfied. Consumers don't have to recognize needs precisely or be able to articulate them in order to function effectively in the marketplace, but marketers definitely should. Perhaps a couple of examples will clarify the necessity:

> **Those marketing medical services almost always suppose patients visit a clinic for treatment to meet biological needs. Yet careful study shows they're more often seeking fulfillment of *psychological* needs for reassurance, attention, or interaction (succorance, affiliation). Regardless of therapeutic effectiveness, they'll be dissatisfied if they're treated mechanically and receive little or no satisfaction for the psychological needs.**

Comparison of television versus movie entertainment provides another very different and graphic example of marketers misperception of consumer needs.

> **With the invention and innovation of television, many predicted that theaters would become obsolete as moviegoers turned to television viewing. In other words, many people thought the two modes of distributing filmed entertainment were both satisfying the same needs. Not so, as the continued success of movie exhibitors indicated. A close look at the needs served by the two media shows why. Although they both provide sight and sound, the activities are very different and they each tend to satisfy a different set of needs. Viewing TV is largely an *individual* experience while going to a movie is a *social* experience.**

Moviegoers are typically young people and a large proportion are unmarried. Movies provide them with satisfaction for *affiliation* and *sexuality* needs. People go to movies together and they're often "dating" or trying to meet and interact with mates. And movies also have more potential for meeting *stimulation* needs with vivid spectacle and dramatic special effects. So they, too, serve rather different needs. But if movie exhibitors continue to shrink the size of the auditorium and screen, deupholster the seating, and handle patrons with crowd-control procedures, more and more young people will turn from movies to congregating in shopping malls and other comfortable places.

Analyzing Consumer Goods Needs

Exactly what needs does your own product or brand, service or store fulfill for your buyers? Don't settle for the obvious; don't rely on conventional wisdom. Dig a little deeper, and do it deliberately! Study the actual activity consumers engage in when they use the goods. Where are they? When do they use it? Who's with them? Why are they doing this instead of something else? When you've identified the different needs that are being met, list them out in your own words. Then determine which ones are the most important—the major needs being satisfied, the main ones.

Next, take a very close look at "the competition," but not just the others in your industry. Who else is *really* competing for those dollars—who else provides goods to meet those same needs? They're your *real* competition!

Now look at the market as a whole. Break it into segments with *common needs*. Which should you target? Which are already well served by competitors? Only at this point can you intelligently adjust the product, promotion, distribution, and pricing to provide maximum need satisfaction.

2

MOTIVES
Silent, Invisible
Engines of Desire

When the bartender opened for business at 9:00 A.M., an elderly, neatly dressed businessman was waiting to enter. He immediately ordered a straight shot of vodka, no chaser. Puzzled, the bartender served him. Removing a folded white handkerchief from his pocket, the fastidious man wrapped it around his index finger, dipped it into the vodka, and scrubbed a small stain from his necktie.

It's not easy to anticipate consumer buying motives.

Consumer buying motives are impelling urges to acquire some product or service. So they're directly associated with consumers' actions in the marketplace. If needs are the soil from which buying behavior springs, motives are the germ of life itself. A need can lie dormant for hours, days, weeks, months, even years. But once it's excited and the person feels an urge to satisfy the need, that creates a motive to act. If needs were heat, motives would be the spark that ignites the fire of action.

THEY DON'T KNOW OR WON'T SAY

Every marketer would love to know what motivates people to buy the goods. If we knew what motives would lead to a decision to purchase, then perhaps we could create a marketing program to instill or intensify those motives among potential buyers in the market. So why not just ask consumers about their motives? The answer is that unfortunately most people don't know exactly what their motives are, and even if they did, they would often be unwilling to report their motives.

Subconscious Motives and Desires

More than any other, Sigmund Freud popularized the notion that much of our mental activity takes place out of sight, so to speak, in the subconscious mind. He viewed the subconscious as a veritable reservoir of dark desires, hidden urges, and buried feelings. He believed them to be based almost exclusively in either sexuality or morbidity. According to Freud, the shapes and forms of this dim, underground landscape are never clearly visible. We get only an occasional glimpse of them in our dreams. But despite their invisibility, the ruminations in our subconscious do often poke through the surface, showing themselves in the disguised form of symbolic behavior or surrogate activity. These ideas led Freudian psychologists and marketers to devise clever ways to ferret out the motives residing in the subconscious mind. By interpreting the inadvertent displays and unintentional actions of people, they sought to understand the vocabulary of symbolic images and activities that arose from the subconscious. But at the core, all behavior was regarded as reducible to sexual or aggressive motives.

While Freudian theories of motivation pretty much held sway thirty years ago or more, most of today's consumer psychologists have moved away from strict adherence to those principles. Nearly everyone accepts the idea of the subconscious mind, but in large measure, they've rejected the notion that motivation is based only on sexual or aggressive tendencies. Contemporary marketers broaden the range of potential motivating factors to include a wide array of motives and desires. Sexual and aggressive motives aren't denied, but they're seen as playing only a part in the broader picture.

THE LEGACY OF FREUD

What does remain of the Freudian theory of motivation is the idea that consumer motives are largely unconscious. In other words, we often don't really know exactly why we do what we do in the marketplace. So when people are asked why they made a particular purchase, the responses they give are often not especially accurate or useful. It might be because they really do know, but they're reluctant to give the real reason. More often, though, it's because they, themselves, actually don't know precisely what their own motives are. So in order to find out about consumer motivation, we often have to make inferences about motives, based on less direct evidence. However, we do have a fairly effective set of tools and techniques for learning about hidden purchase motives. We'll discuss that topic shortly.

Socially Acceptable Responses

Every normal person has a very good idea of what's socially acceptable and what's not. We all learned at a very early age about the taboos and prohibitions of our society. More than that, we know what a "good" person is supposed to want, do, and own. It's extremely important to us to be respectable; to look good in our own eyes and in the eyes of others. But to do that, we have to either follow the dictates of the culture or at the very least, give lip service to them.

So exactly what is a good person supposed to be? What's society's collective notion of a good and noble man or woman? Should we be humble or proud? Restrained or self-indulgent? Self-sacrificing or self-seeking? Independent or dependent? Serious or frivolous? Hard-working or lazy? Any fool knows the answers to those questions! But be honest—is that the way people *really* are? Sure, humility, restraint, self-sacrifice, independence, dedication, and industry are the norms, but not even a saint could or would live up to them all the time or even most of the time. Still, we would all like at least to *appear* to have socially virtuous motives, even when we know we don't.

PLURALISTIC IGNORANCE ABOUNDS

There's a strange phenomenon that psychologists call "pluralistic ignorance" and it's very prevalent with regard to motives. Everybody appears to follow the social norms pretty closely and nobody wants to admit to being different. So people quickly gain the impression that they're the only ones who deviate. Actually everybody deviates all the time, but each person thinks he or she is the only one who's odd. So even when somebody points out that "the king's as naked as a jaybird," everybody else in the crowd ignores it and talks incessantly about his lovely clothes. That's pluralistic ignorance.

Often consumers don't report their real motives, even when they know very well what they are, because they think everybody else's motives are more noble or valid. Each thinks he or she is the only one who wants the product for such "unacceptable" reasons.

> Several years ago one of my marketing students conducted a survey among mothers of young children. He wanted to know why they bought their children certain kinds of cookies. More specifically, he wanted to find out if the nutritional value of the cookies mattered to these mothers. The naive young man asked them about it directly. There was an extremely high consensus that the nutritional value of the cookies (and everything else they fed their kids) was exceedingly important—that this was by far the dominant motive for choosing the kind of cookie they picked.
>
> There's one in every crowd! One brave young mom laughed a little, looked the interviewer in the eye, and declared, in effect, that the king had no clothes. She said, "Look, fella, these cookies are just *bribes*. So the better Joey likes the cookies, the better they work. He gets plenty of good, healthy food, so a few cookies aren't going to poison him, even if they're not the best food in the world. But as far as nutritional value is concerned, I could care less!"
>
> It's hard to doubt that the motives of this courageous young lady were far more representative of mothers in the buying public than were those of the vast majority of respondents. As this became clear to the student, he came away from the project sadder but wiser. Unfortunately there are still many otherwise savvy marketers who don't seem to share that wisdom.

The cardinal mistake that many marketers make is to survey those in their market to determine their reasons for making the choices they do. Only rarely can the genuinely operative motives of buyers be discovered by direct questioning. But this doesn't preclude us from measurement of consumer motivation. It just means that motives must be measured indirectly.

INDIRECT MEASURES OF CONSUMER MOTIVATION

Clinical psychologists have developed a fairly large family of techniques for measuring their patients motives. Many are based on the Freudian concept of *projection*, so they're called "projective techniques" in the trade. Without elaborating on the idea, we can say that projection is the tendency for people to *project* their wishes, desires, and motives on somebody or something else whenever these urges are unacceptable to the individual's superego or "conscience." For example, if you hated somebody but subconsciously couldn't bring yourself to accept the fact that you're a hateful person, you might turn it around and say "That person really hates *me!*" If you did, you'd be projecting your hatred on somebody else to avoid feelings of guilt or shame. But of course in keeping with the Freudian notion of the subconscious, all of this activity would be below the level of conscious thought. You wouldn't know you were doing it.

Many of the tools clinicians use to measure the motivation of patients aren't well suited to consumer psychology and the measurement of buying motives, but a few are useful to marketing researchers. For instance, most people have heard of the Rorschach or "ink-blot" test. It might be an effective instrument for use with people who are mentally ill or emotionally disturbed, but it wouldn't say much about a typical consumer's purchase motives. On the other hand, some projective techniques and other methods of getting around the conscious mind and into the subconscious level of motivation have been used effectively in marketing. For example, word association, sentence completion, picture completion, and depth interviewing have all been used to measure consumer motivation, with varying degrees of success.

Consumers Project Their Feelings

Projective methods of motivation research let consumers project their motives and desires on someone else. That way they can express what they feel without experiencing any bad feelings such as guilt or shame. "After all, it's *her* silly desires, not mine!" So there's no reason to edit what they say or limit their responses, either above or below the level of awareness.

When instant coffee was first introduced, over 35 years ago, it was promoted for it's quickness and ease of preparation; convenience was the main theme. But there was considerable resistance to the new product, despite its obvious advantages over traditional coffee brewing methods. When asked directly, almost everyone who rejected instant coffee said they didn't like the taste and much preferred fresh-brewed coffee. This mystified the manufacturers because blind taste testing revealed that many couldn't tell the difference between instant and fresh-brewed coffee if they weren't told which was which. One usually came out about as well as the other.

In 1950, Mason Haire devised a way to isolate the factors that led to rejection of instant coffee. The ingenious Prof. Haire gave two groups of homemakers two simple shopping lists containing identical items, with one exception. Both lists contained:

> One and one-half pounds of hamburger
> Two loaves of Wonder Bread
> One can of Rumford baking powder
> Two cans of Del Monte peaches
> Five pounds of potatoes

The only difference in the lists was that one included a pound of drip grind Maxwell House coffee while the other listed a container of Nescafe instant coffee.

The women were asked to write down a brief description of the kind of person who would go shopping with such a list. Then the two groups of descriptions were compared. Of course, any systematic differences could be attributed only to the fact that one used instant and the other, fresh-brewed coffee. The differences were dramatic! Take a look at some of the phrases used to describe each shopper:

DRIP GRIND COFFEE BUYER

> A practical, frugal woman
> She must like to cook and bake
> A thrifty, sensible housewife

INSTANT COFFEE BUYER

Likes to sleep late in the morning
She seems to be lazy
She must appear rather sloppy
She doesn't seem to think
The type who never thinks ahead very far
She is fundamentally lazy
Just living from one day to the next
A haphazard sort of life

The results of this projective study implied that shoppers were motivated to buy fresh-brewed coffee by their desire to be good, caring wives, mothers, and homemakers. By contrast, they were motivated to reject instant coffee to avoid the appearance of laziness, thoughtlessness, and inexperience. Instant coffee marketers shifted the promotional appeals from convenience to *appropriateness*. Women serving instant coffee where shown receiving social rewards for it. They were active, caring planners. In similar studies more recently, instant coffee users were viewed positively while the fresh-brewed coffee users were "old-fashioned," a tribute to the marketers' success.

NOBODY'S AFFECTED BY ADVERTISING?

Marketers build promotional appeals around the main buying motives of consumers, or at least they try to do that. For any given product, there's usually a wide variety of optional appeals. But it's just not practical to try one appeal after another in several advertising campaigns until one of them hits. Trial and error is too costly and time-consuming. So advertisers will often sketch out ads with various appeals and pretest them on a sample, using advertising research to discover which is most effective. However, there's often a hitch, if respondents are asked which ad would be most likely to motivate them to buy the product: Nobody wants to admit they're in the least bit affected by advertising! They'll typically claim that they don't pay any attention to advertising, despite the fact that a glance at their pantry or closet, kitchen or garage reveals nothing but heavily advertised, name-brand consumer goods. Often the answer is to use an indirect, projective technique to reveal their potential reactions to various promotional appeals.

> **In our own research for advertising agencies and their clients, we've used an indirect approach to learn what's most likely to motivate people to buy. It's fairly simple and straightforward, but it gets around respondents' defensiveness about being influenced by advertising.**

> **Each respondent is asked to identify a friend or acquaintance they know fairly well, somebody of about the same age and sex, with a similar background and lifestyle to their own. Then they're asked to say how they think "their friend" would respond to each of a series of ads with different motivational appeals. While they might be unable or unwilling to report their own reactions, there's nothing threatening about answering for someone else.**

> **People can more readily project their feelings on someone who's similar than on somebody who's very different or on a fictional person. What's more, asking them to answer for someone they know makes it easier for them to respond with some degree of confidence in their own mind; it makes it plausible, since they are the "expert informants." But the most important reason for identifying a similar other is the ability to break down the reactions by demographic groups and make comparisons—based not on the other person's age, sex, and so on, but on the respondents themselves.**

THE COMPONENTS OF BUYING MOTIVES

Motives may be difficult to identify, but essentially they have a pretty simple makeup. So far as we know, they only have two moving parts: direction and intensity. Buying motives determine two things: what consumers want to do, and how much they want to do it. To market successfully, purchase motives first have to be directed toward your goods, not someone else's. Second, the drive has to be strong enough so that people will act on it; they have to be willing to pay the price in terms of dollars, time, effort, and the like.

The Direction of Motives

A specific type of buyer motive won't lead to sales if it's focused anywhere but on your product or service, brand or store. Marketers in that predicament have two basic alternatives: Shift the motives to focus on the goods in question, or realign the product or service offering to put it in line with the motives—or both. Ordinarily about the only other thing to be done would be to abandon those particular motives in favor of some others.

> About the only thing you couldn't run into with an old, traditional Volkswagen are the motives of sports car enthusiasts or performance car devotees. Economic motives—sure, reliability motives—probably, comfort motives—perhaps, aesthetic motives—doubtful yet still possible, but speed and power motives—never . . . until the VW Jetta.
>
> Volkswagen realigned a product to put it in the motivational mainstream of "performance" by introducing the Jetta, with an aerodynamically designed body, fuel-injected engine, and five-speed transmission. How well they accomplished it, we'll leave to the experts.
>
> The second step was to swing performance-car motives toward their new product. Both print and broadcast media were used to promote the new image, using headlines urging drivers to "Give in to an overwhelming drive," and come in for a test drive of the car. With sleek-looking illustrations and print ad layouts, together with copy references to having ". . . pumped a lot of adrenaline into a lot of hearts," VW appealed unabashedly to the speed and power crowd. Their task is formidable and success is still an open question, but at the very least, it's a valiant try.

The Intensity of Motives

Even when motives are focused directly on a given product or service, their intensity may not be high enough to spark action.

Many potential buyers may have an inclination toward purchase, but lack the drive to go out and buy it or the willingness to pay the price. Since such motives lie in the right direction, the marketer has half the battle won—but not the war. It's not the road to marketers' heaven that's paved with good consumer intentions. For marketers in this position, the options are two: intensify the consumer's drive or make the cost less dear.

"Aren't You Hungry?" Three little words that generated a lot of sales for Burger King. As one of the top purveyors of fast food, Burger King already enjoyed a large and loyal following. So the food-buying motives of a substantial part of the market were directed toward Burger King restaurants. But people are very suggestible when it comes to food, and Burger King found a way to intensify the buying motives of potential patrons.

At one time or another, virtually everybody has found themselves sitting at home in the evening, enjoying their leisure, but feeling just the slightest bit hungry. Maybe just a little nudge— enough to prompt a run to the refrigerator, but not the driving urge that would push them to get up, go out, and get something to eat.

Apparently a lot of people were in precisely that state, when it happened . . . a late-night TV spot showing luscious Burger King goodies, words and music that would alone be enough to excite the appetite of an anorectic, and that provocative, nagging question, again and again: "Aren't You Hungry?" This intensification of the hunger drive was so successful Burger King decided to have many of their outlets remain open later at night, just to accommodate the new trade and take advantage of their promotional success.

THE EASY WAY OUT (IT SAYS HERE)

Marketers who find their buyers lack sufficient desire or drive often take "the easy way out" by making the cost of the goods less dear; in short, by reducing the price. By doing so, they often plunge out of the frying pan and into the fire of direct price competition. And it can get very, very hot, indeed! Unforately, once that happens, it's exceedingly difficult to escape ne fire, even to climb back into the frying pan. So before taking the plunge, it's always advisable to see if there isn't a way to increase buyer incentive.

CONSUMERS' PURCHASE INCENTIVES

People have an incentive to buy when they consciously see a direct connection between their needs and the products or services that will satisfy them. Sometimes this recognition comes from direct, personal experience with the goods. But often the marketer can instill purchase incentives in the minds of potential buyers. The more needs a given product or brand, service or retail outlet can serve effectively, the greater the buyers' incentives will be. But buyers do have to recognize the potential of the goods for need satisfaction or for goal attainment. In brief, this is a very conscious, deliberate process, not something that occurs below the level of awareness. So adroit marketers can literally teach consumers about what they'll get, both through promotion and through direct experience with the goods or services. Not only that, but the marketer can also teach potential buyers to recognize the needs themselves. In other words, incentives can be used to excite dormant needs and make them proactive, rather than merely reactive.

The Cost/Incentive Trade-Off

Buyers consciously evaluate incentives, deliberately studying what they will get and what they'll have to pay. In other words, they take a good, close look at the price/value relationship, seeking the greatest benefit at the least cost. So either a reduction in the cost or an increase in the value will result in exactly the same positive improvement in their motivation to buy. Those who can reduce the cost intensify the motives of potential buyers, but those who can increase perceived value achieve the same end without plunging themselves into direct price competition with rival firms.

> Nordstrom, Inc. department stores enjoyed a meteoric rise in sales over the decade from 1974 to 1984. With over three dozen stores in Alaska, California, Oregon, Utah, and Washington, Nordstrom's sales doubled to over $1 billion during the first half of the 1980s. Most of the gains came from expansion, and they're committed to even more growth in the near future. But that's not the whole story. Their average sales per square foot of selling space are about double that for such notorious retailers as Wanamakers in Philadelphia or Bergdorf Goodman in New York.
>
> Nordstrom's formula for success is based on a strategy of paying salespeople very well and promoting from within the company. In fact, except for the rare, special exception, *all* employees begin on the sales floor, and many elect to continue in that lucrative capacity. The result of this policy is service, service, and more service to customers.
>
> Although some retailers don't seem to be aware of it, retail stores don't sell products—they sell services! The "product" part of every sales dollar a store rings up goes to the manufacturer of the goods. The markup is the store's cut of the pie, and the retailers earn it by providing services. Compared to most other retailers, Nordstrom's takes a whopping markup. And compared to other department stores, Nordstrom's provides a commensurately whopping amount of service. Nordstrom buyers pay for what they get in services, and they get what they're paying for, and more. So they just keep on coming back.

The other side of the price/quality coin can be just as shiny, providing the retailer does it well. Deep-discount, members-only warehouse club stores run a dizzying volume of goods through their dismal, sparsely furnished stores. They employ a singular strategy: volume! And they depend on only one marketing weapon: rock-bottom prices. Their buyers don't get much at all in the way of retail services, if anything, nor do they expect them. On the other hand, markups are extremely low and product manufacturers take all but a very thin slice of the sales dollar pie. It works, just as the high-markup, high-service formula works, because consumers perceive a positive price/quality relationship. Since they neither receive services nor pay for them, their purchase incentives and patronage motives are favorable.

Working Both Sides of the Street

By now it should be pretty clear that some motives reside well below the level of awareness while others are conscious and direct. So which ones provide the most fertile soil for growing consumer demand for your product or service? Often the answer is *both!* In fact, good marketing will engender purchase motives above and below the surface, working in tandem. Of course, there are some situations where only conscious or only subconscious motives apply to the goods. But those cases are few and far between. For most goods, trying to appeal to only one type of motive is about as effective as trying to walk on only one foot.

FROM CAT'S PAW HEELS TO TIGER PAW TIRES

Marketers of very mundane products usually think the only relevant motives for buying their product are strictly the plain, ordinary, everyday, garden-variety conscious kind. But they're wrong. Every now and then, some enterprising promoter of a very common, utilitarian-type product finds a way to evoke images below the level of awareness and excite subconscious motives. Then they spring way out in front of the pack. After the fact, a good marketing idea looks like it was an obvious move—but *before* the fact, it wasn't so apparent. If it were so obvious, then why didn't somebody else do it much sooner?

It's hard to think of a product more basic and mundane than the heel of your shoe. How on God's good earth could such a lowly product as that evoke subconscious motives and desires? Not a chance! That's just what everybody thought, until Cat's Paw came along. But the brand name, together with a little, white-rubber disk imprinted with a cat's paw in the heel, evoke strong animal images in the minds of consumers. Sleekness, power, sure-footedness, grace—it's enough to make the wearer walk a little taller; to quicken the step to a more vigorous stride just at the thought of it. So one tiny symbol says more than hundreds of words of copy because the language of the subconscious mind is the language of symbols, not words; images, rather than logic.

Cat's Paw heels were around a long, long time before it occurred to anyone that the same motivational principle could be applied to a fairly parallel product, the humble automobile tire. Oh, it could be dressed up a little by putting a gleaming whitewall on it, but that was about the limit—or was it? Could a tire be a status symbol? Could it also evoke images of speed, power, and control? A slightly different product design, some raised white letters, and heavy promotion have sold a lot of tires on the basis of motives far more subliminal than conscious.

Who could forget Tony the Tiger? Animal images went from the highway to the breakfast table when Kellogg's introduced Tony to promote Frosted Flakes cereal. Tony became a media celebrity and ended up in a lot of children's cribs as a lovable stuffed animal. Tony the Tiger is over 25 years old now, but you might still notice him today in the window of a toy store—a testament to the creative genius behind that one. Appeals to subconscious motives aren't limited to animal images; they're only confined to the limits of creative imagination.

EVERYTHING I LIKE IS ILLEGAL, IMMORAL, OR FATTENING

For some consumer products, conscious motives go in one direction while subconscious motives go in another. If that's the situation, marketers have to be very careful not to evoke the negative motives at the same time they appeal to the positive desires. Creating a marketing program that will excite both positive and negative motives makes about as much sense as harnessing a team of horses with one animal facing in each direction. You can be fairly sure it won't go anyplace. Here's a glimpse of how three marketers of a product highly sensitive to subliminal repulsion—laxatives—each dealt with both conscious and subconscious purchase motives, in varying degrees.

> **Serutan was heavily promoted as a natural fiber product (the brand name is *natures*, spelled backwards). But it was also billed as a product for "people over forty," resulting in an *elderly* image for the product. Except for the drinking age, nobody wants to be reminded about reaching such benchmarks in life. So consumers had both a conscious, positive buying motive, *natural*, and a subconscious, negative one, *aging*.**

> **In the same product category, Metamucil approached the consumer market through the medical and health care community. While they also tout the brand as a natural-fiber product, the brand name, packaging, and distribution all evoke images of illness and medicine.**

> **The FiberAll brand of the same basic substance uses a name that indicates the nature of its contents, and also promotes the fact that it's free of sugar. The makers approached the consumer market directly, using TV spots with a natural, "almost food" theme while they carefully avoid symbols that might evoke negative subconscious images of either aging or illness.**

How to Unchain Motives and Desires

Most consumers—in fact, *all* consumers—have motives and desires that are shackled tightly by cultural and social norms and by their own self-images. If we could take a peek into the mind of a typical consumer we would be spectators to the granddaddy of all bowl games: Motives on the left, motives on the right. The liberal team in splashy-colored uniforms, leaping up and down and screaming *"Go for it! Go for it! Go for it!"* The conservative corps, standing proudly in rank and file, pin-striped suits over their bulletproof vests, with authoritative voices chanting in unison *"Hoooooold on! Hoooooold on!"* But the really bizarre fact about the whole game is that they're both the home team!

A good part of the art of marketing is to unchain favorable purchase motives, or at least somehow to persuade the potential buyer that these desires are actually worthy and legitimate. So consumer marketing isn't so much a job of instilling motives and desires as it is of opening up the ones that are already there, of freeing up strong, vital, but closely fettered urges and impulses. (Of course, any similarity between this description and a seduction is purely coincidental.)

How many people would pay a doctor to inject cow fat under their skin to get rid of wrinkles? The answer: Well in excess of a quarter of a million people, that's how many!

It sounds absolutely horrific, doesn't it? It's hard to think of a more difficult "sell" than Collagen Corporation was faced with in the beginning, over a decade ago. Yet with marketing strategy and execution we could describe only as brilliant, the marketing team at Collagen has pulled it off. And all indications are that they'll continue to succeed.

Initially the company was faced with a double-sell; both physicians and their patients had to be convinced. After clinical tests lasting for years, Collagen spent $3.5 million during the early 1980s to sell the medical profession on the product and teach them how to use Zyderm, a soft gel obtained from the hides of calves. Facing a group not prone to jump at innovations with purely cosmetic value and no therapeutic function, Collagen courted them with a very dignified, professional approach that largely (over 70 percent) succeeded.

The next step was even more challenging, and that was to generate consumer demand for a product that can only be administered by physicians, mostly dermatologists, plastic surgeons, and head-and-neck specialists, rather than general or family practitioners. A physician-to-patient sell-through of this sort was unprecedented.

With a profit margin of over 80 percent, consumer demand for Zyderm Collagen Treatments was absolutely critical. It was targeted to five groups: feminine status-seekers, mature women entering the work force, beauty specialists, public figures such as entertainers, and those scarred by acne (who number well over 10 million). With an advertising budget in the millions, Collagen used print media, turning first to slick magazines such as *Town &*

Country and *Vogue* to reach 35 to 54 year old women with incomes upward of $25,000. Later, they slid down a bit on the socioeconomic scale with such media as *Woman's Day* and *Ladies' Home Journal.*

But the key factor in the Collagen story is their ability to tickle the right motivational nerves among their affluent, well-educated target consumers. This, after all, is a fairly conservative lot. How do you get such people to go out and spend $300, $600, or more on their appearance when they don't even want to admit that they're aging and wrinkling by the minute in the first place?

Most consumers would think it was frivolous and self-indulgent to spend a few hundred dollars just to look a little younger. The last thing in the world Collagen wanted was a "look younger overnight" image. So the ads claimed the product "can smooth certain skin imperfections—not necessarily to make you look younger, but to look better." Defensiveness about age wrinkles was approached even more obliquely by turning their acquisition into something of a status symbol itself: With a classy photo of a lady's dressing table strewn with signs of activity, affluence, and success, the headline comments, "She's successful enough to have earned a few wrinkles and smart enough to know what to do about them." To really nail it down, the tag line reads, "Just because you've earned a few wrinkles doesn't mean you have to wear them."

ALWAYS GIVE THE BUYER AN ACCEPTABLE PURCHASE MOTIVE

A big, flashy car is an acceptable purchase because it's a good investment or because it's safer for the family. A body massage is an acceptable purchase if it's for health's sake. If a prestigious and expensive racket or country club membership will lead to business contacts, then it's acceptable. And if buying the frozen mocha tart is a well-earned reward for a responsible, hard-working woman, then it, too, is acceptable. Acceptable, as well, are the health club fees to work off the excess poundage from justifiable mocha tart rewards—providing that a trim appearance is necessary to a professional image.

You owe it to yourself. You deserve it. You need it. It's expected of you. In fact, it's required. There's a good sound reason for buying it. You need it because _____. Good consumer marketing will fill in that blank with an acceptable motive, regardless of the *real* one.

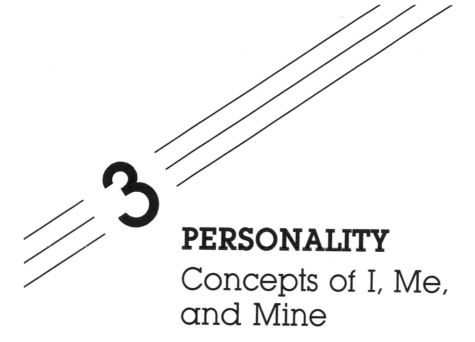

PERSONALITY

Concepts of I, Me, and Mine

Bill drives a sports car; Bob, a station wagon. Jane wears housedresses; Joan likes sexy clothes. John shaves with a Schick razor; Jim with a Norelco. Kevin plays tennis; Ken is a skier. Suzy loves to cook; Sally eats fast foods. Alice and Andy live in the suburbs; Ann and Art in a high-rise condo. Terri loves the opera; Trudy collects rock records. Rick smokes and drinks; Ray does neither.

The things people buy often reflect their personalities.

51

Personality consists of the entire package of durable values, habits, attitudes, and predispositions that consumers take with them from one life situation to the next. A normal individual's personality is internally consistent, even though it might not appear that way from the outside. It's also pretty durable; it ordinarily doesn't change a great deal over the months and years of a person's life. When we say we "know" someone, it's because we're familiar with that individual's personality traits or characteristics.

VALUES HELP DETERMINE PERSONALITY

Consumers' values are stable convictions about what is good and desirable. Learned early in life, values often endure for an entire lifetime. Values incorporate a lot of assumptions and conclusions about the goals one should pursue in life. They also suggest personal policies and strategies for reaching those goals and fulfilling important needs.

Consumer values reside in clusters, rather than in isolation from one another, and some are far more important than others. Psychologists sometimes refer to a person's "value system" or "value structure." That suggests a close relationship among different values, and it indicates that some values dominate over others. So even though we all share the same basic set of fundamental values, we share them in greater or lesser degrees. Different people put more emphasis on some values than others, and so they also have different goals, different strategies for reaching them, and different motives than those whose value system takes another shape. We'll take a look at six distinct types of central core values and describe the personality of a consumer who puts the greatest emphasis on each type of core value.

Economically Oriented Consumers

People who place the greatest emphasis on economic core values are pragmatists. They're most interested in what's useful and applicable. Often they're very practical people who appreciate and respect the accumulation of wealth and material goods very strongly. They're typically more interested in engineering and technology than in pure research, something intellectually oriented people would value more highly. They're likely to pursue luxury, rather than beauty, as aesthetically oriented people would. Materialists would usually rather compete with others in terms of accumulation of material goods than serve and support others, as socially oriented people do, or direct and control other people like politically oriented people.

In the marketplace, materialists respond well to the logical, practical approach. They're rarely very impulsive, so they really value a sound, well-organized program, rather than just a potpourri of things from which they can select. Here's how one firm appeals to these pragmatists:

> The headline of a black and white print ad for Merrill Lynch declares: "In case you don't have any plans for tomorrow." Listen to the first part of the copy follow-on:
>
>> "Sure, you have goals for tomorrow—a home, a European vacation, an investment portfolio. But goals without plans are dreams that don't come true." *The Catalog of Investments* from Merrill Lynch shows you how to achieve your goals by approaching your financial situation from an informed and organized point of view. Topics covered range from how to get started to managing your savings dollars to task-saving tactics. We've even included helpful cash flow and net worth worksheets.
>
> The approach is money oriented, but also practical, organized, and programmed for the materialistic consumer.

Intellectually Oriented Consumers

The consumer who places the greatest emphasis on intellectual values is keenly interested in knowledge and truth. These consumers are mostly concerned with observation, empiricism, and abstraction, rather than with aesthetic appreciation, as aesthetically oriented consumers are, or evaluation of utility, like the materialists we just described. Intellectual types are usually inclined toward rational and critical thinking. They try to identify the similarities and differences that distinguish objects or people from one another. They like to compare and contrast things, and they may use both analysis and synthesis to make judgments. Intellectual types show a strong preference for abstract ideas and concepts, over more concrete, tangible things. They usually respect rational, deductive conclusions more than intuitive forms of insight. These people like to soak up information and then make their own judgments.

> In one full-page print ad for Johnston and Murphy's shoes there are over 14 column inches of copy, with a photo of a pair of shoes and illustrations of a humidity gauge and a last for making shoes. With a play on words, the headline refers to "Johnston & Murphy's Law," defined by the copy as "What could go wrong— won't."
>
> The ad goes into detail, describing some of the 165 steps in making the shoes; explaining that there are 18 stitches to an inch; noting that "Stitching needles are a science"; and so forth, on and on: Insoles and outsoles. A special cork formulation. Overlap. "Skiving." The "mulling" room. Eight working days to this point. Ten steps to that.
>
> Johnston and Murphy's buyers aren't likely ever to make a pair of shoes, so they really don't need all that technical information. But intellectually oriented consumers value information for its own sake. The data may be a little much for other personality types, but not for intellectuals who want to do their own analysis and judgment.

Socially Oriented Consumers

Consumers who put the most emphasis on social values are motivated by their love of people. Affiliation and support are often viewed as the only acceptable way of relating to others and interacting with them. Socially oriented consumers don't much like contest or competition and they usually abhor direct conflict among people. Often altruistic and unselfish, consumers in this group are frequently characterized by empathy, kindness, and sympathy for others. They see other people as fundamentally and essentially good and worthy, in and of themselves, rather than for their behavior, position, or possessions. Cooperation among people is of primary importance and competition or efforts to exert influence have serious negative connotations for this personality type.

> "You're in good hands with Allstate." That slogan along with the logo of a pair of cupped hands say it all. People who value nurturance and social service couldn't help but respect a company that takes care of its people. Visions of claim agents rushing to the scene of a natural disaster to help the poor victims restore their lives are strongly appealing to most consumers, but especially to those for whom social values dominate. While they may not think it will ever happen to them, these vivid images exert a strong pull toward the company as *people* with whom these consumers would like to affiliate.

Aesthetically Oriented Consumers

People who emphasize aesthetic values seek out and focus on the harmony and grace of their perceptions and experiences. Whether they're actively creative and inventive or passively observant and appreciative, those who dearly value beauty are most often directed to the symmetry and form of the objects in their environment. They're likely to value and respect the artistic episodes and experiences of life and hold beauty and charm as more desirable than correctness and accuracy, as an intellectual would, or utility and potency, as would a pragmatic materialist. These consumers may also equate truth with beauty or confuse peak sensory experiences with the purely spiritual elevation of consciousness. They might enjoy and appreciate the pompous rituals of political or religious institutions, but at the same time denigrate any repressive or dogmatic aspects of such institutions.

> While the vast majority of cars are promoted to the buying public on the basis of speed, power, handling, technology, and similar appeals, the Lincoln-Mercury division of Ford has advanced in another direction—sheer beauty! They commissioned top designers (Givenchy, Bill Blass) to create special editions of the Continental and Mark VII, inside and out. Slick, two-page spreads in *Architectural Digest, Town & Country*, and other top-scale magazines picture the designers with their creations, describing the niceties of the interior and exterior design. Throughout the ads there is not a word about anything technical or mechanical. Color, texture, line, and form only. The entire appeal strategy rests on beauty and that alone.

Politically Oriented Consumers

Consumers who assign great importance to "political" values are oriented principally toward *power*. This doesn't apply only to the field of politics, itself, but to the general expression of power and influence in any occupation or profession, in personal life, and in the marketplace, as well. Oriented toward competition and struggle, leaders in many fields place their major emphasis on this core value. Highly competitive strivers, they appreciate the ability to influence, direct, and control the activities of others, though they may not be at all coercive or seek to dictate other's thoughts or beliefs. Power-oriented people tend to enjoy imposing their own will on situations. They'll often seek to persuade or convince others to adopt their views and opinions. To this group, status is defined by *position*, rather than by material wealth or the elegance of their possessions. Affluence and material goods are valued more to symbolize position than for their own sake.

> An elementary school classroom, every student but one, slouched, pensive child with hands raised high, anxious to respond. And the headline:

You've always had a lot of competition.
Now you can have an unfair advantage.

This promotional appeal for the Commodore Amiga in *Fortune* magazine isn't actually directed to parents to sell them a computer for their children. Instead it conjures up a few frightening memories of childhood inadequacy, if not outright failure. Subtle, but effective; especially for power-oriented consumers with an inclination to compete and a strong need to win. With an introduction that says "Nobody ever said it was going to be easy," and a tag line stating "Your competition is gaining on you. Is that fair?" this ad paints a picture of the world as an extremely competitive battleground. Then it hooks the product directly into the fight as a *weapon* with which to vanquish the enemy. Is it any wonder that power-oriented strivers would want it for their own personal defense department?

Spiritually Oriented Consumers

Consumers who mainly stress spiritual values are keenly interested in the religious or the philosophical aspects of life. They may be devoutly religious people, agnostics, or even atheists, but they focus on the mystical or spiritual aspects of life. Whether they're intensely involved in active participation or relatively withdrawn and reclusive, they focus on unity, symmetry, and fundamental causal forces in the universe as a whole. Such people feel they have a profound and *essential* relationship with others and with the world, rather than merely an interactive or juxtapositional posture. They usually display far more interest in the primary source of animation and the principal source of life's energy than in the inanimate or material objects in their environment.

Consumers' core values are in large measure culturally determined. We tend to value not only what our parents taught us to value, but also what our culture teaches us to value. People's values, in turn, influence the kinds of personalities they have. So some societies have a higher proportion of people of one personality type than others. For example, our society places a lot of value on individuality and not very much on obedience. By contrast, in the Japanese culture the emphasis is exactly reversed. Americans are more individualistic than Japanese consumers, while the Japanese have more authoritarian personalities in their society than we do.

In terms of the personality types based on core values that we just described, the most common consumer orientations are *economic* (possessions), *political* (power), and *social* (service). *Aesthetic* (beauty) and *intellectual* (knowledge) orientations are less prevalent among consumers, and *spiritual* (religious) orientations are by far the least common. Consequently, some types of marketing appeals are also used far more than others.

THE SOCIAL CHARACTER OF CONSUMERS

Some consumers are heavily dependent on the opinions and choices of other people when they make buying decisions. Others depend mostly on their own understanding of the world; their personal values and attitudes. This tendency to either look inside one's self or to look outward toward others is called *social character* by consumer psychologists, who refer to *inner-directed* and *other-directed* consumers. It's difficult to say just what proportion of the buying public takes each view, but there is some evidence that Americans are becoming more other-directed. If so, we could expect to find more inner-directed people among mature consumers, whereas younger buyers may include more other-directed people.

The social character of those in the target market should also have effects on the way that they respond to different promotional appeals. We expect people who are other-directed to be more sensitive to the attitudes and behavior of their peers. They require more information about the social acceptance and meaning of the product or service that's being promoted. By contrast, inner-directed people depend more on their own perceptions and judgments. Since they'll judge the product on its own attributes and merits, they need more technical information, data about the physical or chemical nature of what they're buying.

The typical buyers' social character also helps determine *who* should present the message or be presented in an advertisement. Showing the product in a social setting or using endorsements by famous people is more likely to win a favorable response by other-directed consumers. On the other hand, an inner-directed audience is more likely to be responsive to "hard data" presented by technical experts such as the man in the white clinic jacket or the well-recognized race car driver or athlete.

Table 2 lists several consumer products and services of various kinds, together with typical promotional appeals to inner-directed and other-directed consumers. Notice the difference in the amount of technical versus social information listed.

THE INTERPERSONAL STYLE OF CONSUMERS

Another way to view the personality of consumers in relation to their social environment was provided by psychologist Karen Horney. She suggested a typology that identifies three distinct *interpersonal styles* of behavior: those that go *with* the crowd, those that go *against* it, and those that go *away* from the crowd, identified as *compliant, aggressive,* and *detached,* respectively. As the following sketch indicates, those in each type have different attitudes about others and each exhibits a distinct pattern of behavior toward those around them. Because of the different meanings other people have for consumers of each interpersonal style, their reactions to social buying motives also differ significantly.

Compliant. Goes *with* the crowd; conventional and conformist; accepts social norms; sensitive to expectations of others; preference for cooperation over competition; trustful of others, avoids interpersonal conflict; values love, affiliation, and belonging.

Table 2. Appealing to Social Character

Product/ Service	Inner-Directed Appeal	Other-Directed Appeal
Automobile	A thrill to drive, handles beautifully, well-engineered, holds its value for resale.	A car you'll be proud to drive, an impressive machine that typifies your lifestyle.
Wine	Superior vintage, fine bouquet, bright, fresh taste.	Share it with your closest friends on special occasions.
Compact disk player	Excellent response across the entire sound spectrum, technically superior design, highly reliable.	Fills the room with delightful music to create an atmosphere of grace and charm.
Department store	Superb service, wide selection, comparable prices, very convenient location and hours.	The store that everyone's raving about, the talk of the town in the very best circles.
Mouthwash	Tastes good, kills germs, helps prevent colds.	So you never need to worry about offending someone close.
Fine restaurant	World-class chef, a five-star rating, ambience of an old-world country manor.	A delightful place to bring the boss for lunch *and* your companion for dinner.
Diamond ring	Judge by color, cut, clarity, carat weight; will appreciate in value, an excellent investment.	It's hard to tell if she'll be more astounded by your gift or her friends by her appearance.
Personal computer	IBM-compatible, 2MB memory, internal 10 MB hard disk, color monitor, RS-232 interface.	Communicate worldwide, create graphic color presentations, generate lovely music. Do it all!
Hair stylist	Wide selection of styles to fit your personality, professional, and social position.	Where you'll find the styles you've so often seen and admired on gracious ladies.

Aggressive. Goes *against* the crowd; unconventional and nonconformist; resists the expectations of others; preference for competition over cooperation; distrustful of others, unthreatened by controversy or social conflict; values power, status, and prestige.

Detached. Goes *away* from the crowd; antisocial and self-governed; ignores expectations of others; preference for independence over either competition or cooperation; skeptical of others, uninterested in social conflict; values solitude and isolation.

Sometimes the only thing more important for a marketer to know than what to do is what *not* to do! This is especially true for creating marketing appeals for those with different interpersonal styles. A common appeal such as "everybody has one" will be greeted hospitably by *compliant* types, but it will fall on deaf ears among consumers who are *detached*. But since *aggressive* people actively resist the expectations of others, a conformity appeal will often alienate them completely from the product.

Marketing appeals to status and prestige, filled with references to "winning," "coming out on top," and "showing them who you are," will simultaneously turn *aggressive* consumers on and *compliant* consumers off to the goods. The relatively small group of *detached* consumers will probably be indifferent to that appeal.

Our culture values individualism very highly, and so you might get the impression that appeals grounded in being different, or unique, or displaying individuality would win everyone's hearts. Not so—there's no middle ground here, either. While the *detached* consumer may respond well, those who are *aggressive* might ignore the appeal while *compliant* types are likely to be hostile toward it.

Some companies with products that must be marketed to all three groups at once find it necessary, or at least advantageous, to introduce two or three brands so that each can be marketed to buyers of different interpersonal styles. This is especially true for products with a masculine gender where the brand differentiation is more psychological than physical or chemical. Ordinarily this isn't the only reason for multiple branding. But by providing multiple brands of beer, men's cosmetics, sports and athletic equipment, or even automobiles, the appeal strategy for each brand can be tailored to buyers of one interpersonal style, as well as other important differences.

THE INTERACTION STYLE OF CONSUMERS

Social character and interpersonal style typify people based on their attitudes toward others: whether they judge by others or on their own, and whether they go with, against, or away from other people. We can also identify three different personality types based on their *interaction style*. Some people deal mainly in *emotions*, some with *actions*, and some in *possessions*. *Emotional* consumers focus primarily on people's *feeling*, while *technical* people are interested in what they're *doing*, and *material* consumers are basically concerned with *owning*.

Feeling Type. Concerned with emotions, focuses on the past, likes to see connections, values continuity. Evaluations are based on subjective interpretations of pleasure or discomfort, people are judged for their social contributions, goods are valued for their emotional meaning.

Doing Type. Concerned with actions, focuses on the future, likes to understand processes, values progress. Evaluations are based on the dynamics of how things run or work; people are judged by their activities or occupations; goods are valued for their technical sophistication.

Owning Types. Concerned with possessions, focuses on the present, likes to see distinctions, values diversity. Evaluations are based on comparisons of relative economic worth, people are judged by their wealth and property, goods are valued for their monetary or exchange value.

The interaction style of the prospect is very important in a personal selling encounter where the salesperson interacts with the potential buyer for more than just a brief moment. For instance,

those selling insurance, financial and investment services, cars, or homes often have a chance to get to know their customers to some degree. If they're sensitive to the recognition signals, the cues they get from the prospect, they can tailor their presentation to fit the interaction style of the potential customer.

RECOGNIZING EACH INTERACTION STYLE

Feeling Oriented. They display their moods and personal reactions more than others. They talk about how they feel about the deal and express their emotional reactions. They often take their time and they pay more attention to the salesperson's own personal reactions.

Doing Oriented. They talk about processes over time; about trading the stock, living in the house, or driving the car, as opposed to just owning such things or to what they mean. They often hurry things and talk much more than they listen, sometimes interrupting the salesperson.

Owning Oriented. They stock more closely to the dollars and cents issues, to what the goods are worth in a monetary sense. They're more interested in the physical condition of things than how they work or what they mean. They're slower to respond and they sit back and study.

SALES PRESENTATIONS TO EACH TYPE

The three types live in three different "worlds": emotions, actions, or possessions. So it's important for the salesperson to get into the same context as the prospect.

Let's take a look into the mind of a prospective buyer of each type, then suggest some responses from a salesperson who can empathize well with the potential buyer:

Buyer's Emotional World. I'm really excited about this. It's a tough decision for me. I'm worried about making the right choice. Will I feel secure with this insurance plan? I wonder how my kids will feel about this car. What kind of home do *you* live in? I know you really want to make this sale and I'd hate to disappoint you. Do you know how hard I worked to get to the point where I can afford this?

Empathic Sales Responses. You're going to love this! As soon as I saw it I knew it was perfect for you. I want you to go ahead with this. You'll definitely feel good about this choice. There's no doubt in my mind that you'll be very happy with it. I want you to know you're special and it's important to me to help you do the right thing. I know how you feel. I feel the same way about it as you do.

Buyer's Technical World. Give me a thumbnail sketch of this whole process. Let's get into it and get on with it. I don't have an awful lot of time. Are you sure this will work out the way you say it will? How much does the cash value grow? What kind of appreciation can I expect over time? How would the kids get from here to school? Where are you going from here? Will you call back?

Empathic Sales Responses. I took a run at this from three different directions. Here's how this whole plan works. You can appreciate what we've done for you here. This won't take very long. We can get this handled right now. Give me a hand here and just jump in if you have a question. This is a very functional home; a technically superior car. This plan has flexibility. It will grow and change as you progress.

Buyer's Material World. I'd really like to own this. It looks like it's really worth something. What's the cost? I know there's a way to get the price down. I do hope I can make a deal on this. I wonder what this will be worth in five years. This house is in excellent condition. Will I get good gas mileage? What will repairs cost? I'd sure like to know how much you get in commissions from this.

Empathic Sales Responses. This fits well with what you already own. You've acquired some good property. Add this to what you already have. You know your way around the business world. This is a valuable plan. Study this carefully and give me your own appraisal. Can you see its worth? It's a sound investment for you. You'll have pride of ownership for years. It's rare; there's really nothing exactly like this in the world.

Every buyer has some concern for the emotional, the technical, and the material aspects of the goods. But the salespeople who discover the *dominant* world of their prospects and talk in those terms are far more effective.

SPECIAL CONSUMER PERSONALITY TRAITS

The different ways to look at consumer personality described previously are only four among a multitude. There seem to be as many identifiable personality traits as there are psychologists to discover them. But among all these different traits and types, one fairly general configuration is especially useful to marketers, and particularly those who market innovative new products or services. These special traits have to do with *rigidity* and *control.*

Some people are very concerned with maintaining control—control over themselves, control over others, and control over the physical things that surround them. Others, by contrast, are willing to pretty much take things as they come, provided things don't get out of hand. This is what we might call the "general control syndrome." But to make things simpler, we'll create a couple of acronyms. People who need to have a lot of control are HiCon types and those who are more relaxed about controlling things are LoCon types.

The HiCon trait seems to affect just about everything the person does, at least to some degree. Society regards some aspects of HiCon behavior as positive, but other aspects of it are often viewed as negative. For example, HiCon people tend to be very neat and clean, well-organized, and frugal; all much valued by society. On the other hand, they're also likely to be rather closed-minded and dogmatic; things that society doesn't really appreciate. But this isn't a social commentary and we're not as concerned about what society thinks as we are with the way that HiCon and LoCon traits affect consumers in the marketplace.

Innovators and Laggards

Whenever some new product or service is introduced, it spreads through the market in stages ranging from initial acceptance by the innovators to final capitulation by the laggards.

Surely when some creative genius of his or her day invented
the wheel, a few brave souls jumped on it immediately, a lot of
people stood back to see how well it worked, and a few catego-
rically declared that it never would amount to anything. (And
when it did, they probably felt it adversely affected the
weather.)

HiCon types avoid risks and they're slow to innovate. They'll
stay with the tried-and-true product or service until the innovation has been well-tested and accepted by others. It's the Lo-
Con type who's willing to take a chance on a new product or
service.

> Yugo, a boxy little three-door hatchback sedan from you-know-
> where, made its debut on the American scene in 1985, selling for
> under $4,000. Less than 4000 cars had been delivered to the
> United States that year, while there were orders for twice that
> many waiting to be filled at year's end. By the end of the decade
> the company hopes to sell 200,000 cars a year in this market. It
> won't be easy!
>
> A car purchase is laden with perceived risk for the prospective
> buyer: functional risk (maybe it won't run well), monetary risk (it
> might depreciate rapidly), physical risk (it might not be safe),
> social risk (people might laugh at it), and psychological risk (buy-
> ers may feel remorse and regret). Yugoslavia doesn't enjoy a
> high-tech image in the minds of Americans; the car is small,
> plain, and costs about $1,000 less than it's closest price rival.
> Consumer doubts will be high and it will be a difficult sell.
>
> But the Yugo is in almost precisely the same predicament the
> VW Bug was in about twenty or so years earlier. And the man at
> the helm of the promotional campaign, Leonard Sirowitz, is also
> the fellow who did the trick with the Volkswagen Beetle, way
> back when.
>
> Now, as then, the chances hinge on the car's acceptance by the
> initial LoCon innovators. If the car is promoted and sold to those
> who can't afford anything more, it may well earn an image as an
> "inferior good" and it won't go very far in the United States. But
> if, like the VW, it's marketed to fairly affluent, innovative yup-

pies, it may thrive as a negative status symbol, an icon of under-consumption.

. . . And Now the Good News

HiCon consumers are the backbone of the market for anything related to cleaning or being clean: shampoo, floor wax, deodorant, hedge trimmers, razor blades, roach traps, laundry detergent, and air spray, to name just a few products. It's the same with services: a car wash, hair styling, dry cleaning, pet grooming, rental carpet cleaners, and that shoe shine at the airport, for example. It's not that everyone doesn't purchase such things, it's just that HiCon consumers are the really heavy users.

But HiCon types are also the quintessential organizers of things. So they buy everything from appointment books to shoe racks, trash compactors to drawer organizers. A real, dyed-in-the-wool HiCon type will buy anything matching, in pairs, or in a set. If they get into a "continuity program" at the supermarket, they'll return again and again, dutifully purchasing the item-of-the-week, whether it's children's encyclopedias, dinnerware, or whatever. You don't have to sell them a chess set, just sell them (or give them) one humble pawn, and you can be sure they'll purchase the rest—and the board, if it matches.

HiCon consumers even tend to match brands! So in that sense, they're brand loyal across products: they like to own major and countertop appliances of the same brand, his and hers cars of the same brands, and if they happen to buy one brand of pickles, they'll probably look for the same brand of olives, as well, even though it doesn't show when they're served. The pros and cons of family branding and brand extension may be arguable, but there's an indisputable advantage when it comes to HiCon consumers. For HiCon types, the "buy-words" are *neat, organized, clean, orderly, bright, sparkling, shiny, coordinated,* and *matching.*

Nobody has seen him on television or in a personal appearance in over a decade, yet in a poll, over 90 percent knew his name

and could describe him very well—that's the image of a real superstar! In fact, there are strong indications that he's better known than the current Vice President of the United States. So what do you think of his chances for a comeback, after all this time? We'd say excellent! Who is this celebrity? Why, Mr. Clean, of course. And he's the perfect—the *absolutely* perfect—HiCon icon.

Joking aside, Procter & Gamble has decided to return this popular figure to the nation's TV screens because of tremendous identification among the buying public. And why not? Procter & Gamble knows a lot about selling to HiCon buyers, the heaviest users of many of their product lines. And the attributes personified by Mr. Clean are precisely what HiCon buyers go for in a big way.

The figure of Mr. Clean is powerful, and he looks clean with the clean-shaven head and tight-fitting tee shirt. The single gold earing adds a tough of dash—images of pirates and adventure, maybe. He's mature, authoritative, and in control, yet soft spoken and nonthreatening. Even children find him fascinating. But most of all, he's on the HiCon type's side, because his first, last, and middle name is Clean!

The secret to using effectively what we know about consumer personality in marketing is often to determine the dominant personality traits or characteristics that are at the very *core* of the target market. As we saw, HiCon consumers are the heavy users of cleaning products, but they're rarely innovators. Nor do compliant types like appeals to individuality. So when a single product must be marketed to multiple personality types, it may be necessary to introduce multiple brands to serve those of conflicting traits.

4

PERCEPTION
What You See Is
What You Taste

For many years, Miller High Life, the "Champagne of Bottled Beer," was perceived as *lighter* tasting than others. It's no coincidence that it was bottled in clear glass while the others were in deep amber bottles. Today, lighter, low-calorie beers seem watery to many because they *know* they're lighter. To avoid that image, brewers might compensate by tinting their light beer a deeper color.

Consumers often "taste" with their eyes and ears!

Consumers' *perceptions* are what really counts! There's a cardinal rule about choices in the marketplace that marketers often find difficult to accept:

> **The physical properties of the goods are important only to the degree that they affect consumers' PERCEPTIONS!**

Consumers learn far more from words and images than from sensations. Their perceptual acuity isn't nearly as sensitive as marketers usually think it is.

THE CONSUMER INFORMATION PROCESS

Perception is actually just one step in the entire process by which people become informed about alternative consumer goods. It's a very important step, to be sure, but it has to be considered in context with the process. (See Figure 1.)

The consumer information process starts when the consumers selectively *expose* themselves to some source of stimulation. Watching television, going to the supermarket, and driving past a particular billboard are all examples. In order to start the process, marketers either have to *attract* the consumer to the source or else put the source squarely in the path of the people in the target market. This involves selection of the most effective advertising media and/or distribution outlets, those that will reach consumers in the target market.

The second step involves some form of energy to stimulate the senses: light, sound, pressure, or chemicals that are inhaled or ingested. If the energy reaching the eyes, ears, skin, nose, or mouth of the receiver is in the right form and within the right range of intensity, then it creates *stimulation,* the second step in the process.

Marketers don't have direct control over any of the steps that follow in the consumer information process. The only things they can control are media for transmitting the messages and the characteristics of the stimuli themselves. But the stimuli

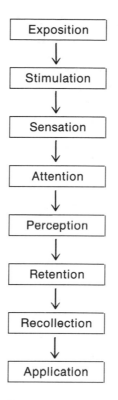

Figure 1. Steps in the consumer information process.

can be adjusted and modified so they affect consumers in different ways. Manipulating the stimuli to which prospective buyers
will be exposed indirectly controls what the person will experience and what will result during later steps in the consumer
information process. To do that effectively, marketers have to
understand something about the way the stimuli are processed
at later phases. If we know how certain stimuli affect the later
steps in the process, there's a chance that we can get the message all the way through in the form we want it to take.

> Take a quick look at the jacket or cover of this book. If you
> bought it off the rack, would you have noticed it or looked
> through it if it were black with plain white lettering? What if it
> were purple and chartreuse with pink polka dots and orange

lettering? In fact, you probably wouldn't be reading this, even if someone gave the book to you, if it were three inches wide and eighteen inches tall, printed in very tiny type! But the book is designed to create pleasant sensations, get your attention, make it easy to perceive what you read, store some information, recall it when you need it, and apply it to your work. The only way the book designer could do any of that was by manipulating the stimuli that would emanate from the book.

The third step in the train of events when consumers process information is *sensation*. The sensory organs transform the signals into electrochemical impulses the nervous system can transmit to the brain. These impulses last for only an instant, while the central nervous system transmits the signals to the brain and initiates perceptual processing. This storage of information is called "sensory memory" and it lasts for only a brief fraction of a second, until the brain itself begins processing.

If the information received by the brain makes sense to the person, it constitutes an *attention* signal and results in what psychologists call an "orientation response." It's at this fourth step that the person may orient toward the source of the stimulation. That's what happens when a colorful package catches the eye of a passing shopper in the supermarket or drugstore. It's the same if a spot announcement captures the attention of a radio listener or television viewer. This is a very important step in the process because if attention doesn't result, the rest of the message will be lost. Since it's so important, we'll consider attention more closely a little later.

Step five of the consumer information process is *perception*. It's a very elaborate process that involves classifying the incoming signals into meaningful categories, forming patterns, and assigning names or images. For example, the sight of a four-legged animal and the sound of a bark while watching a TV commercial get translated into the dog category in the viewer's mind. In the meantime, a lot of other stimuli are ignored or cast aside, while the viewer focuses on the animal for a brief moment. And the conversion of the sights and sounds into words and images is far from perfect. The end result of the perceptual process is only a crude representation of the pattern of stimuli that come into the senses. The images that result are highly *personalized;* they differ from one person to the next and from one moment to the next. Later we'll examine some of the most common and prevalent forms of perceptual distortion.

The sixth step of the information process is *retention,* the point at which the images are stored for later reference. Some of the data will be dropped rather than retained. What is retained goes into *short-term* memory, kind of a temporary stopping place or holding room for information. For example, a television viewer might mentally note an "800" telephone number she saw and heard just long enough to call and inquire or order the merchandise. Some information that's put into short-term memory will eventually be transferred, so to speak, into long-term memory. It can then be evoked at a much later time. For instance, the pictures and facts about a new model of automobile might be retained for several months, until the prospective buyer gets around to visiting a dealer's showroom for a test drive.

Rote retention of a series of unrelated things is facilitated by repetition. By repeating the telephone number many times, radio listeners or television viewers are encouraged to continue the repetition at least until they jot down the number or make the call.

Memory is also assisted by using two or more kinds of stimuli. Simultaneous multiple stimulation of both hearing and vision is perhaps TV's greatest advantage over radio (only audible) or print media (only visible). Recent technical developments now allow perfume and cologne marketers to impregnate magazine ad inserts with the scent of their product. The verbal description, illustration, and scented paper work together to provide multiple stimulation.

Another important factor for short-term retention is *chunking.* A series of letters or numbers can be retained more easily and accurately if they're presented in chunks. For instance, it's diffi-

cult to retain, or even to read a telephone number listed as
8005557924. But by chunking the number as 800-555-7924, it's
more easily retained.

The seventh step in the process is *recollection*. At some point
after the information was stored, the consumer may recall the
facts and images, bringing them to the conscious mind. This is
analogous to retrieval of information from a computer information system. Recall is easy if the information has been stored in
a systematic way. If it were stored in a specific place, so to
speak, the person has access to the information by mentally
going to the correct internal location. There's an "address" that
facilitates recollection. That's why it's easier for people to recall
information if they're prompted by some hints or cues. For instance, people will *recognize* many more brand names for a
particular product category if the brands are listed for them than
they will recall if merely asked to list all of them they can
remember. With the suggestion, they can mentally look inward
to see if the information resides there. Without the helpful cue,
they would have to sort through a much larger storage area, to
use a physical parallel.

The eighth and final step of the information process is actual
application of the information. Assuming that everything went
reasonably well during all of the earlier stages, the consumer
can bring the relevant information about a product or service,
brand or store to mind when it's needed to solve some problem
or meet some need. But even after fetching the data, the consumer need not necessarily *act* on it. In other words, only a
portion of everything consumers learn about the goods in the
marketplace is ever really applied, resulting in a purchase.

SELECTIVE BARRIERS TO COMMUNICATION

The ghost of Dr. Murphy (Murphy's Law) can and does visit
itself on every and any phase of consumer information processing. Often only a small fraction of what the marketer had origi-

nally intended when communicating with consumers actually takes place. We'll take a brief look at the *selective* barriers that disrupt the processing of information.

SELECTIVE EXPOSURE

Only a part of the audience for any message from marketers to consumers will be exposed to the medium used. Any one ad medium will reach a part of the target market. The same holds true for the messages contained on packages and at the point of sale of the goods. So marketers have to strive hard to select the best media, timing, placement, and the like, to reach as many of their intended audience as possible within the constraints on the promotion and distribution budgets. High repetition rates also help get exposure to a large part of the market.

SELECTIVE ATTENTION

Before presenting the substance of the message, the marketer first has to get the attention of the audience (and to hold it, as well). But the consumer's world is chock full of different stimuli, all screaming for attention. So among the cacophony of sights and sounds, the marketer has, somehow, to rise above the maddening din. Now that's no easy task, and often a very large proportion of the space in a print ad or the time in a broadcast announcement is used merely for one purpose: to gain the attention of the reader, listener, or viewer.

SELECTIVE PERCEPTION

As we'll shortly see, perception is a highly individualized process. People hear what they want to hear, see what they expect to see, and perceive what they need to perceive. When data are input to a computer, the internal representations are virtually always precisely what's entered. Human perception is far more complex. A computer is extremely literal, but humans can tolerate a great deal of ambiguity when perceiving the inputs to their senses. On the other hand, the internal representations that result are only *approximations* of what comes in.

SELECTIVE RETENTION

A large part of what the brain processes is lost after only an instant. A split second later, there's no trace of the signal, figuratively or literally. Actually, much more is stored than people think, but nonetheless, much is also lost—discarded after the original impulse. Nor is this a conscious process. Even when we try very hard to retain some information, a lot of it escapes our efforts to save it.

SELECTIVE RECOLLECTION

People actually recall only a small fraction of all the words and images that find their way to short-term or long-term memory. For example, what are your reactions when you see an old movie on TV that you've seen before, perhaps several times? You probably remember certain scenes very well, others are only a little familiar, and most you can't even recall. They may not have been retained, but many were saved in memory, only to be lost as time passed.

SELECTIVE APPLICATION

Consumers don't have to act on what they can recall. Instead of diligently applying what they've learned, they simply choose to ignore the recollection. For instance, they may have been exposed to an ad, learned about the positive attributes of some brand, and believed it. Yet they may choose to go with another brand, simply because they feel it's superior or for any one of a myriad of other reasons.

All of these selective factors may appear to present a pretty dismal picture for marketers striving hard to communicate successfully with consumers in their target market. Yet people's ability to comprehend information is nothing less than astounding. The average consumer can recall several thousand brand names, learned over many years' time. If the typical consumer were to write out everything he or she had learned about the goods in the consumer marketplace, the report would probably take up half a library. And most of the information would have been gained from messages from marketers.

FIVE SENSATIONAL OPERATIONS

Each of the five senses has its own unique characteristics. Sight and sound are admittedly most important to marketers, but touch, taste, and smell are often drastically underrated. In fact, while anyone would recognize a reference to the *visual* or *auditory* senses, few would even know what the *tactile, gustatory,* or *olfactory* senses are, let alone how they work.

Vision and the Camera of the Mind

The human eye and the visual system as a whole are marvels of complexity and capability. Unlike most other animals, humans can visually perceive stationary objects clearly. So the eye captures not only images, but the printed word as well. Sighted, literate humans probably gain more information from their eyes than from any of the other senses. The images captured by the eye are distinguished by the intensity of the light, by the color or hue, and by the shade or tint, from pastel to solid. But aside from mere recognition of colors, the various hues and tints also have strong, subconscious psychological affects on people. So marketers are well advised to consider carefully the affects the colors they use will have on the consumers of their products and services.

> Can a $500 million operation go wrong? You better believe it. Just about everybody stumbles now and then, and this time it was General Foods Post cereal division. Over 15 years ago Post created Pebbles, a cereal associated with the Flintstone TV cartoon show, which was popular at the time. The cereal was a roaring success and outlasted the television show by many years.

In the early 1980s, Post noted the rapid rise to fame of the humble Smurfs—little, blue, fuzzy television characters. Thinking along the same lines, Post introduced another brand associated with the popular TV show: Smurfberry Crunch. But rather than sailing like a Pebble, the new product proved to have all the buoyancy of a concrete zeppelin. When David Hurwitt, the man who runs GF's Post operation, was asked why the cereal didn't succeed, his terse reply was simply "It was blue."

Auditioning the World Around Them

One of the most distinctive features of the ears and hearing mechanism is that they can't readily be turned off. The eyes, and to a lesser degree the other senses, can be pretty thoroughly cut off from sources of stimulation. But during every waking moment, and to some degree even during sleep, the ear continues to capture sounds and the brain continues to process them. Sensitive to intensity or volume, to pitch or tone, and to purity or density of audible signals, the ear conveys meaning to listeners at both the conscious and the subliminal levels of awareness. So sounds often have meaning to consumers far beyond the obvious interpretation of audible words and music. Jingles and melodies associated with products are often far more memorable than merely a verse or slogan. But aside from the sounds presented in audible advertising, the sounds present at the point of purchase and sounds emitting from the product when handled or used also convey meaning to consumers.

The sound of a car door closing has long been thought to indicate the quality of construction of the vehicle to prospective buyers: A "tinny" sound indicating poor quality and a quiet, whispered "thud" suggesting strong, durable construction. So car makers work hard to insulate the doors and seals to attenuate unnecessary reverberation.

Noise within the moving vehicle is also a sign of the quality of the machine. Capitalizing on this, celebrated ad man David Ogilvy created one of his most legendary ads: "At 60 miles an hour the loudest noise in this new Rolls-Royce comes from the electric clock." To which one of the manufacturer's engineers is reputed to have commented, "We've just got to do something about that bloody clock!"

A Touching Experience for Consumers

Humans probably learn more from their tactile sense than do any other animals. Our hands and skin are exceedingly sensitive to pressure, texture, and temperature. One of American retailers' most significant contributions to world marketing was the creation of stores and displays that allow consumers to touch and handle the merchandise freely before they bought it. Shoppers have an extremely strong tendency to touch and handle goods even when there's no obvious meaning to be gained. If you've ever walked through a china shop with a small child in tow you've had a graphic and probably unforgettable demonstration of that urge to touch. But it doesn't disappear with maturity. Why car buyers have a compulsion to kick the tires remains an inexplicable mystery.

> How can you convince shoppers that your brand is softer and more pleasant to the touch than others? Well, obviously you can tell them, or better yet, package it in a soft wrapping so they can feel it. But that won't do it because everybody else does the same thing. Enter Mr. Whipple, the friendly corner grocer, and Procter & Gamble's now familiar slogan: "Please Don't Squeeze the Charmin." It's absolutely amazing how a brilliant idea seems so patently obvious—after the fact. After all, it's so basic, isn't it? Yet "back to basics" may be a movement with more promise for marketers than for educators.
>
> Touch has a certain suggestion of intimacy, especially for the American consumer. That's why squeezing a package of toilet tissue hints, just a little, of indecency. And that's also why Mr. Whipple and the others presented in Charmin ads are as harmless and unthreatening as they could possibly be. But the intimate suggestion associated with touch can also be the basis for a conscious appeal such as the slogan "The skin you love to

touch." At a more subtle level, the Pillsbury Doughboy's "Squeeze Me" theme also provides a bland but provocative suggestion.

The Consumers' Uncultivated Taste

Gustatory sensations are created in the mouth, where both the flavor and the consistency of solids and liquids are gauged. Just as there are only three primary colors but an infinite variety of combinations, so, too, with flavor. The primary sensations are *sweet, sour, bitter,* and *salty.* But between the combinations of these four basic flavors and those of different consistencies, the conceivable pallet of tastes is indeed vast. But in fact, the consumer's sense of taste is greatly overrated. Research consistently demonstrates that people taste more with their eyes than their mouths.

Almost everybody has a favorite brand of each of the beverages they drink: liquor, beer, soft drinks, coffee, tea, and so on. And they'll defend it vehemently, insisting that their preferences are based on their perceptions of the differences in flavor. *Nonsense!* Remove the labels and rarely, if ever, can they identify their favorite brand, or even distinguish which of several pairs of unlabeled drinks are the same substance and which are different brands. In fact, if ginger ale is colored as darkly as a cola, about a third of the people who try it along with unlabeled cola drinks fail to recognize that it's not a cola beverage, let alone tell what soft drink it really is.

Manufacturers and marketers of beverages and a wide variety of solid foods often spend vast sums of money to make subtle improvements in the taste of the product. In the vast majority of cases, those funds could better be invested in *promotion* to "improve the taste."

The now famous experience of Coca-Cola has been widely misinterpreted by both critics and proponents of the change in formula for that beverage. Coca-Cola Classic, the old formula, was outselling the new by about two to one within a year after the change. But wait: *The mistake was not in changing the for-*

mula—it was in PUBLICIZING it! Unfortunately, the owners of
the most famous brand name in the history of the world failed to
appreciate the insensitivity of gustation and the hypersensitivity
of the consumer to verbal declarations about a new flavor for an
old favorite.

A Consumer's Nose in Your Business

Much of what people think is gustation, their sense of taste, is
actually olfaction, their perception of aroma. When people
come down with a common cold, they often proclaim that their
food doesn't taste right. But colds don't inhibit the taste buds in
the mouth; they just congest the passages in the nose. So what
they miss about their food is the smell of it, not the flavor.
Compared to most other mammals, humans have a very crude
sense of smell. While a dog can distinguish thousands of different odors and uses the nose more than the eyes for many close
encounters, humans are relatively insensitive to different va-
pors and aromas in the environment. On the other hand, consumers' perceptions of odor have only a small conscious meaning compared to the subliminal affects of scent. Another rather
peculiar characteristic of the nose, compared to the other
senses, is the fact that it's far more prone to *revulsion* than to
attraction—a fact that the marketers of deodorants have capitalized on to maximum effect. So why have they been so blatantly
successful, compared to those who market perfume and cologne? It appears that our sense of smell has developed almost a
protective specialization, to repel us from potentially poisonous
or infectious substances, rather than attract us to desirable contacts.

A local food store chain initially thrived by offering a wide variety of fresh produce and "healthy" foods of other sorts, rather
than the sterotypical fare of strident health food advocates. They
carried only about 5000 items—about a third the selection of a
supermarket—but they offered significantly more in both selection and selling space than a typical convenience store. They
enjoyed a brisk trade among both young shoppers looking for a

more healthy diet and the elderly patrons who appreciated the wide array of fresh produce and the less routinized, mechanical modes of displaying the merchandise. We, too, frequented the store.

Then one day as we entered, we immediately perceived an odorous difference: the store had begun to handle fresh fish. Uninitiated in the ritual necessity of perpetually wiping down any surfaces the fish touched with an acidic wash, their store soon took on the olfactory ambience of a fishing schooner in dry dock. But the managers and staff were completely unaware of the repulsive odor because they were constantly in that environment and quickly habituated to the fishy scent. They literally drove their customers away, and are perhaps to this very day wondering why they suddenly failed after such original promise.

By contrast to this dramatic example of the repulsive potential of odor, such attractively aromatic things as in-store bakeries and barbecues need not necessarily pay their own way in sales. The subconscious effects of the pleasant aroma tends to intensify people's appetites and encourage impulse purchases of many food products quite aside from the actual source of the scent.

PERSISTENT PERCEPTUAL PROCLIVITIES

There are several perceptual biases that cut across the senses. They cause what's perceived to differ from what's presented in the stimuli themselves. We'll take a brief look at those most relevant to marketers.

CONTRAST, FIGURE, AND BACKGROUND

With visual stimuli such as an illustration of a product in an ad, the main element of focus is the figure, set on a background referred to as the field. The greater the contrast between the figure and field, the more likely the eye will move to and concentrate on the figure. The same holds true for the other senses as well. So when there are words-over-music, the words should be distinctive enough to gain the attention of the listener. The musical field merely sets the mood and enhances the glitter of the words, just as a setting enhances the gemstone it holds. It's often desirable, if not absolutely necessary, to devise a package for consumer goods to contrast with the competitive products close by.

ORGANIZATON AND GROUPING

Things that are in close proximity to one another or that share readily perceptible characteristics are usually grouped together in the consumer's mind. Such things are seen as "belonging" together and they're put into the same classification. So products in close proximity to one another on the store shelf are all viewed as belonging to the same general class of merchandise. An inexpensive item among more expensive goods will take on additional value in people's minds; an expensive product among cheap goods loses perceived value. Sometimes consumers will *impose* organization on a chaotic assembly of stimuli. In other words, they'll assign some commonality to obtain a more orderly picture.

IMPOSITION OF CLOSURE

Consumers don't wait for the other perceptual shoe to drop—they'll usually drop it for you. It's difficult to hear a "Bump ba-ba-bump bump" without adding the last couple of "bumps." Those who recall when cigarettes were still advertised on broadcast media may remember that Salem ads ended with the slogan in jingle form: "You can take Salem out of the country, but . . . ." Invariably the listener's mind would finish the jingle: ". . . you can't take the country out of Salem." Marketers sometimes use this tendency to seek closure to get the attention and the involvement of their _____ .

INTERMITTENCY AND ATTENTION

A dynamic stimulus will gain people's attention much more readily than constant ones. A moving figure on a point-of-sale display, a blinking light, or a sound that varies in pitch are great attention getters. That's why emergency vehicles use varying sirens and warbling horns, rather than constant tones. But while such devices get attention, it's also difficult to study or concentrate on them. It's not easy to read a moving page, or even the moving credits at the end of a TV show. So that which consumers are to attend continuously should be stationary.

CONSTANCY AND HABITUATION

Our senses quickly become accustomed to constant stimuli—they habituate to them. At that point, stimulation and perception are lost. Only when there's a shift in the stimuli will the perceiver again experience it. Even though it's there, few will hear the noise of ventilators in the building because it's constant. People become "blind" to the noise until it suddenly stops; then everybody wonders what happened to get their attention. Similarly with scents: Women often put on perfume again and again when they wouldn't need to do so, mostly because they've habituated to the scent and don't think it's there. Meanwhile everyone's eyes water at the strength of the aroma.

EXPECTANCY AND MENTAL SET

Consumers see what they expect to see, hear what they expect to hear, taste what they expect to taste, perceive what they expect to perceive. If their learning or initial experience was extremely positive, they're likely to continue perceiving the goods very favorably, despite minor deteriorations in quality. That's the "halo effect," but it also works in reverse: One bad experience may jaundice their perspective even when the following episodes are positive. Once people have adopted a particular mental set, they're likely to continue in that frame of mind with subsequent exposure to the same set of cues. Perceptual primacy effects of this kind highlight the old axiom: First impressions are what counts!

PERSPECTIVE AND FRAME OF REFERENCE

We usually adopt a particular standard or frame of reference that affects our perceptions on later occasions, where we adopt the same perspective. For example, how much does a loaf of bread or a pound of butter cost? Once shoppers have an idea of the price, they'll ordinarily assume that's what it *should* cost. If it's a few cents more, they'll *assimilate* the price toward their standard. But if it deviates too far from their benchmark price, they'll perceive the difference and make a distinction; they'll recognize a shift or change and react. The same applies to brand names, store price levels, product composition, and service quality. So if such marketing variables are to be changed, it's advisable to change them just a little at a time and allow a sufficient amount of time to pass before the next change, to let them adopt each step as their new standard.

NEED AND PERCEPTUAL VIGILANCE

When consumers are in a high-need state—very hungry, thirsty, tired, ill, and the like—their perceptual merchanism becomes more sensitive to things that will meet their needs. Perhaps you've skipped breakfast and missed lunch, then driven down a street you've traveled many times before. Since you were starved, you may have noticed dozens of restaurants and grocery stores you never noticed before. Your ravenous hunger made you perceptually vigilant. Usually food ads also get much more notice when they're broadcast *before* mealtime than when they're scheduled shortly afterward. Similarly, motel signs are noticed more when they're located well into or toward the end of a long, desolate stretch of freeway than just after the traffic has passed through a populated area.

THREAT AND PERCEPTUAL DEFENSE

People will often block out or distort their perceptions of stimuli that are *psychologically* threatening. (They pay *more* attention to physically threatening things—that's for survival.) When an ad or even the product or service itself is threatening, people usually don't want to deal with it perceptually. The two categories that are most likely to be threatening are things that involve *sexuality* and *morbidity*. There is also some repulsion or threat associated with what the society regards as dirty or unclean, with things that are bloody or with internal organs, and with some snakes, rodents, and crawling bugs such as roaches, ticks, and lice. But the principal threats are sexual or morbid, so those who promote products or services such as tampons or contraceptive devices, funeral services, care for the terminally ill, charity for destitute, starving victims, and the like, must be careful to avoid presenting highly graphic or descriptive stimuli, lest the audience misperceive or block out the message.

EMOTIONAL EFFECTS OF STIMULI

What's perceived often has emotional overtones, conveying certain feelings that may be well below the awareness level. High complexity and/or variation are "busy" and agitating. Curved and smooth shapes are feminine, comforting, and relaxing; sharp angles and rough surfaces are more masculine and exciting. Loud sounds, especially if they're sudden and close, are alarming and will startle or shock people. They may create rage as almost a reflexive reaction. Low intensities such as "soft" music are relaxing: Muzak and similar sounds sometimes serve as "white" noise, soothing the nerves and masking other sounds. Nature's sights, sounds, and aromas are more pleasing and tranquilizing than are artificial stimuli. "Hot" spices and strong flavors tend to exhilarate the taster while bland food and drink are more restful. Bright red, orange, and yellow colors are "hot" colors and intensify activity. Quick-serve restaurants use them to move people through the dining room more rapidly, for more sales. Bars and cocktail lounges use deeper, softer, "earthy" color tones to encourage patrons to relax, stay put, and drink, for more sales. These are only a few of the emotional effects stimuli are known to have on consumers.

JUDGMENTAL EFFECTS ON STIMULI

What consumers perceive has a strong effect on their judgments and assessments, just as it does on their emotions. For example, dark-colored containers are perceived as both heavier and smaller in size than light-colored packages of the same size and weight. Goods of metallic color are judged to be stronger than the same products in a pastel hue. As noted earlier, blue food is suspect, and may be judged as less palatable than another color. A large male announcer with a deep voice is perceived as more credible and authoritative than a small female announcer with a high voice. She'll often seem to be childlike. The list is infinite, but there is one principle that seems to underlie these perceptual effects: Consumers tend to generalize from one set of stimuli to another. If the object in question shares *some* of the characteristics of another object (or person), they assign the attributes of the second to the first. Small women with high voices share some characteristics with children, who aren't authoritative, so they see *her* the way they see a child. There aren't many edible blue foods in nature, so "blueness" is judged to indicate a nonfood, distasteful at best.

MARKETERS' PERCEPTION OF PERCEPTION

Consumer *misperceptions* can be as lethal as a razor's edge; you can cut your own throat and not even know it until you try to drink your orange juice! But perception is also a complex subject that even consumer psychologists only partially understand. Marketers don't have to know all the details, but it's also a mistake to ignore the whole area. We'd like to suggest three simple steps along a more practical middle way.

First, know the basics and recognize that there's often a big difference between what you intend your consumers to perceive and what they actually do perceive. When you're creating or changing the marketing program, focus on consumer perception; on how it will look in the eyes of consumers. That way you won't miss any remarkable opportunities and at least you'll know when you're in trouble.

Second, don't be afraid to get help when you need it. When production managers have some problem or need some assistance, they usually don't hesitate to go out and get expert help from good, reliable engineers or physical scientists. But when marketing executives are in the a same boat, they only rarely seek out a consumer psychologist or other behavioral scientist to lend a hand. They should.

Third, check it out! There are two kinds of marketing research to check consumer perceptions. One is specialized, measuring the details of the *process* of perception such as eye flow or pupil dilation. The other type of research measures the *results* of consumer perception. It provides *image profiles* that indicate the pictures consumers hold in their mind's eye. We'll talk more about images in a later chapter.

Finally, never forget the basic axiom we noted at the start:

>   *The physical properties of the goods are important only to the degree that they affect consumers' PERCEPTIONS!*

5

LEARNING
Painless Injections
of Information

Before his wife put the ham into the oven to bake, she cut about two inches from the small end and set it aside. He asked what it was for, and she said that's the way it's always done. Months later he received exactly the same answer from his mother-in-law when he saw her do it, too. A year later, in the kitchen of his wife's maternal grandmother, he observed the same thing and asked the same question. "I have to," the old lady said, "otherwise it won't fit into the biggest roasting pan I have."

Consumers often learn to do things, not knowing why!

In today's highly complex and sophisticated marketplace, consumers don't know how to function—what to buy and what not to—until they've *learned* to relate products and brands, stores and services to their various needs. Product preferences, brand loyalty, patronage habits, even the criteria for evaluating goods: They're all end products of one or more of the consumer's learning processes.

LEARNING ABOUT LEARNING

The mention of learning conjures up images of a school classroom, but certainly not all learning occurs in school (and some suspect that none of it does). Since people often associate attempts at learning with formal education, they also tend to think of it as a conscious, deliberate, tedious, and often painful process. People may or may not take delight in learning to be consumers, but they rarely find it uncomfortable or painful. In fact, learning is typically an unconscious activity; consumers don't usually even know when it's happening. But it does happen, starting early in life and continuing throughout.

If consumers are students of the marketplace, then marketers are their teachers. But any instructor would tell you that it's difficult to be an effective teacher if you don't know anything about how your pupils learn. Without an understanding of the learning process, a teacher is stuck with the trial-and-error method. And you know full well how expensive and time-consuming trial-and-error can be in marketing. So it's the marketers' responsibility to teach consumers to accept and use their goods. Actually that's exactly what marketers do, although usually consumers are unaware of it. Consumers usually think they're doing it all by themselves, and it's a good thing they do, because they often share Winston Churchill's view: "I am always ready to learn, although I do not always like being taught."

The consumer learning process takes on several different forms, depending on the individual, the situation, and what's to be learned. We'll take a good look here at the most important kinds of learning for consumers: *association, conditioning, modeling,* and *reasoning.*

ASSOCIATING THE GOODS WITH NEEDS

One of the most common ways of learning is simply associating one thing with another. This kind of learning is based on *proximity* in time or space between the two things. And the more closely to one another they're presented, the more likely consumers will learn the association. But we don't automatically associate one thing with another simply because we've seen or heard them together on one or two occasions. So another key to this type of learning is *repetition.* The more often the pair appear together, the more people will learn to associate them with one another. Finally, learning the association between two things depends on the *consistency* of the pairing. If the two almost always appear in conjunction with one another, consumers more strongly associate the two. But if one or the other, or both, are often found in isolation or paired with something else, that weakens the association between them in the minds of consumers.

The Kinds of Associations

The associations marketers are most eager to teach consumers are those between some kind of consumer goods, some brand or product, service or retail outlet, on the one hand, and some category of consumer needs, on the other. For instance, Procter & Gamble strives to teach consumers to associate Tide detergent with laundry and the need for clean clothes. Beginning over forty years ago with sponsorship of daytime radio soap operas such as Ma Perkins, Procter & Gamble drummed at the association between Tide and laundry. That's a lot of repetitions. But Lever Bros. with Rinso was with them most of the way, so the consistency has been less than perfect.

The Kinds of Goods

Associative learning sometimes applies to major product purchases, items such as appliances or cars. But it's most effective for small, consumable items such as snack foods, toothpaste, or flashlight batteries. Retail stores and frequently purchased services also teach consumers to associate their services with specific consumer needs. This means of learning is greatly assisted, if not completely dependent on, heavy promotion. Since it's based on repetition, saturation advertising with a dense schedule of many very brief ads is more effective than a more sparse schedule with protracted copy content. Because proximity and consistency of pairing also facilitate association, mentioning the need within the brand name or along with it is ideal. Short of that, a logo or slogan that presents the association would be helpful.

> Many companies incorporate the type of need the goods meet right into the brand name, so the two are consistently paired, and by association they become almost synonymous:
>
> L'eggs—hosiery
> NutraSweet—sweetening food
> Mr. Clean—cleaning
> Minute Maid—quick preparation
> Die-Hard—dependable batteries
> Kool-Aid—a cool beverage
> Windex—window cleaning
>
> Others devise a logo or slogan that closely associates the goods with a consumer need:
>
> Allstate—"You're in Good Hands with Allstate"
> McDonald's—"You Deserve a Break Today"
> AT&T—"Reach Out and Touch Someone"
> Yellow Pages—"Let Your Fingers Do the Walking"

ASSOCIATING THE GOODS WITH A STIMULUS

The associative learning we just outlined pairs goods with some consumer need. But marketers can teach consumers to depend on the product or service by pairing it with some stimulus or cue that already suggests some response or reaction. By doing so, the name of the brand or product, store or service "takes the place" of the original cue or stimulus that leads to action. This is often referred to as "classical conditioning." It was originated by nineteenth century Russian physiologist Ivan Pavlov. In his now-famous experiments, Pavlov sounded a bell each time he presented a dog with meat powder. The dog naturally begins to salivate when it perceives that food is present, even though it doesn't actually eat the food or get a reward. Just the presence of the food prompts the automatic reaction of salivation. By pairing the sound of the bell with the presence of food, the bell and the food become associated with one another in the creature's mind. Later Pavlov noted that he needed only to sound the bell to make the dog salivate. In other words, he got the same reaction from the *conditioned stimulus*, the bell, as he did from the *unconditioned stimulus*, the food.

Marketers were quick to pick up on the potential of classical conditioning for promoting consumer goods. This method of conditioning became popular in the mid-1920s when commercial radio was also gaining in popularity among consumers. It was a natural combination and a marriage of convenience. (In many other countries around the world, radio was exclusively or largely noncommercial and remained in the hands of the government.) Often-repeated radio commercials with singing jingles employed classical conditioning, and this mode of advertising dominated for many years.

The Types of Associations

Classical conditioning in advertising works by a fairly simple process. The brand name is paired with some other cue that automatically will generate a response in people's minds that's favorable to the goods.

> During the era when cigarettes were advertised on broadcast media, Salem cigarettes were associated with pleasant, relaxed country scenes with the jingle and slogan we mentioned earlier: "You can take Salem out of the county, but you can't take the country out of Salem." In magazine print ads and on billboards, the Salem cigarette package was shown together with pleasant country scenes. The objective was to associate the brand name, logo, and package (conditioned stimuli) with other kinds of (unconditioned) stimuli; a quiet picnic with a friend out in a country woods or field. Natural settings automatically evoke pleasant emotional reactions in people, and especially among the urban crowd, who are largely deprived of such relaxing natural environments. By pairing the brand with scenes that evoke pleasant emotions, the advertisers sought to condition smokers to associate Salem with relaxation and contentment—powerful inducements to choose that brand.

The Types of Goods

The associations used for classical conditioning are most effective for small, heavily advertised, often-purchased consumables. The goods most frequently promoted this way are things that don't differ much in their physical properties from one brand to the next. So most of the brand differentiation has to be created by the marketing and promotion of the goods. Often each brand within a product category will "stake out an emotional territory," so to speak, and strive to associate the brand with a particular type of favorable feeling.

> Both Beecham Product's Bounce and Procter & Gamble's ClingFree fabric softener sheets for dryers contain similar substances and provide almost identical product benefits. But each takes a different classical conditioning approach.
>
> ClingFree uses the typical slice-of-life commercial. They show Mom and Junior or Sis in the laundry room, where mom first tries a different brand and finds the clothes still have that dreaded

plague, "static cling." Then she uses ClingFree and lo and behold—no cling! They push the main product benefits: "Makes clothes super soft, eliminates static cling, gives clothes a fresh, clean smell, and fights body odor on clothes." The conditioning revolves around the association between brand acceptance and successful parenting and homemaking.

Bounce takes a very different tack, using sound-alike versions of popular rock hits such as the Pointer Sisters "Jump for My Love," with lyrics stressing such cues as "Feel the touch" and "Jump." TV spots feature a breathtaking sequence of quick-shots showing energetic young dancers spinning, twirling, and jumping with their light, airy clothes. Such sights, together with the sounds of an already-popular song, evoke joyful, pleasant feelings among the audience. The advertisers hope to condition their audience to associate the brand with youthful joy and exuberance through this emotional shorthand.

Notice that with classical conditioning, there needn't be a logical, rational connection between the unconditioned and the conditioned stimulus. There's no connection between the smell of meat powder and the sound of a bell for Pavlov's dogs, except that they're paired together in time and space. Similarly, there's no connection between joyful music or an exuberant dance, and a fabric softener sheet. The two are only connected through association.

CONDITIONING CONSUMERS WITH REWARDS

With classical conditioning, there's no explicit reward, it's only implied. Pavlov's dogs didn't eat the meat powder, they just saw and smelled it. But operant conditioning, the kind marketers use most today, is based on specific rewards that lead to learning and subsequent responses. In fact, there are four key concepts involved with this kind of conditioning: *drive, cue, response*, and *reinforcement*.

Four Principal Elements

People are in a *drive state* when they have some need that's crying out for satisfaction: when they're hungry, tired, bored, lonely, sick, or in some such condition. Drives often create internally generated stimuli—an urge to act or do something to alleviate the drive or satisfy the need. When they're in a drive state, consumers are most susceptible to this kind of conditioning. A *cue* is a signal of some kind. It's a stimulus that's generated externally and it tends to trigger or direct the activity that's prompted by the drive. The *response* is the thing that consumers learn to do in order to satisfy their drive. Finally, positive *reinforcement* is a reward of some kind. It's something people receive as a direct result of the response, something that satisfies the need and alleviates the drive.

Most of the early work on operant conditioning took place in the psychology lab, where Algernon, the hungry (drive) little white rat, was put into a cage with a light that blinked (cue), a bar to press (response), and a food pellet hopper (reinforcement). If Algernon presses the bar when the light comes on, he gets to eat. He soon learns to watch for that light!

There's a lot of difference between a rat and a consumer, but it didn't take operant conditioning long to make the leap from the psych lab to the marketplace. Consumers are often in a drive state of some kind. Brand advertising, store signs, point-of-sale displays, and product packages serve as the cues. The response takes place at the cash register or checkout counter, and the reward comes when the goods are consumed. People *can* learn by conditioning, just as rats can, but of course consumers aren't limited to this mode of learning. Rats may be.

> **The classic example of conditioning is the case of snack food such as candy. It's ideal because eating candy is very rewarding. Sucrose (beet or cane sugar) goes into the blood stream very quickly, the nibbler gets a real "hit" almost immediately, and it lasts for only a little while. Then the blood sugar level drops**

precipitously, introducing a new drive state and the need for another "shot" of what the industry promotes as "quick energy."

This process of drive–response–reward, then even more drive with sugar, is exactly parallel to what happens with nicotine, alcohol, and caffeine: when a smoker lights a cigarette, the drinker at the bar has a beer, workers take a coffee break, or a thirsty kid drinks a cola. Any wonder that the promotions for all these products depend heavily on operant conditioning?

This little four-factor model of operant conditioning looks pretty simple at this point, but we've only seen the bare bones of it. It gets more complex as we flesh out the skeleton, but not terribly so. There are a few rules to the conditioning game that are mostly intuitive, unless we muddy it up with the obscure terms psychologists use. We'll try not to.

The Consumers' Drives

The stronger the drive state, the quicker people learn through operant conditioning, unless the drive is overwhelming. But when we condition consumers to buy and use our goods, we like to approach them when they're most susceptible to conditioning: when they're hungry, uncomfortable, lonely, or whatever. That way, they really want the reward.

The television commercials for Nyquil cold medication depict cold-sufferers who look and sound as though they're about to die! After watching for only a few seconds, the viewer might gain the impression that the common cold can really be a terminal illness. And even if it isn't, the poor victim of the cold bug is so uncomfortable he or she almost wishes it was!

These dramatizations are so vivid that they evoke an empathic response from the viewers. And they represent an exceedingly strong drive. To the degree that viewers put themselves in the victim's place, they'll feel impelled to buy some Nyquil—"Just in case it happens to me, God forbid."

Highly Distinctive Cues

The more distinctive the cue, the better. What we seek is a *unique* association between "our" cue and the response we want: purchase of our brand or from our store. If the ads don't really accentuate our brand, or if our brand or package looks a lot like the others, the response to our efforts to condition people might result in the purchase of their brand, rather than ours. People would be conditioned to buy the product, not the brand, and we'd be promoting the industry, rather than our own company's product. That's no good at all. So we strive for highly distinctive cues.

> Each of the leading fast-food chains has developed its own distinctive set of cues. Then they drum these symbols into the minds of consumers with extensive advertising. But what's more, they make their many store locations so obvious, nobody could miss them. Passersby don't need to see the McDonald's sign, they only need catch a glimpse of the golden arches. The Jack-in-the-Box clown face plays the same role. Pizza Huts are shaped like huts, and the unique architecture sets them apart from any other store. So, too, does the white-bearded face of "The Colonel" for Kentucky Fried Chicken, along with their distinctive colors.

A Very Easy Response

The easier it is for consumers to respond, the more quickly and thoroughly they'll be conditioned to use our goods. If it's difficult, they may not respond often, and it weakens the conditioned learning. When they respond by buying, it intensifies the learning. So if the goods are widely distributed, located nearby, and easy to find, that facilitates learning. It's also necessary to tell people *exactly* what it is they're to do; make it easy!

> Consumer goods such as candy, gum, and cigarettes are distributed as widely as possible—supermarkets, convenience food stores, drug stores, liquor stores, delicatessens, gas stations, bars,

restaurants, and vending machines in any high-traffic location. And notice where these products are stocked in stores. Often they're right at the checkout stand or on the counter by the cash register. Since people are largely conditioned to purchase such things, the marketers make it as easy as possible for the consumers to *respond* with a purchase of their brand.

The Reward They Get

The reward is very important to operant conditioning, and it should come as close to the response as possible; preferably immediately. The longer consumers have to wait for a reward after they make a purchase, the weaker the link between buying and being rewarded will be.

> Except for the drummer selling hot dogs at the ball game, it's usually almost impossible to put the drive, cue, response, and reward right next to one another in time and space. There's usually a lag between purchase and consumption, and reward is obtained from consuming the product, not just buying it. So marketers focus on consumption as the response they'll condition. But that often means a separation between the cue, the brand name or logo, and the response. Fortunately there are ways to cope with that, as well.

> Mars' M&M's candy is shaped in little, brightly multicolored pills. Originally the unique shape helped candy eaters associate consumption with the cue. But to ensure the association, M&M was also printed on *every piece*. For a long time, they had that distinctive shape pretty much to themselves. When Hershey introduced rival Reese's Pieces, they had some problems with consumer acceptance. The pill-shaped signal had become so associated with chocolate M&M's, when kids tried Reese's peanut butter-flavored filling, it just didn't seem to taste right to them.

> Reese's Pieces finally came on strong with a boost by *association* with ET, the lovable movie character who was fond of them. M&M's had declined a movie endorsement by a reptilian animatron, as well they might. Nonetheless, most kids still associate brightly colored, pill-shaped candy with the originator, M&M's.

THE STRONGER THE BETTER

The stronger the reward, the greater the learning. Weak rewards don't provide much incentive for consumers to repeat exactly the same behavior: to buy the same brand of the product.

> Here's a riddle for you: When do you want the consumer of your product to forget half your brand name? We won't print the answer upside down at the bottom of the page, because if you've seen many TV commercials, you probably know it already. General Foods' Post Fruit & Fibre brand of ready-to-eat breakfast food cereal was faced with a fairly difficult problem—and they found a unique answer to it.
>
> A substantial proportion of consumers are concerned with fiber intake, especially since President Reagan's highly publicized medical problems. Yet eating fiber isn't especially rewarding. But eating fruit with your cereal sure sounds good, and it is. So what about a cereal called Fruit & Fibre? The idea proved sound, and it's one of the few new entries into that tight market that thrived.
>
> But to increase the *perceived* reward value (perceptions are what counts, remember?) Post has promoted the "invisibility" of the fiber and accentuated the emphasis on the fruit with heavy TV advertising. In the slice-of-life commercials, the couple eating the cereal remember only the "Fruit & . . ." part of the brand name. They can't even recall the rest of the name when challenged! This highlights and intensifies the reward value of the cereal.

Punishment: Reward in Reverse

What happens when reinforcement is negative, providing punishment rather than reward? It will result in learning, but unfortunately the wrong kind. They'll learn *not* to buy and use the goods.

THE NATURE OF THE BEAST

Some consumer products and services are things that people need and want, but by their very nature they're punishing to consume, rather than rewarding in the visceral sense of the word. If that's the case, the marketer is virtually shut out from using operant conditioning—there's no way! Can you imagine your friendly family dentist trying to appeal on the basis of conditioned learning? Not hardly.

> **Listerine is a brand of mouthwash with a distinctively *unpleasant* flavor. Introduced in 1879, it was originally intended for treatment of dandruff, cuts, and athlete's foot, and it's changed very little since then. Sales skyrocketed in the 1920s when it was promoted to prevent bad breath. A prisoner of the brand's history and stuck with a distinctive, medicinal flavor that couldn't really be changed, Warner-Lambert was forced to rely on appeals focusing on other modes of learning—association, modeling and reasoning, rather than operant conditioning. In the 1930s they switched to a health appeal with a distinctively rational learning approach: Use Listerine twice a day, every day, and you'll have fewer and less severe colds. But this rational approach left them vulnerable, in the 1960s, to market intrusions by what they disparagingly referred to as "soda pop" brands such as Procter & Gamble's Scope mouthwash. Since the rivals were pleasant tasting, they could and did depend heavily on operant conditioning.**
>
> **Warner-Lambert retaliated by openly admitting Listerine tasted terrible (punishment, not reward), but tried hard to use it to their advantage: It tastes so bad it must be *good for me*. That *rational* appeal, tied to the cultural norms of the puritan ethic, was effective so long as consumers believed in the medicinal benefits of the product. Then in 1970, the Food and Drug Administration ordered the makers to stop making the medical claims. To add insult to injury, five years later, the Federal Trade Commission insisted on corrective advertising. With the medical mystique thoroughly dispelled among consumers, Listerine was back to appeals only to bad breath, back to the same footing as the pleasant-tasting rivals. And brand share plummeted.**
>
> **Then came the coup de grace: "Medicine breath!" Scope commercials made Listerine the *cause* of bad breath, rather than the**

cure (presumably). Listerine users were shown as rejected by loved ones because of their "medicine breath," then strongly *rewarded* by social acceptance when they switched to Scope and their breath was "minty clean." Although Listerine is still around and maybe always will be, Warner-Lambert finally capitulated and introduced Listermint, a mouthwash they could condition consumers in the $350 million-a-year breath-freshener market to use.

OOPS! SORRY ABOUT THAT

Unfortunately there are other situations where the product is punishing not by nature but by *accident*. If negative experience with the product conditions consumers to avoid it, they are removed from contact with any subsequent reward value. A failure in quality assurance may cause consumers to be "burned," and once they are, they're just not at all likely to return. The important point here is that they were *conditioned* to reject the goods. So rational appeals that explain in detail that the problem has been handled and the situation rectified usually don't work. Even though consumers believe and accept those facts, psychologically they'll have "a bad taste in their mouth" that will *block* them from buying. It just won't seem right, and with close competitors, they'll buy another brand. Despite the cost of such a painful move, the marketer may be forced to withdraw the brand (cue) and start over with another.

MODELING: MONKEY SEE—MONKEY DO!

One of the most potent ways marketers have for teaching people to use their goods depends on consumer modeling. One of the most peculiar things about this mode of learning is the fact that people learn to do things, usually without the slightest idea of *why* they're doing them. It was modeling that taught the young lady mentioned at the beginning of the chapter to cut the end from the ham before baking it. Originally there was a valid *reason* for doing it, but when modeling took over from mother to daughter, over two more generations, the reason was lost in antiquity. While conditioning doesn't depend on conscious understanding, consumers who learn through operant conditioning are usually aware of the reward and can identify it consciously. But with modeling, they may never know why. That's because they let the model do the thinking and make the choices. True, they may see the outcomes of the model's behavior and understand the rational basis or the reward value, but it isn't really necessary. All that is required is a model that they respect and admire; someone they would like to be like.

Look what great opportunities this opens for marketers! It's absolutely remarkable. All they need to do is find some model their audience will look up to and show them using or praising the product. Don't confuse this with *expertise;* these models aren't necessarily experts on the products they represent or endorse. And don't confuse it with *fame,* either. It may help to have a famous figure, but the model doesn't necessarily have to be a celebrity. Just plain "folks" will do, providing they're people consumers can respect and with whom they can identify. Examples are rampant. Here are a few famous models and the products they've promoted:

> **Joe Namath selling panty hose**
> **Arnold Palmer selling pool cleaners**
> **Joe DiMaggio selling coffee-makers**
> **Paul Newman selling health foods**
> **Bill Cosby selling gelatin dessert**
> **Cathy Crosby selling orange juice**
> **Anita Bryant, also selling orange juice**
> **Elizabeth Taylor selling mink furs**
> **Linda Evans selling hair coloring**
> **Angie Dickinson selling avocados**

These celebrities have no special expertise concerning the products they promote. In fact, they needn't even *use* the product, as the first example so aptly demonstrates. Now some campaigns that use "slice of life" depictions of models who are "ordinary folks just like you and me":

> **AT&T promotes overseas telephone service with attractive models of parents and sons or daughters, lovers or spouses, friends or business associates happily keeping in touch with one another.**

> **Wamsutta bedding is promoted with the slogan "After all, it's one-third of your life" and a picture of an attractive, anonymous model sleeping peacefully and comfortably.**

> **Benson & Hedges cigarettes magazine ads show an attractive, anonymous couple, each pursuing a different activity or showing a different preference: "He likes (this), she likes (that). But there's one taste they agree on."**

> **Many brands of laundry detergent are advertised with neat, respectable homemakers obtaining spectacularly clean clothes by using the brand.**

RATIONAL CONSUMERS: A DYING BREED?

The frequency of marketers' dependence on association, conditioning, and modeling modes of learning suggests that few consumers rely on conscious reasoning. In fact, *all* consumers use reasoning to evaluate goods in the marketplace. But they don't do it all the time or even the majority of the time. Very little reasoned learning takes place for often-purchased, small-ticket items, especially when the brands or alternatives are almost identical in most respects that really count. Such purchases don't deserve that much of the consumers' time and attention. Marketers of these goods don't depend on rational learning because there are just too few concrete physical differences among brands on which to base rational appeals. Instead association, conditioning, and modeling are used to create psychological brand differentiation.

When Rational Learning Applies

Rational learning is usually reserved for important purchases or for selection of a policy that will apply to an entire string of purchases. Major purchases that involve an extended decision process usually lead to rational learning. For consumer durables such as major appliances, cars, furniture, homes, and the like, consumers spend substantial time and effort learning about the alternatives and trying to reduce perceived risk. So, too, for important service purchases: selection of a physician or dentist, a decision about education, or selection of a religious affiliation. That's when consumers are most likely to consider very carefully the reasons, pro and con, for making a particular purchase and rejecting others. The attributes of these alternatives differ enough to warrant reasoning and evaluation.

The Extended Decision Process

Rational learning typically occurs when consumers have consciously identified specific needs to be satisfied or goals and objectives to be obtained. When they're aware of where they want to go, they'll consider the products and services available, to see what alternatives will help them the most to attain what they want. In other words, this is the classic case of problem solving: (1) identification of a *goal*, (2) multiple *alternatives* to reach it, (3) *uncertainty* about the path to take, (4) *evaluation* of the alternatives, and (5) implementation of a *choice*.

Marketers can contribute at every step in the consumers' extended decision process. They often suggest goals and objectives or help consumers identify desirable goals. By relating their goods to specific goals, they inform consumers about the alternatives open to them. They help people reduce uncertainty and perceived risk by furnishing product information and by providing guarantees and warranties. By describing the attributes and characteristics of the goods, marketers help consumers to weigh the merits and determine relative value. And when consumers make choices, selecting some product or service to meet their needs or reach their goals, marketers facilitate the implementation of the decision by helping with the transaction and perhaps by providing credit, delivery, installation, or after-service.

Rational learning is a conscious process that leads to cognitive development as well as the acquisition of tastes and preferences. These are the "ingredients" of images and attitudes, topics we'll discuss in some detail in Chapter 6. But it's important here to note the information acquired through reasoning is often fairly *durable*. Rational learning takes place over time, and the results may also affect consumer choices over time.

Table 3 contains a sketch of each of the five basic modes of consumer learning discussed here. It should help to identify how each type works, how it differs from the others, and what goods are most often the focus of each kind of consumer learning.

HELPING CONSUMERS TO LEARN

We've been speaking about the five modes of consumer learning as though they were mutually exclusive, when in fact they typically complement one another. Ordinarily consumers learn about some brand or product, store or service in at least a couple of ways, and maybe all five kinds of learning have taken place. But this doesn't suggest a "shotgun" approach to teaching consumers to use your goods. As you can see, some kinds of learning are especially suited to certain types of consumer

Table 3. Modes of Consumer Learning

Learning Mode	Description of Process	Typical Application
Association	The brand name of the product or service is associated with a particular kind of consumer need that can be met by using the goods. After many repetitions, the two concepts, the brand and the need, become associated and almost synonymous in the minds of consumers.	Laundry detergents with distinctive brand names are often advertised repeatedly in close conjunction with kids wearing soiled clothes, · laundry rooms, washing machines, and clean, folded clothes to "link" any form of laundry activity with the brand.
Classical conditioning	By pairing the brand name of the product with stimuli that naturally elicit positive emotional responses from people, over many repetitions, consumers learn to associate the brand with the positive emotions. When they think of the brand, they'll have good feelings about it.	Many brands of beer are promoted by showing them in highly congenial or affiliatory settings that those in the market would ordinarily enjoy occupying, while the beer is an integral part of the friendly, comfortable social scene.
Operant conditioning	While in a *drive* state, when some need is highly excited, consumers are presented with a distinctive *cue* indicating a purchase *response*. If they are quickly and strongly *rewarded* for buying, they will learn to respond in the same way on similar occasions.	Soft drink marketers spend huge sums to design highly distinctive can labels, so that the brand name will be linked with the strong rewards thirsty consumers get when they open and drink the beverage. They're then conditioned to buy it again.

Table 3. (*Continued*)

Learning Mode	Description of Process	Typical Application
Modeling	Consumers are presented with attractive models, who are not necessarily experts or famous, but who can be respected and emulated. Consumers learn to buy and use the goods as the models do, through positive, vicarious experience, though they may not know why they do.	Clothing designers advertise their garments with large, color ads in slick magazines, using extremely attractive models. The readers who would dearly like to look that good often model the models and buy the clothes.
Reasoning	The consumers are consciously taught how the goods can help them fulfill their needs or reach their goals. The benefits of the goods are described to provide reasons for buying. Credibility is important, so perceived experts can be used, generating positive attitudes.	Financial service companies often cite typical investor goals—security, retirement, luxuries, and so on—and provide detailed descriptions of how their services will ensure that investors reach them in a safe, timely manner.

goods, while others couldn't be expected to contribute much. The trick is to discover what kind of learning will work best for your particular offering, then do what's necessary to facilitate that kind of learning among your target market.

We've talked a bit here about advertising and promotion, and certainly they're important, even vital to consumer learning. But the *promotional* component of the marketing mix is actually only part of the whole story. Consumers learn about a company's products or services from a wide variety of sources, including all kinds of different messages sent by the marketer.

The *pricing* of the goods says something to prospective buyers about quality, value, and potential benefits. The mode of *distribution* indicates a good deal about the goods as well. And perhaps the most important in many cases, the *product or service* itself and what the consumer learns from direct, personal experience with it also play a role.

The point here is not to send conflicting messages. All of the inputs you provide to your consumers' learning should be highly consistent. If some messages conflict with others, whether provided directly or gleaned by inference, the conflict will seriously inhibit consumer learning.

ATTITUDES
The Pictures in the Mind's Eye

Fruit drinks in funny little squat aseptic boxes, about 1.5 billion of them this year alone. Over the past few years, they've found their way into kids' lunchboxes, but adult men have rejected them. Why? *Bad attitude.* OK for kids and women, maybe, but not macho types—real men don't drink through silly little straws. With that discovery, one maker, Sunglo, installed a new foil pull-tab to improve the "gulpability" and the pack's image among men.

Consumer attitudes are closely linked to actions in the market-place. A good attitude leads to product acceptance and pur-chase—a bad one results in rejection of the product or brand. So marketers are constantly concerned with the consumers' atti-tudes toward their goods. Accurate, positive, potent attitudes mean consumers will seek out and buy the goods. But inaccu-rate, negative, or weak product attitudes signal danger. The goods aren't likely to sell until marketers change the attitudes of potential buyers.

DURABLE RESPONSE TENDENCIES

Attitudes are the consumers' reservoirs for holding onto facts and beliefs about goods, for storing tastes and preferences, and even for indicating how best to act. An attitude *always* has a topic, something that provides a focal point for the beliefs, feel-ings, and action tendencies. And the topic is often a brand or product, store or service.

ATTITUDES ARE ENDURING

A consumer's attitude toward some product or service may last for days, weeks, months, or even for years. Sometimes it can go into hibernation and lie dormant, only to be excited again by the marketer of the goods.

> The baby boom generation grew up with Kool-Aid. Who could possibly forget that frosty pitcher with the "happy face" etched on it by a child's finger? But it's a kids' drink, and fond memories don't sell products. Or do they? The astute marketers at Kool-Aid knew those images and attitudes were still there, in the minds of all those babyboomers who drank gallons of Kool-Aid as chil-dren. Now these former consumers were themselves parents. But their childhood attitudes and images were long dormant. Even so, they represented an important investment by the com-pany over the years and they were a valuable asset today, if they could only be tapped. Kool-Aid updated the product by replac-ing the now unpopular sugar with NutraSweet. Then they used

nostalgia ads to evoke happy childhood memories in the minds of modern moms, encouraging them to provide the same precious memories for their own children—by serving Kool-Aid, of course. The campaign made already existing product attitudes more salient, positive, and potent.

THEY'RE NOT INBORN TENDENCIES

Nobody is born with a set of attitudes. Consumers learn them in the course of daily experience in the marketplace and while consuming the goods. But since they learned them, they can also change or unlearn them, or replace them with new ones. Whatever attitudes exist at the moment predispose consumers to act in a certain way. So attitudes come before actions and condition or direct behavior in some way. Then a new or different attitude may result from the behavior.

THEY HAVE DIRECTION AND POTENTIAL

Attitudes have a positive or negative valence: a good–bad, like–dislike, or attract–repulse dimension to them. The valence might come from being rewarded or punished for using the product, or the direction can come from evaluations or judgments about the product or service, brand or store. Consumer attitudes also have potential: power to encourage or discourage people to act on what they know and feel. But they don't all have equal potential. Some are "heavyweights" and some are "bantamweights." Some attitudes are much more likely to lead to action than others.

ROLES ATTITUDES PLAY FOR CONSUMERS

Consumers wouldn't have attitudes if they didn't serve some purpose in their mental or emotional lives. But of course, attitudes are functional. They usually play one or more of four principal roles: value expression, ego defense, knowledge integration, and/or instrumental utility. There are no hard-and-fast rules, but usually if we know what role a product attitude serves for most consumers, it tells a lot about marketing the goods.

Attitudes Express Consumers' Values

Each consumer holds some values because they represent and display the person's distinctive personality as a unique individual. Value-expressive attitudes help consumers define themselves to themselves and to others in their social world. Attitudes playing this role indicate what people stand for and identify the things they believe to be important in life.

Many product- or service-related attitudes are value-expressive in nature, especially those toward "socially visible" goods, things like clothes, cars, homes, and furnishings. These products make a statement about the consumer's status in life, but they also symbolize the consumer's values. After all, if you know how someone dresses, what kind of car he drives, where he lives, and what his home is like, you probably feel you know a bit about that person's personality as well as lifestyle. So the goods provide personal identity and "put handles" on who a person is.

To create positive attitudes toward a brand or product, service or store that also express personal values, the consumers have to recognize the symbolic value of the goods. People have to know what the goods stand for and what values they represent. Marketers often provide that symbolic meaning for the products and services they sell. In effect, they "teach" consumers what the product or brand means by associating it with a particular set of values. Often the production of the product furnishes the *utilitarian* value, while the marketing provides the *symbolic* meaning.

> **The rise and fall of designer labels in the early 1980s is an excellent case in point. Designer names such as Bill Blass, Ralph Lauren, and Pierre Cardin were once sold only at such prestigious stores as Saks Fifth Avenue, Neiman-Marcus, and Bloomingdale's. Both the store name and the designer labels**

"meant something" to the buying public and "said something" about the people who wore such clothes.

The craze for designer labels swept the nation early in the decade. As demand skyrocketed, clothing manufacturers scrambled to put a designer label on their garments, a flock of new designers came on the scene, and many well-established designers with well-recognized names began licensing their names and images for a variety of goods they hadn't even designed or been associated with previously.

By 1983, famous-name designer labels had found their way into price-off stores like K mart and Target in a big way. With so many labels and so many people wearing them, designer labels lost much of their meaning and symbolic value for consumers. Why should a Marshall Field's, an I. Magnin's, or a Dayton's store carry designer clothing that's available at J. C. Penney's or Mervyn's at far less?

The large, prestigious department stores quickly began to shift to their own private designer labels, whose image they could control. By offering private labels, the stores maintained their own exclusivity of supply. That permitted them to associate the private label with the prestige and symbolic value of the store name itself. Today, the Saks or Bloomingdale's label has far more social meaning and symbolic value to consumers than do many of the formerly "big name" international designer labels.

Attitudes Defend Consumers' Egos

Some attitudes protect a fragile ego, warding off feelings of inadequacy for the consumer. They protect the personality from threat, attack, or feelings of insecurity or inferiority. These attitudes help people identify with hero figures. They also permit consumers to disassociate themselves from groups they regard as inferior or conditions they see as undesirable. These ego-defensive attitudes don't provide as many opportunities for marketers as the value-expressive kind. Yet ego-defensive attitudes protect people from unpleasant feelings, and many products and services also play a protective role. Attitudes about goods that shelter consumers against adverse social or psychological conditions are sometimes ego-defensive attitudes. They can be reinforced by advertising, to generate greater consumer acceptance of a particular product.

People fear embarrassment and humiliation more than just about anything else. Most of us will undergo severe physical discomfort before we'll suffer the agony of humiliation in the eyes of others. Advertising that presents "fear appeals," scaring the audience into buying the product, sometimes engenders ego-defensive attitudes. Show an audience a model with whom they can identify, cast into an embarrassing situation, and it will strike terror in their hearts.

> **Procter & Gamble's Head & Shoulders shampoo uses both magazine and television advertising appeals based on fear of embarrassment. With headlines such as "Every time you scratch your head, you could be telling someone you have dandruff," they show people in a social setting, not with dandruff flakes on their shoulders but, rather, *inadvertently scratching their heads*. The message is that you're telling people you have dandruff when you scratch! By depicting the shocked expressions and reactions of others to merely scratching your head, they hope to evoke fears of ego-loss. They promote the product more for ego-protection than for health maintenance or hair care: "Show off your hair, not the itch of dandruff."**

Attitudes Integrate Consumer Knowledge

Attitudes are storehouses of ready information about the consumer goods in the marketplace. Attitudes that play this role are especially important to marketers because promotional messages don't often reach consumers exactly at the time they're considering a purchase. Most of the knowledge consumers bring to the marketplace has been acquired much earlier, long before the need actually arose, and stored in the form of attitudes. When consumers gather and store market-related information, it isn't usually just the facts that they retain. There's also some evaluation of these bits of data, some interpretation of their meaning, and perhaps some anticipation of future actions. Often they develop and then store a tentative, ready-made decision in the form of an attitude toward the product. This means that promotional information isn't entirely perishable. It allows marketers to build favorable attitudes toward the goods in the minds of potential buyers well before a need arises. Then, when consumers actually see a need that the goods can satisfy, they're likely to act according to those attitudes.

The promotional objectives and messages used to create these attitudes differ a bit from others. The goal isn't to get the audience to rush out and buy the product, because actually most of the audience won't need it at the moment. Instead, the objective is to instruct and inform them in a way that helps them to store the information and recall it later, when they have a need for the goods. These ads usually have a "when you're ready" element to them. They stress how the goods fit into the picture and describe a lot of signals that indicate when the product or service should be bought and used. That way, the promotion facilitates need recognition, so that when consumers see the cues, they'll go out and act on the attitude.

> **Long before most people were ready to make a decision or had received their "ballot" from the local telephone company, AT&T, MCI, and Sprint, the three long-line industry giants, were locked in a promotional battle to engender favorable, knowledge-based attitudes toward their services. While the other two and a flock of lesser contenders stressed cost of service and only mentioned quality of sound, AT&T took the leading "instructor" role. Represented by the distinctive, credible-sounding voice and image of Cliff Robertson, the AT&T ads carefully articulated one service feature after another, everything from operator assistance to instant refunds for wrong numbers to long-distance information to service in smaller communities. They didn't solicit immediate response—they did point out that local customers would be randomly assigned to a long-distance service if they didn't make a choice in time, and it just might not be AT&T!**

Attitudes Are Instrumental to Consumers

These attitudes are instrumental to people for obtaining rewards, and they usually result from positive conditioning.
When experience with the product rewards consumers for making a particular purchase, their attitudes become more positive.
When they're punished for buying something because it
"turned out badly," their attitudes toward the goods turn sour.
Product preference and brand loyalty for small, often-purchased consumables such as food and beverage are based on
this kind of attitude. So marketers strive to "build in" as much
reward value as they can, and to facilitate the operant conditioning process. That way, positive attitudes toward the goods
are reinforced every time the buyer consumes the product.
Brand or store loyalty will increase with each positive reinforcement the consumer experiences.

> Over 2600 Merle Norman cosmetics studios across the United
> States and Canada feature a "try before you buy" policy to create
> positive attitudes toward their complete line of feminine cosmet-
> ics. Prospective Merle Norman customers need only call a
> nearby store for an appointment, then drop in for a demonstra-
> tion makeover or makeup application. This allows the cosmetolo-
> gists to match the products with the characteristics and needs of
> the client, and to teach her to use the various kinds of cosmetics.

> The studios aren't as much interested in the single sale as in
> establishing a continuing relationship and winning a long-time
> customer. The initial demonstration makeover is highly reward-
> ing to the new visitor, since women are accustomed to receiving
> personal services of this kind and enjoy being catered to and
> pampered a bit. What's more, the trained professionals invari-
> ably do a more expert job of selection and application than the
> customers would be able to accomplish by merely selecting and
> applying the makeup on their own. So prospective clients get
> additional social rewards from the compliments they receive as a
> result of the makeover. With such conditioning and reinforce-
> ment, they develop positive instrumental attitudes toward the
> studios and merchandise; the mention of Merle Norman is likely
> to evoke pleasant feelings and reactions.

WHAT CONSUMERS KNOW, FEEL, AND DO

Consumer attitudes aren't terribly complex—they only have three moving parts: What consumers know or believe, how they feel or evaluate something, and how likely they are to act on it. Yet when marketers try to change attitudes, they have to consider each individual component.

The Knowledge Component

To have an attitude toward some product or service, consumers must have some minimum amount of information: know the name and a little something about it, at least. Consumers have many opportunities to learn about products on the market. Yet there are over twenty-five thousand brands advertised to consumers, and most people are exposed to several hundred advertising messages every day. Nobody could absorb that much information. Much is lost, and the knowledge component of an attitude is never perfect. A couple of things might go wrong: What they know or believe may be incomplete, inaccurate, or both. When measuring attitudes, marketers want to know if potential buyers have *enough* information, and whether the information they have is *correct*. If they don't know much about the product or hold the wrong beliefs, they won't buy.

Consumers have to be informed and reminded about the goods more or less constantly. That's most often done with advertising, but other forms of communication will also work. It's usually easier to furnish additional information when knowledge is incomplete than to correct or modify inaccurate knowledge or unfavorable beliefs. Clarity and credibility are important; the audience must understand the message and believe what they're told.

INCOMPLETE KNOWLEDGE

> **Problem.** Prospective customers are unaware of several relevant facts about the product or service.

Solution. Use ads providing additional facts that are positively related to the consumers' values

Emphasis. Take special care to make messages as clear, understandable, and relevant as possible.

INACCURATE KNOWLEDGE

Problem. Consumers hold some negative ideas about the product or service which are incorrect.

Solution. Use promotion to correct the misconceptions or inaccuracies in the minds of the audience.

Emphasis. Be sure to make the messages as credible, acceptable, and authoritative as possible.

The Feeling Component

Almost everyone will have some feelings, positive or negative, concerning just about every product they've ever heard of and can recall; complete neutrality is a rare exception. These feelings develop in one of two very different ways: by evaluation or by conditioning.

EVALUATION

Product evaluation might be conscious or subconscious. Either way, a positive or negative feeling results. Direction and strength of the feelings depend on the evaluation, where consumers compare what they know about the product with what they value. If the product information they have is positively related to their core values, the attitudes pick up a positive valence; feelings are favorable. But if the data at hand are negatively associated with the values, negative or unfavorable feelings result.

CONDITIONING

Direct, personal experience with consumer goods usually turns out to be either rewarding or punishing to the person. If the experience is satisfying or pleasurable, the person's feelings about the product will be favorable. But if the experience proves unpleasant, disappointing, or painful, then unfavorable feelings toward the goods will result. So in this mode, the positive or negative valence of the attitude depends on the kind of reward or punishment that resulted from the experience.

Changing Evaluations. When Miller introduced its Lite brand of beer in 1973, most industry analysts were very skeptical. "Diet" beer could hardly be expected to go over well with the macho males at the core of the beer-drinking market. A casual glance into any neighborhood bar showed that these people don't much value a slender figure, the typical appeal for a diet food or beverage.

If Lite had appealed to such values, the campaign would certainly have fallen as flat as others in the industry had expected. Instead, Miller changed beer-drinkers' attitudes toward what is basically a "diet" beer by associating Lite with *different values.* They used famous athletes to endorse and promote the brand, and the appeal was subtle but compelling.

Despite diligent practice, how much beer can any one person hold in an evening? Instead of "filling up" on heavy beer, why not choose Lite, the "less filling" beer? The ads strongly implied that you could drink more if you drank Lite. It worked. Sales soared, until today over 20 percent of all beer sold is light beer, and Miller holds over half that market, despite the 40+ brands now available.

Changing Conditioning. Burger King discovered that many people don't find fast food very *rewarding* because the burgers are all made the same way, and not exactly the way the individual buyers wanted them. To increase the reward value of the food, they modified their in-store routine to facilitate making hamburgers "to order." Then they introduced the slogan "Have It Your Way." When people got exactly what they wanted, it was more rewarding. But even those who *don't* order their food a special way benefit and receive greater reward value. Everyone likes to have choices, even though they don't exercise them. Merely knowing they had a choice made a Burger King visit more rewarding and attitudes more positive.

Action Component

The chances that consumers will act on the basis of their attitudes depend on several factors, but perhaps the most important are *relevance* to goals, *centrality* of the value basis, and
integration with other positive attitudes. People are more
likely to act on attitudes if they're directly related to obtaining
important goals. Attitudes based on values that are central to
consumers' value structures are also more likely to be acted out.
And when an attitude is closely linked with other important
attitudes, consumers are more likely to act according to the
attitude.

Marketing appeals based merely on peripheral values or
amorphous objectives may result in favorable attitudes. Yet
when it comes to making a purchase, the action component of
the attitude may not be strong enough to prompt action. In
other words, the consumer may buy from a competitor who
happens to be more convenient, or merely buy nothing at all.
By contrast, if the appeal is closely tied to important goals and
objectives, if it's based on core values very central to consumers, and if it's tightly knit to other attitudes that reinforce
action, then consumers are much more likely to behave in the
marketplace in accordance to the attitudes they hold.

> In the women's fashion world, *beauty* is everything, and every-
> thing else is nothing. But today's executive woman has an en-
> tirely different set of values, goals, and priorities regarding her
> wardrobe. An afternoon tea on the patio is a frivolity to a young
> woman attorney, more likely to spend her afternoon in a frigid,
> air-conditioned office, preparing a brief for tomorrow's hearing.
> She's far less concerned about "pretty" than she is about "credi-
> bility," and old fashion dictates no longer apply.
>
> Hartmarx Corp., the $1 billion clothing maker, understands the
> executive dress code. Their well-known Hart Schaffner & Marx
> line for men carries the headline "The right suit might not insure
> your future. But the wrong suit can certainly hurt your pres-
> ence." The appeal to central values and goals has resulted not

> only in a positive image for the clothing line, but in attitudes that lead directly to sales.
>
> Well aware of the fact that most businessmen would far rather look competent than just handsome, Hartmarx recognizes that businesswomen share the same career-oriented values, goals, and attitudes. So they're introducing a new line of high-quality women's suits under the Hart Schaffner & Marx label. They'll continue to concentrate their ads in magazines other than those devoted to fashion and to use appeals to professional, rather than merely cosmetic goals and values.

Customers buy consumer goods because they have favorable attitudes toward them, whether the attitudes are expressions of their values, protection for their egos, instrumental in getting them rewards, or storehouses for their information (or all of the above). To have a favorable attitude toward the product or service means they're well-informed about it, they have good feelings about it, and they feel strongly enough about it to act accordingly. Those who don't buy usually have attitudes that are lacking in some respect—their knowledge is inadequate or inaccurate, their feelings or evaluations have turned negative, and/or they don't feel strongly enough to behave in the marketplace in accordance with their attitudes. We can predict consumer response by measuring attitudes, but we can ensure it by improving them.

IMAGES IN CONSUMERS' EYES AND MINDS

The image of a product in the mind's eye of a consumer is both more than an attitude, and less. It's more than an attitude because it fills in or completes or enhances the picture. Consumers round out the picture and fill in the gaps in their information, based on what they *have* learned about some consumer product, service, brand, or store. But unlike an attitude, an image doesn't have three distinct components. Instead, images have multiple dimensions. What consumers know or believe, what they feel about the object of the image, and their likelihood of acting in accordance with it are all combined and reshuffled into many different categories and dimensions.

The Basis of Images

The image that consumers have of a particular product, brand, service, or store is largely *their own creation!* The marketing program can influence the image, but the picture is "developed" in the consumers' minds. So no two people are likely to hold precisely the same image of any one kind of consumer goods. That's because the image is based only in part on what each consumer learns about the goods in the marketplace, and partly on their own personal history and experience in general.

Virtually nobody has perfect information about any particular product or service on the market. So consumers depend on cues that are just hints about other features or attributes of the goods. Facts about the goods imply other things as well. Consumers reach a conclusion about the goods and form an image by inferring things that are important to their decision, even though they don't know them for sure. So if they aren't sure about the quality of the product or service, they might infer it from the price: high price, high quality; low price, low quality.

Why would consumers assume that a high price connotes high quality? Mostly because they've been taught to expect it. That's what they've found to be true in the past, for a wide variety of things. And statements such as "You get what you pay for" also reinforce that general belief. So consumers generalize what they've learned about other products to the particular one in question. Of course they're not always right, but they'll live by that rule as long as it proves to be true in most cases.

The cues consumers use and the inferences they make from them aren't usually as obvious as they are with the "price/quality syndrome." Sometimes they will cue off of things the marketer wouldn't even suspect. There may not be a direct connection between what they look at and what conclusions they reach. So prunes might have an "old" image merely because they are dark and wrinkled. Or a bank might not be seen as very safe and sound, merely because it's housed in a wooden building. It's difficult to guess the image of consumer goods without hard data. Often guesswork isn't very accurate or precise and it can be downright misleading. Marketers who are uncertain about the image of their goods in the minds of consumers are well advised to do some research, rather than just speculate about it. Then the marketing program can highlight some of the positive aspects of the image and reduce or eliminate the most serious negative factors.

The Dimensions of an Image

Marketers tend to think about and talk about *"the* product"— as though it was one single entity. But in fact, what we call one product or brand, one store or service is actually a package of utility containing many different "goodies." When people buy tangible products such as personal computers, it's not the physical product that they want. It's the service it provides or the function it serves that they're seeking. They don't want the machine, itself, they want what it will do for them. Yet without much other information, they're very likely to cue heavily off of the appearance and physical characteristics of the machine.

So, too, for the service sector. When mom takes the kids to a fast-food drive-through, she's buying a service in the form of food. But what's she *really* buying? Not the hamburgers and fries. She's buying satisfaction for hunger, entertainment for the kids, or ease and convenience for herself. So the image that people hold of some particular product or service is dimensioned in terms of the attributes the goods include. The image profile shows what consumers glean about the entire package.

MANAGING PRODUCT AND SERVICE IMAGES

The image of the goods in the consumer's mind can not only be monitored, it can also be *managed.* By modifying the marketing program—the product or service, the pricing, the distribution, and the promotion, marketers shape and reshape the picture of their goods and firms in the mind's eye of consumers. Some marketers do it very adroitly, making changes that range from minuscule to gargantuan. Others focus more on what they feel consumers *should* see, rather than what they *do* perceive about the goods. And of course the degree of marketing success varies accordingly.

TWO "MAC'S" IN CONTRAST

After rave reviews from the media and from a good friend (who was selling them), I was finally going to try an Apple Macintosh computer for the first time. As soon as I laid eyes on it, my reaction was instantaneous: *This is IT?* It looked awfully like one of those little video games. "Ahhh," he said, "but wait until you see what it *DOES!*"

The Macintosh did everything they said it would—and more. I found it absolutely revolutionary—the mouse, the graphics, the pull-down menus, everything. But despite all that, I still didn't *like* the machine. It worked like a computer, but it didn't *look* like a computer. That first glimpse hung in my mind, and its appearance jaundiced my entire image of the other, very positive attributes.

I wasn't the only one to feel that way. Later, as Apple began efforts to enter the business market, the Macintosh found little acceptance, despite its sophistication and power. One business publication cited a remark about the "little avocado toy for Yuppies and their kids." Technical analysts cite the closed architecture, the incompatibility with IBM, and other technical inadequacies.

Despite their advantages, three-wheeled cars have never been successful—they don't *look* like cars. Many products are packaged in squeezable tubes in Europe and they sell well. Not here. To Americans, they all *look* like toothpaste. Say what you wish about a "small footprint" and more desk space, but it seems unlikely that Apple's Macintosh will find it's way into many offices until it *looks* like an office machine.

An Image, Reborn. During the past few years, fast food outlets have steadily gained a larger and larger share of the total food market. In the early years, the emphasis was on speed and economy. Stores used hot, bright colors—reds, oranges, yellows. Each chain developed its own symbols and logo: the more garish, the better to be recognized. The menu was strictly limited and much of the food was prepared in advance to save time.

The image that developed was less than desirable. The public felt fast food was quick and economical, but they viewed it as markedly inferior to "sit-down" restaurants or the meals they prepared at home. So fast food developed the image of an "inferior good," something you accepted if you had to, but nothing you'd relish very much.

The industry has changed markedly and rapidly over the past few years and its image has changed with it. McDonald's, the industry leader, switched from the slick, sterile surfaces and bright, gaudy colors to a more sedate decor. Rough wood and brick replaced many of the metal and plastic surfaces, to introduce a softer, more textured look. Earth tones, browns and deep ambers, replaced the more vivid colors in many areas. The logo and signs were reduced in size and stylized to fit the new image.

The "walkup only" stores are a thing of the past. Today, these stores feature tastefully decorated, well-fitted dining areas. The food and service changed right along with the decor. The menu was broadened dramatically, including such things as salads and separate entrees, rather than just sandwiches. Prices were adjusted accordingly. Hours were extended and a complete new breakfast menu introduced. To compensate for longer food preparation time, in-store production procedures were tightened and drive-through service was offered at many stores.

The firm was very successful in achieving the image it sought in the public's eyes: that of an American institution. Rather than a place where one goes for quick, cheap food, a new identity has been created. Today, it's not only an integral part of the core culture in this society, it's also become a symbol of Americana in the eyes of the rest of the world as well—so much so that the mere appearance of the golden arches in other countries often brings cries that they're being "Americanized!"

What do McDonald's and others like them really sell? Certainly not just food! For much of the public, eating at their stores is socially acceptable, even expected. It's an experience, and the customers have fun, they get entertainment from their visit. They play games and get prizes. There's often a place for the kids to entertain themselves. But perhaps what they don't get is even more important: There are no rude surprises, practically no perceived risk, and rarely a disappointment. So familiarity and certainty are an important part of the total package of goods. The image in the minds of the public is traditional, positive, and multifaceted. It was created by careful manipulation of the marketing mix to include the cues and symbols which lead to a favorable image.

In The Mind's Eye of the Consumer

Business managers and executives operate on the basis of the physical realities associated with the goods they sell. Consumers in the marketplace operate on the basis of the *psychological* and *social* images of the goods they buy. The distance between the two is often great, and marketers have to bridge the gap. Consumers are often far more interested in the symbolic value of the goods they buy than in purely functional utility. Social and psychological factors often dominate. We can see the physical and chemical production of consumer goods, but what about the "soft" characteristics of these products? What governs the images consumers hold? Attitudes and images are the domain of marketers. They are the "stuff" of which marketing success is born—or dies.

SOCIAL ROLES
Playing Out Life's Drama

Whether alone or with others, consumers play out their special roles in the drama of life. Society has written the script, some authority figure may be the director, the physical environment is the stage, the current situation the setting, the others in the group the players, outside observers the audience, clothing the costumes, each consumer a star actor. *Consumer goods are merely the "props."*

This isn't a way that marketers are used to seeing the world. They don't usually think about consumers in terms of the roles they play, but play them they do! What does it mean, to "*act like a lady*"? How does a man "*act* his age"? And who has "the right stuff" for the job? Consumers are far more aware of their role requirements than one might think. Role-playing not only tells people what to do and what not to do, but also makes the behavior of others around them predictable and understandable. Roles are important!

ACTORS PLAYING THEIR SOCIAL ROLES

With a clear, simple understanding of social roles, marketers can use them as a unit of analysis for making decisions and managing the marketing program. Consumer goods can be designed for a specific role and marketed to all those who play it. Advertising will provide some of the script, to give direction for the social performances of buyers and users of the goods.

> Few companies know the *homemaker* role or market to it as effectively as Campbell Soup Company, whose red-and-white label soups alone hold about 80 percent of the entire canned soup market. But how can a group of mostly male corporate executives understand the role of a female homemaker? Campbell chief executive Gordon McGovern has his own formula—go where they go, do what they do, and talk to them as much as possible. That's his key to understanding the homemaker role.
>
> McGovern carries it to what many top executives would consider the extreme. He not only does the weekly grocery shopping for his own family, he insists that top executives and managers do the same. Company executives routinely visit some 300 homes in every part of the country to study homemakers in their own kitchens. He went so far as to hold a board meeting in a supermarket, allowing the directors to wander through the store to see and talk with shoppers buying Campbell's products.
>
> With such well-recognized brands as Campbell's gold-label soups, Swanson and Le Menu frozen dinners, Mrs. Paul's frozen

foods, Pepperidge Farm baked goods, Prego spaghetti sauces, and Vlasic pickles, Campbell focuses mainly on the homemaker. Closely monitoring changing homemaker and family roles, Campbell successfully launched 42 new products in 1984 alone. And McGovern has ambitious aspirations for the firm. But thorough understanding of the role of the company's main consumers will certainly contribute to his chances to achieve corporate goals.

THE FUNCTIONS OF SOCIAL ROLES

Consumers wouldn't engage in role-playing if the roles didn't have important functions in their lives. But role-playing isn't just functional for individual consumers, it's also pretty necessary for society as a whole to work smoothly and effectively. So roles have a personal function, an interpersonal function, and a broader social function, as well. They all work together to make role-playing a major part of our lives.

The Personal Value of Role-Playing

Consumers' social role requirements are more often a blessing than a curse. While it may be troublesome at times, people usually accept their roles willingly and play them enthusiastically. In fact, people often judge themselves and others according to how well they play their roles—parent, executive, neighbor, friend, and so on. The more roles people play, the more social satisfaction they seem to get. So to see social roles as a burden on consumers is to miss the point.

If there's one thing that people hate, it's *uncertainty*. Uncertainty about how we're to behave or what we're supposed to do in a social situation is especially abhorrent. Everybody needs to know what others expect of them. The benefit people get from social roles is that they *provide guidelines for individual behavior in social relationships*. Effective role-playing helps consumers avoid embarrassment or humiliation and gain the acceptance, approval, and appreciation of others around them.

Consumers welcome social role prescriptions when they know exactly what to do and what not to do in a social situation. This is where marketers can really help—and benefit from it, at the same time. The promotional messages marketers send to consumers often flesh out the role prescriptions and requirements. They make plain to people what's expected of them: what others expect and how they should behave. And often an acceptable role performance involves the purchase and consumption of consumer goods.

> A decade ago all but an extremely small minority of men wouldn't go near masculine skin care products—it just wasn't in the male role prescription. Facials, moisturizers, creams, and masks still aren't a part of most men's lives, but their popularity is growing and offering more opportunities to cosmetics marketers. The fitness and health movement suggests more attention to skin care. What's more, the high divorce rate results in a larger population of single, middle-aged men, concerned about their appearance and also buying their own toiletries.

> But there's still one big problem: *the macho obstacle.* To get around it, Faberge has tied its new facial soother in its Brut line to something that's squarely at the core of the masculine role— the shaving ritual. The Interface line of masculine facial cosmetics follows a similar path, but links its products to the physical workout, rather than to shaving. By linking their products to existing aspects of the male role, these marketers and others are gradually but persistently broadening the masculine role prescription.

The Roles' Interpersonal Utility

Another major purpose of social roles is to *make the actions of other people predictable.* It's important for consumers to know what to expect of others with whom they interact. If a person knows what role somebody else is playing, then he or she can forecast the other person's behavior fairly accurately. There are many differences between individuals, but when they play the same role, it levels things out and makes for a more predictable social situation.

> This interpersonal aspect of role-playing has a special meaning for marketers, different from the one we mentioned previously. In this case, it means that marketing people, themselves, have to play their own roles effectively or they'll blow their prospective customers right out of the water. The simple rule is this: *You have to meet the role expectations of the people in your market.* When marketing or salespeople act in exactly the way that consumers expect them to, things go smoothly—when they don't things go badly. If you're a salesperson (and in a way, we all are), you have to *look* like a sales professional, *talk* like one, and *act* like one when you're in that role.

The Roles' Broader Social Meaning

Aside from telling consumers what they should and shouldn't do and telling them what to expect of others in a given role, social roles also contribute importantly to the way that we all live and work with one another. They *mask individuality and provide the lubricity for smooth social (and professional) interactions.* We use this in dozens of ways in the day-to-day activity of marketing to consumers.

The last time you went through the checkout line at a supermarket, what did the clerk say when you got to the checkstand with your groceries: "Hello, how are you today?" Did you answer that question the same way you would if you had gone to see a physician and the doctor just came into the examination room and asked the same question? Certainly not! If you started describing your physical condition to the checkout clerk, it wouldn't go over very well with either the clerk or the people waiting in line behind you. But of course you didn't because you knew that it wasn't really an inquiry, just a signal that the clerk was going to start checking your groceries; you knew the role and so you knew how to respond. This might seem like a trivial point, but it's not. There's an elaborate, though almost invisible set of rules for doing business in the consumer marketplace.

> **Living so close to Mexico, we often have the opportunity to visit and observe other Americans shopping in the Mexican marketplace. Unfamiliar with the differences in cultural, social, and business norms, they often act as though they were still in Chicago or New York. They expect the Mexican merchants to play the same roles as salespeople in the United States. They'll ask the price of an item in a shop. The Mexican salesperson will give them a price. Sometimes, to the utter amazement (and delight) of the merchant, they'll simply take out their wallet and pay it!**
>
> **The roles of Mexican buyers and sellers include *negotiation* far more often than for Americans. Here, that applies only to certain things—new and used cars, real estate, or goods at a local swapmeet or neighborhood garage sale, for instance. To operate effectively, both the seller and the buyer have to know the rules of the game and the roles of the players.**

CONSUMERS' ROLES ARE ACQUIRED

There are two fairly different kinds of roles that consumers routinely play: those that are *acquired* and those that are *ascribed.* Acquired roles are more voluntary. They result from the choice of some position or relationship. For instance, the roles of salesperson and customer are both acquired roles. Some roles aren't really acquired, they're ascribed by society, based on a person's characteristics. The most important ones are age roles and sex roles, and we'll discuss them a little later.

Role-Related Consumer Goods

The products and services consumers buy and use are the "props" on which they depend during their role performances. Consumer goods relate to acquired roles in four fairly distinct ways: they're *required* for performance, they *improve* performance, they *facilitate acquisition* of the role, or they *symbolize* a role relationship.

Goods Required for Role Performance

Groceries and food preparation appliances for the family cook; sports equipment for the athlete; playing cards for the bridge player; tools and materials for the do-it-yourselfer.

Goods to Improve Role Performance

Tennis or golf lessons for the amateur player; a food processor for the family cook; high-performance auto parts for the sports car enthusiast, a word processor for the secretary.

Goods to Facilitate Role Acquisition

Finishing school for the socialite; fashionable clothes for the singles bar patron; a new house for the social climber; golf clubs for those soon to retire; vitamins for the mother-to-be.

Goods to Symbolize a Role Relationship

Engagement ring for the bride-to-be; the badge of a law enforcement officer; a clinic jacket for the physician; a bumper sticker for a political party member; a pennant for the sports fan.

GOODS ARE REQUIRED BY SOCIAL ROLES

When a consumer product or service is absolutely necessary to perform some role, everybody playing the role needs some type of the goods. Marketers of such goods can monitor the number of consumers who play such a role, as well as the rate at which the goods are consumed during role performance. Such data provide a good estimate of the total market for the goods in a particular category.

> **Mrs. Olson has, for many years, been teaching new homemakers how to make a good cup of coffee by using Folger's Mountain Grown coffee: "It's the Richest Kind." The TV ads point to the**

ability to make a good cup of coffee as an absolutely essential part of the homemaker's role. But they carefully avoid any hint that the novice might be incompetent by identifying other aspects of role performance that she can do very well.

GOODS IMPROVE PERFORMANCE OF ROLES

Some consumer goods aren't really required by the role but they improve the role-player's performance in the role. So purchase and consumption of the goods won't vary in lock-step fashion with the number of people engaged in the role. But as noted earlier, consumers are often vitally concerned about their role performance. They really strive to do it well, and that's especially true for the most important roles they play: parent, spouse, breadwinner, homemaker, friend, and the like. Marketing appeals to consumers based on the ability of the product or service to improve role performance are extremely potent.

> Picture this scenario: You finish your jogging for the day, then come home and plug one of your running shoes into your computer to see how you've done! Unbelievable? Not if you have a special shoe from Puma to help you improve your performance. It records and later displays physiological data such as time, distance, and calories expended during the run.

> Wilson, a subsidiary of PepsiCo Inc. and the nation's largest sporting goods manufacturer, is also working zealously on new product development to give the klutzes of the sporting world more balls—a golf ball with more accuracy and distance, an easy-to-hit tennis ball, and a basketball with a texture that can be held more easily. Consumers are highly motivated to buy products that will improve their role performance, especially in areas where there are obvious standards of performance.

GOODS FACILITATE ACQUIRING ROLES

It often takes some time and effort for consumers to acquire a social role. People who are looking forward to taking on a new role may engage in anticipatory buying while they're getting ready to take their place in the role. The gifts given at a wedding or baby shower are typical examples, but there are many others. We'll take a closer look at the *role adoption process* a little later. At this point we should note that it's the rate of entry into the role, rather than the total number of players, that governs the demand for consumer goods to facilitate role acquisition. These consumers who anticipate acquiring a new role are especially good markets because they're very sensitive to appeals for role-related goods. They want the right things to do the job. Marketing appeals for these products and services stress the desirability of the role and the way that the goods will help consumers to get into the role and get started.

> **Newlyweds assume several new roles, aside from those of "husband" and "wife." The acquisition of new roles is more intense for women who assume the major part of the homemaking responsibility. One magazine, *Modern Bride*, caters specifically to women soon to marry. It's interesting to note that the average annual household income of their readers was $31,300 in early 1986, up from only $13,000 in 1973. Changing readership patterns may account for some of the increase, but it may also reflect later marriages and an older, more affluent population of newlyweds.**

> **Not only advertising media, but also retailers are very sensitive to the newlywed market. Consumer goods purchases for the new roles aren't confined only to the couple; friends and relatives join in with gifts for the new household. Many department and specialty stores feature bridal registries to help select styles and patterns desirable to the bride and to avoid duplication of gifts.**

GOODS SYMBOLIZE A SOCIAL ROLE

Many of the roles consumers play provide some degree of social status, recognition, or prestige. Brides love to have their weddings documented in local newspapers: parents send out graduation announcements for their children; professionals taking on new positions or receiving promotions make sure the event is listed in the trade journals. Yet the new roles may not be socially visible or observable by others for very long. To make sure other people know they're incumbents in certain prestigious or respectable roles, consumers often buy and use products and services that symbolize the role and display it to others. The recent appearance of signs in the back window of cars indicated that there's a "CHILD IN CAR" are, perhaps more to symbolize the parenthood of the driver than to ensure that those who would otherwise crash into the car would swerve to avoid it, knowing of the juvenile occupant.

> **Engagement and wedding rings epitomize the use of consumer products to symbolize a role relationship. The pride and zeal with which a bride-to-be displays her new stone to her friends doesn't seem to vary, regardless of whether her diamond is dimensioned in microcarats or multicarats. While more impressive stones are desirable, the ring's value lies not in displaying social status, but in symbolizing a role relationship.**

The Role Adoption Process

When consumers acquire a new social role, they typically go through a four-step role adoption process: *anticipation, acquisition, actualization,* and *accommodation.* Their motives for buying and using role-related consumer goods differ from one phase to the next. So at each phase, they're likely to buy different goods and to be sensitive to different marketing appeals. This implies that marketers can benefit not only by considering what roles those in their target market play, but also where they're at in the role adoption process, from eager anticipation to veteran incumbent.

> *Anticipation.* The consumer has an *idealized image* of the role requirements based on observation or media stereotypes, strives to fit the mold as closely as possible, and prepares by acquiring the goods appropriate to the new role.

> *Acquisition.* The consumer learns the *essential requirements* of the role from direct contact and instruction, including the conventional wisdom and traditional postures, and obtains the goods needed to initiate role performance.

Actualization. The consumer assumes tenure in the role and gains comprehension of the *pragmatic requirements* from direct personal performance, obtaining the goods to continue as time progresses and they are needed.

Accomodation. The consumer, completely familiar with the role after much experience, strives to tailor the role to *personal preference* and reestablish *individual identity,* obtaining goods to customize role performance.

THE ROLE ANTICIPATION PHASE

When consumers aspire to a role from afar they develop an *idealized image* of what it takes to play the role. Their information is usually based on common social stereotypes of the role. They often concentrate more on ovbious signs and the most visible signals associated with the role, rather than the more essential aspects—more on form than on substance. They'll often engage heavily in *anticipatory buying* to prepare for the new role and display their intentions and expectations to others. They're heavily dependent on marketing media and they're responsive to promotion of the most visible goods associated with the role.

> **Hart Schaffner & Marx promotes "The Right Suit" line of men's businesswear with two-page color spreads in magazines such as *Forbes* with the headline "The right suit might not grant entree to the Boardroom. But the wrong suit could very well keep you out." Those who aspire to a higher position may not fully grasp the nature of a director's role, but they can at least adopt what they perceive to be the proper dress code. If they lack contact with those already in the role to which they aspire, they're likely to take their cues almost exclusively from media images such as this.**

THE ROLE ACQUISITION PHASE

At this stage, consumers take on the mantle of the role and begin the on-the-job indoctrination process: what we might call an *internship* for the role. They're beginning to practice the actions associated with the role, but they're still relatively unfamiliar with many of its characteristics and requirements. During this phase they acquire the so-called tools of the trade and absorb the instructions and directions provided to novices by those with more tenure in the role. Perceptions of the need for goods and services are likely to be more conventional and traditional than they are pragmatic, as in the next phase, or idiosyncratic, as in the last stage.

> **McGraw-Hill Training Systems promotes their FastStart software with a "Why Waste Time . . . the old way?" theme. The software allows those already familiar with microcomputers to learn to use conventional programs such as Lotus 1-2-3 or operating systems such as DOS while actually performing their regular tasks on the computer. Such products are ideal for those in the role acquisition phase, but those still anticipating the role would lack the prerequisite familiarity, while those with tenure in the role would already have mastered fairly basic software tools.**

THE ROLE ACTUALIZATION PHASE

At this point consumers become completely aware of the products and services associated with the role. Through continued practice they become thoroughly familiar with the performance of the role and the goods that serve as the props for it. Their criteria for evaluating role-related goods are more pragmatic than symbolic or formal. They want to know if the product or service will get the job done and do it more effectively. The level of demand for role-related consumer goods depends on the number of role incumbents, not the volume of incoming novices or aspirants. These consumers respond best when marketing appeals address them as experts at role performance.

> **Dale Carnegie Sales Training services are promoted in business-oriented magazines such as *Business Week* with a simple slogan: "It Works!" The copy stresses the practical, workable, hands-on nature of the training and refers to quick, measurable results. They seek only those who are already experienced in sales and currently working in the field, so that the students' job situations**

become part of the training workshop. The no-nonsense, get-the-job-done approach in both the promotion and the course itself is highly appealing to those in the actualization phase of the salesperson's role.

THE ROLE ACCOMMODATION PHASE

At some point during tenure in a social role, the incumbents have become thoroughly familiar with it, sometimes to the point of boredom and ennui. They may feel a bit constrained by the norms associated with the role. So they tend to adjust role requirements to make them accommodate their own personal preferences and individual style of performance. They don't value the stereotypical model of the role any more, and they'll resist it's homogenizing effects by differentiating themselves from other role-players. They "customize" the role performance and tailor it to their own personal identity. They'll judge consumer goods by dual criteria: Will it meet the *essential* needs of the role, and does it also vary a little from the standard goods used by "everyone else"? This creates demand for more specialized products and services associated with the role and more variation in the cosmetic or peripheral attributes of the goods. Rather than susceptibility to "role conformity" appeals, they become sensitive to appeals to individuality.

Over the past few years, a relatively new service has been created for high-level executive women—personal shopping consultants, wardrobe managers, and personal wardrobe buyers. At the accommodation phase of the business or professional role, these women are long-familiar with the requirements of executive dress. Yet they are often completely dedicated and engaged in what they regard as more essential aspects of their roles. If evenings or weekends are to be given over to work-related activity, it's more likely to be poring over reports or budgets than shopping for business attire. Enter the shopping consultant, to relieve the executive of an unwelcome chore while meeting her needs for a distinctive style of dress.

There are several personal shopping service businesses throughout the country, located only in major metropolitan business centers where there's an abundance of both women executives and professionals and also sources for fashionable women's business attire. But upscale department stores such as Saks and Robinsons also provide personal shopping consultants. Service offerings vary, and some have annual fees, but most don't. The essential ingredient is providing business and professional women with a distinctive wardrobe to fit their tastes, positions, and personalities, while relieving them of the shopping burden.

Consumers of role-related goods behave differently according to the stage of the role adoption process at which they reside. The demand for role-related goods varies more with the volume of incoming role-players during the early phases but depends more heavily on the number of incumbents during later phases. Promotional appeals to the symbolic and cosmetic aspects of the role are most effective at the first stage, to conventional and traditional role performance at the second, to practical and functional role requirements during the third, and to individualization and personalization during the last phase of the role adoption process.

Social Role Transition Points

Purchase and consumption of role-related products and services are often directly related to the adoption of new social roles. Consumers who take on important new social roles often make dramatic changes in their purchase and consumption patterns. For example, assuming the role of parent with the birth of the first child means less expenditure on vacations, recreation, clothes, and luxuries, and at the same time, acquisition of a host of childcare products and services. Many acquired roles are adopted at different times by different people, but there are some very common transition points that apply to the majority of consumers.

Transition Point	Typical Situational Change
Emancipation	From family to individual
Majority	From child to adult status
Graduation	From high school to college
First job	From student to wage earner
Marriage	From single to married status
First child	From nonparent to parent
Job separation	From employed to unemployed
Midcareer change	From one job role to another
Divorce	From spouse to divorcee
Late job entry	From homemaker to employee
Last child gone	From full to empty nest
Retirement	From employee to retiree
Death of spouse	From married to widow(er)
Disability	From unlimited to handicapped

When consumers reach these transition points, the differences between the old and the new social roles are dramatic and comprehensive. Many will change their entire lifestyle to conform to the new role requirements. At the same time, personal and disposable income ordinarily changes substantially, exaggerating the changes in purchase and consumption patterns. Role-related consumer goods marketers find it effective to identify and define their markets in terms of these role transition points. The number of consumers reaching each transition point determines the nature of new demand. It also indicates potential decreases in demand as consumers abandon the social roles that have become obsolete for them. Fortunately a large amount of demographic data to measure the rate of these role transitions are readily available to marketers.

Purchase and Consumption Roles

While role-playing often results in the purchase and consumption of certain products and services, the converse is also true: The necessity to buy and use products and services requires consumers to play roles that are directly related to consumer choice. Here are nine roles commonly required by the purchase and consumption of consumer goods.

Name of Role	Type of Purchase- or Consumption-Related Behavior
Filter	Regulates the flow of consumer goods information
Influencer	Helps shape other people's evaluations of goods
Decider	Makes the actual purchase or consumption decision
Buyer	Implements the decision and purchases the goods
Preparer	Converts the goods to a form that can be consumed
Consumer	Actually uses or consumes the products or services
Monitor	Regulates or controls consumption by other people
Maintainer	Services or repairs goods so they're ready to use
Disposer	Discards goods that are no longer wanted or needed

The same person may play several or all of the roles simultaneously, but we can't really speak of "*the* buyer" or of "*a* consumer," as though only one person and role are involved. Most family purchases involve multiple role playing by different individuals. Promotion to create awareness or introduce goods should be directed to the *filter,* while evaluative information should be routed to the *influencer* or the *decider.* Store or service information should go to the *buyer* and instructions should go to the *implementer* or *consumer.* When consumption by children is regulated, the *monitor* has to be considered the target. Service information goes to the *maintainer,* and promotion of replacement goods can be directed to the *disposer* who will substitute the new merchandise. Marketers can really benefit by studying these nine purchase roles and relating them to the purchase of the goods.

CONSUMERS' ROLES ARE ASCRIBED

The acquired social roles we've been discussing are a matter of choice—those who play them do so voluntarily. By contrast, *ascribed* roles are attributed to people by society, based on personal characteristics such as sex and age. When consumers perform their acquired roles effectively, they're usually rewarded by society. Not so with ascribed roles, since we're all expected to follow them. On the other hand, those who deviate from ascribed roles are often punished for doing so. So marketers promoting goods associated with acquired roles often stress how they'll help the role-player get rewards. But consumer goods associated with ascribed roles are ordinarily promoted as proper, appropriate, or required by the role. The implication is that the person will suffer if they don't adhere to the role, and that's often the case.

Those who really believe in the ascribed role and want to follow it seek the goods that are associated with the role and respond to this kind of promotion. Yet those who dislike the role stereotype and don't want to adhere to it resent society's attempts to get them to conform. They not only reject promotional appeals based on the role, but also resent the stereotypes used in the ads. They may develop very negative attitudes toward the goods and the companies that market them. So marketers who are considering promotion of their products or services on the basis of ascribed age or sex roles have to know which groups will accept the role stereotypes and which will reject the stereotypes and resent role-related promotions. Ascribed role stereotypes can be used effectively in some markets, but not in others.

Sex Roles and Gendered Products

Some products and services are appropriate to one sex or the other, but not to both. Such goods are inherently "gendered" and marketers don't have any choice. But many consumer products are basically asexual or "unisex" goods: cigarettes, deodorant, cars, vitamins. Marketers can give them a gender image only by associating them with one or the other role stereotype. Let's see what those stereotypes include.

THE MASCULINE SEX ROLE

There are two basic aspects to the male role. The first is a set of *requirements* concerning masculine potency and responsibility. To meet the male sterotype, a man must be tough, strong, aggressive, decisive, and a good breadwinner. The second aspect is a set of *prohibitions* regarding traits that are viewed as feminine, including limitations on emotionality, sentimentality, tenderness, sensitivity, expressiveness, the need for help or support, and interest in young children.

THE FEMININE SEX ROLE

There are two corresponding aspects of the female role, things that are *required* and those that are *prohibited.* To fit the feminine sterotype, a woman must observe feminine etiquette and demeanor, "act like a lady," put her family first, accept household chores, and be weak and submissive relative to men. The second aspect includes prohibitions against dominant or aggressive behavior, active physical sports, or strong interests in scientific or technical occupations or pursuits.

The vast majority of the buying public—male or female, young or old, better or less educated, wealthy or poor, upscale or down, accept the first part of both the masculine and feminine sex role prescriptions. We all adhere pretty closely to the *requirements* of the sex roles. (Many find that very regrettable and would like to deny it, but we'll have to deal here with the data about what *is*, rather than what should be.) Now adherence to the *prohibitive* aspects of each role is a very different matter!

Generally the younger and better educated consumers are more likely to reject the prohibitive aspects of both sex roles and to resent promotions using such stereotypes. The typical profile of the consumer most likely to *reject* the prohibitive aspects of both sex roles is *a young, single woman, well-educated and employed outside the home in a relatively high-status occupation.* Conversely, the consumer most likely to *accept* both the requirements and the prohibitions of each sex role and adhere closely to such sex role prescriptions is *an elderly, retired male, married, little education, and a former occupation that required little skill or training.*

The lesson for marketers of consumer goods is clear: Given a choice, you may gain something by gendering the goods if your market is mainly downscale and/or largely male. But you won't gain much and you could lose out by gendering goods for an upscale market, especially if it contains a significant proportion of women. In order to gender the goods, you'll have to employ sex role stereotypes, and that can create negative attitudes toward both the goods and the company among upscale audiences.

There's another general rule about gendering products that's certainly worth noting: *Women will usually accept goods with a masculine image, but men always reject goods with a feminine image!* Women often wear slacks, but how many men have you seen in skirts lately? The fact is that men are *very* sensitive and protective, even defensive about their sexual identity.

Women, by contrast, are more secure in their sexual identity and don't see purchase and consumption of a masculine product or service as a threat to their femininity. So giving the goods a masculine identity may capture a larger part of the male market without losing the distaff buyers. But give the goods a feminie gender and you automatically say goodbye and take leave of your prospective male buyers.

> Philip Morris began marketing their Marlboro brand of cigarettes over 60 years ago, with either a red beauty tip or an ivory tip. The Marlboro name was in a soft, fancy script and the cigarette was feminine, indeed. After 30 years with that image, Philip Morris made a big change in the 1950s: The name stayed, but the product blend, the package, and the promotion were redone entirely, to focus on the heavy-smoking male market.

> The stark red-and-white colors, sharp, angular design, a "crush-proof" box, a new type of filter, more robust tobacco, and promotion of the cowboy image and later the "Marlboro Man" propelled the brand to the rank of a best-selling cigarette, well accepted by male smokers. Yet today the brand enjoys a very substantial brand share among women smokers as well. By contrast, how many male smokers have you noticed smoking Eve or Virginia Slims? Probably none. Women will accept a masculine-image product, but men universally reject consumer goods with a feminine image.

Consumers Act Their Age

Socially ascribed age roles prescribe what those in each age cohort are and are not to do. "Age-marking" a product or service image is the age role equivalent to gendering goods by associating them with a sex role. The product is positioned on the age spectrum by associating it with important aspects of the age role stereotype for a particular cohort group—teenagers, retirees, young parents, and so on. Some young consumers may object to the "frivolity" aspect of their age role stereotype while some elderly consumers might resent stereotypes of poverty and infirmity. But when marketers age-mark their goods, they don't include such negative images. So age-marking a consumer brand isn't likely to ruffle as many feathers as gendering it might.

Just as there's differential acceptance of opposite-gender products between men and women, so, too, do those of different ages respond differently to age-marking. The general rule is that consumers in the marketplace are more willing to move *down* on the age spectrum, toward youth, than to move upward, toward seniority. Juveniles are the exception; kids want to be older and they like goods associated with maturity, but children and especially adolescents will avoid any goods strongly associated with their juniors. Aside from that, adults tend to welcome products with a "younger" image and to find goods with an "older (than they are)" image unattractive.

Age-marking a product or service image is far less popular among marketers than gendering, and for good reason: it limits the market across a broad spectrum of ages without gaining much additional acceptance from the targeted cohort. While it's usually desirable if the goods have a fairly youthful image in this society, any one age group won't reach for consumer goods that are *too* far down the age spectrum from their own age cohort.

CONSUMERS, ON-STAGE FOR A CURTAIN CALL!

Let's return for a moment now, to the theatrical metaphor with which we began. As marketers, we operate behind the scenes. We don't direct the play—the performance is largely an improvisation by the consumer–actors themselves. But we can do our own casting and select the players we want by targeting certain segments. We can audition them informally, merely by getting into the audience and watching their daily role performances very closely. If we decide it would be more effective, we can hold a formal audition, using marketing research. And there's one thing about which we can all agree: It wouldn't make much sense just to choose our players at random or invite everybody onto the stage at once. We can rule out *mass* marketing in favor of intelligent segmentation.

More than casting directors, we marketers are the prop men and women of the theatrical marketplace. We're the ones that design and often stage-manage the properties the players will use. But it's a tough job, because there's *no way* we can force them to use what they don't want. We don't have an "exclusive" at this theater. There's always plenty of competition. What to do? *Know the play—know the roles.* It's not so much the individual players we want to understand, but rather the parts they're playing. Sure, some players' performances will be different from others. But since they're in the same role, there's a lot more commonality than there are distinctions. So know the roles they're playing; then give them props to fit their roles exactly. Give them things that will really improve their performance; get them standing ovations; make them stars. By doing so, we may not get very famous, but we could certainly get very wealthy!

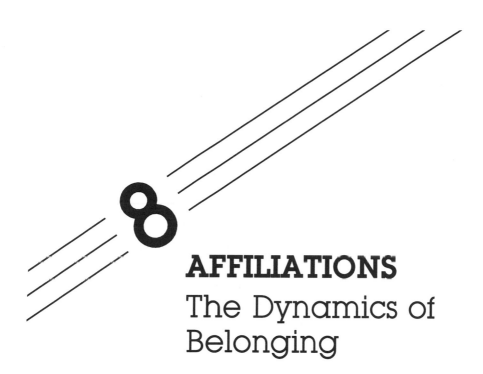

AFFILIATIONS
The Dynamics of Belonging

Innovations such as microwave ovens spread from one household to the next along the same side of the street. Several families on one side may have one, but almost nobody on the other side, even though the houses across the street are closer than some down the line. Why? Consumers copy the people they know—they often get acquainted through their children—and small children aren't supposed to cross the street! So the "Joneses" live next door.

You can't overestimate the importance of social influence on consumer choice. Faced with any uncertainty, consumers almost invariably turn to those around them for guidance and direction. Even when they buy something because of advertising, the ad probably presented it in a social setting and used social appeals. Only a small fraction of consumer purchases represent entirely independent actions by consumers. And only a small fraction of those rare cases would be contrary to what the person regards as socially acceptable.

We don't want to suggest that people are aware of how much social influence affects them. They're not usually aware of it and probably wouldn't admit it if they were. We all like to think of ourselves as very independent and almost completely self-determined. But in fact, our decisions are only rarely free from social influence. We just don't recognize it because social influence is so common it's almost invisible to those affected by it. But that certainly doesn't reduce its potency in our lives.

SOCIAL GROUPS THAT INFLUENCE CONSUMERS

All of us are members of several different groups. We're not really influenced or affected very much by society at large. We don't have that much contact with all the peoples of the world, but we are affected by others in the same group. The thing that distinguishes a particular group is the fact that all the people in it *share* something; they all have some *commonality*. They might differ in a lot of ways, but there has to be some common thread that runs through the group and distinguishes it or sets it apart from other groups. The following is a list of a dozen different kinds of groups. Each one is based on some common feature or characteristic. Since those in each group have something different in common, each one exerts a different type of influence on its members—on what they buy and use and on the way they behave in the consumer marketplace.

Familial	Avocational
Regional	Recreational
Political	Religious
Educational	Ethnic
Occupational	Racial
Demographic	Subcultural

Three Stages of Group Influence

When a group to which a consumer belongs has an effect on the person's behavior in the marketplace, the group influence goes through three different stages: *conformity, identification,* and *internalization,* outlined in the following list. At the first step, the members follow the norms to get something from the group or avoid being punished or rejected. At the second stage, they do what the group wants or advocates because they cue off of the group and see themselves as belonging to the group. At the third level, the members have adopted the group's standards as their *own;* they feel it's right for them, personally. At this last stage, the person might not even belong to the group any more and probably won't be aware of the fact that the idea originated in the group. The influence becomes invisible at this point.

Marketing appeals that depend on group influence can be pitched at any of the three levels or stages, but not usually to more than one at a time. If it's based on *conformity,* the message to consumers is that the group will love them if they buy and use the goods or reject them if they don't. If the appeal is to be *identification,* then the goods are promoted as something that people of this type normally use. But if the marketing appeal is based on *internalized* standards, then it doesn't even have to mention the group or refer to anybody else. It can be addressed only to the individual because the audience has probably long since forgotten that it was the group from which they learned the norm or standard in the first place. But even at this third level, the group is relevant to the marketer, even if it's

Stage	Motivational Basis	Behavioral Maintenance
Conformity	The members adhere to the norms and standards of the group to obtain rewards and avoid sanctions.	The behavior will be maintained only when the group can observe the member and issue rewards or punishment.
Identification	The members follow the norms because they see themselves as sharing and belonging to the group.	The behavior will be maintained in the group's presence regardless of rewards or punishment.
Internalization	The members adhere to the group norms because they accept them as their own personal ethic.	The behavior will be maintained even in the absence of other members or during isolation from the group.

not to the consumers. That's because the appeal is rooted in some common feature or characteristic of the group. For instance, it's based on something that everybody in that regional, occupational, or ethnic group values or does.

> **The three advertisements described here are all directed to the same recreational group, photographers. But each is pitched at a different level of group influence.**

> **Television commercials for Kodak processing paper and products show fictional characters receiving and examining their prints, then zero in on the pictures while those in the group chide the photographer, "The color is wrong!" And it obviously is wrong: green sky, purple faces, pink dogs, and the like. If only**

they had specified Kodak paper, "For a Good Look." The appeal is aimed at *conformity*.

In one magazine ad, Nikon uses the headline "If you're considering the pros and cons of various cameras, consider that Nikon has most of the pros." The copy points out that "Nikon cameras are used by more professional photographers than all other 35mm SLR cameras, combined." The ad is pitched at *identification* with the pros.

In another magazine ad, Nikon's headline reads "Presenting a camera that has more in common with the human eye than with other cameras. See?" The illustration shows two sets of four photographs each, allowing the reader to compare those taken with the Nikon FA with identical shots taken with other SLR cameras. The judgments are left to the reader and there's no reference to emulation or social influence. This appeal depends on *internalization* of the norms that define good photography.

Main Characteristics of Groups

The way groups are organized determines how much they affect the consumers that belong to them. A group doesn't affect all of its members in the same way. A member's *position* within the group governs how much the group will attempt to influence the person, as well as the person's desire to conform to or deviate from the group norms.

GROUP NORMS

Every group has some norms which are *standards or rules of conduct* for its members. Some group norms may be clearly spelled out, but more often they're just informal and somewhat ambiguous. For instance, a party invitation may state that formal attire is required, but that's a special case. Most invitations are likely to be either verbal or a handwritten note, saying nothing about what to wear. But that doesn't mean that the partygoers can dress as they like and get equal acceptance. Everybody will know that. Some people might call the host or hostess and ask what he or she is wearing, just to get a feel for how to dress.

Usually that isn't necessary, and nearly all the people who attend will probably be dressed about the same or at the same level of formality. If they're even vaguely familiar with the group, they'll have a pretty good idea of the unstated dress code.

Some group norms are *universal:* they apply equally to all the group members. The main reason for universal norms is to make the entire group distinct from those who don't belong—to separate the "in-group" from the "out-group." That helps people to identify with the group and increases the solidarity and cohesiveness of the group. Just about every group has some norms like that, whether we're talking about street gangs, supreme court justices, sewer workers, bishops, drug addicts, professors, pickpockets, psychiatrists, or astrologists. The people in the group tend to take on many of the same characteristics: they look similar, dress similarly, act like one another, and especially they *talk* in a similar vocabulary. If you've ever stayed at a hotel where there's a convention or conference going on, you could probably tell in a minute, just by seeing and hearing the conventiongoers in the lobby, whether it was for X-ray technicians, funeral directors, or stamp collectors.

GROUP NORMS AND CONSUMER GOODS

Such universal group norms are important to marketers because some purchase and consumption patterns will be shared among most or all of the group's members. Everybody in the teen subculture tends to buy and listen to the same kind of music, lawyers all buy and wear basically the same kinds of clothes, and you won't find many born-again Christians in the local bar. They *avoid* the same kinds of products and services, too. Whether it's as broad as a racial or ethnic group, or as narrow as a tiny interest group such as butterfly collectors, to appeal to the group effectively, marketers have to know three things about the group norms: what's *required,* what's *acceptable,* and what's *prohibited.*

Marketers selling things that are required by the group need only point that out and show how the use of the goods will meet the requirement. If it's acceptable, that takes a little more effort, but the group membership might help and at least it won't inhibit acceptance of the goods. And marketers have to watch out for prohibitions, as well. It's wasted effort to try selling liquor to members of AA, the WCTU, or MADD.

> **Johnson & Johnson, a company generally associated with juvenile products, took a leap at the other end of the age spectrum with its Affinity shampoo. In an attempt to grab a piece of the $1 billion plus shampoo market, Johnson & Johnson avoided the 18-to-34 year old age group, the "boomer" subculture that just about everyone else has targeted heavily. Noting the special hair-care needs of those who are greying, they designed the product and promotion to meet the special, shared needs of the over 40 age group. But their age and hair condition aren't the only things that these women have in common. They also share a strong concern about aging and often resent what they see as the tyranny of being young. To appeal to this group, Affinity adopted the line that "Now there's no age limit to looking good." If Johnson & Johnson can first grab the attention and loyalty of this age group, they may then be able to broaden their sights in the highly competitive shampoo arena.**

GROUP NORMS AND ROLES

Some group norms apply equally to everybody in the group, but others apply only to certain group members, with special roles. For example, in a project team, there might be unofficial but recognizable roles: the boss, a lieutenant or two, an egghead, a clown, an arbitrator, a gofer, an organizer, a worrier, and several grunts. The names identifying these roles aren't very flattering, but they readily call to mind the stereotypes you've seen in many group situations. What's more, they're very real! Nobody in the group would expect a brilliant idea from the jester, accept direction from a grunt, or send a lieutenant for coffee and donuts. Individual roles were discussed in the last chapter. These group roles are virtually the same as broader social roles, except that they apply to members of a particular group rather than everybody in the society.

Marketing appeals to a particular group often use role models who represent the most attractive and successful consumers in the group. Nobody would choose a perfect klutz from the group as a role model. But effective marketing appeals sometimes do use models who are very different from those in the target market, as noted in Chapter 5. That's often effective, providing that consumers don't perceive much *risk* in buying the goods. When there is some social risk—when consumers in the group are likely to wonder if it's "right for them"—they're more likely to emulate an attractive model who is within their group than someone equally attractive who is an "outsider" to the group. They can identify more easily with models who share some of the same characteristics.

> In the Johnson & Johnson case noted previously, Affinity shampoo greeted the market in early 1984, amidst a rash of new shampoo brand introductions: Revlon introduced Hair's Daily Requirement, Andrew Jergens came forth with Dimension, Clairol brought out Essence, while giant Lever Bros. announced a $60 million campaign for Dimension shampoo. Johnson & Johnson had earmarked only about $12 million for Affinity advertising and a similar amount for a sampling campaign.

> To court the target group they had identified, Johnson & Johnson chose an attractive mother–career woman, over 50, to represent them, rather than a young celebrity. She traveled to over 20 major metropolitan areas to hold press conferences and give instore seminars on issues of concern to women over 40. Both she and the mature models used in their TV commercials were typical of attractive leaders in this age group. By using such in-group role models, they hoped to secure a following among the nearly 50 million American women over 40.

CONSUMER GROUP INTERACTIONS

Consumers belong to many groups, groups of different size and cohesiveness. Some are very large and loosely knit, with little or no interaction among the members. For instance, people of the same ethnicity or religion will share certain views and characteristics, but they don't routinely interact with one another. The group may help to shape the frame of reference of an individual member, but aside from that, the group has little or no *direct* influence.

There's usually regular interaction among members of smaller, more closely knit groups: family, neighbors, friends, coworkers. These closer, more cohesive groups have a much stronger, more direct influence on the way that members behave. Usually the purchase and consumption patterns are more similar within smaller groups than within larger. But the influence the group has on its members isn't equal. The group has more power over some members than others.

Position Within the Group

Some members are more important to the group than others. It depends on what each member has to contribute to the group as a whole. Some groups have an *extrinsic* purpose: people come together to jointly accomplish some external purpose. A project group or work unit is a good example. The key members, those who can do the most to help the group reach its objective, are more important than those who have only very little to offer. The more important members are more *central* to the group, while the least important are *marginal* members. Ironically the group has more power over marginal than over central members.

Many groups to which consumers belong have an *intrinsic* rather than an extrinsic purpose. In other words, people gather into groups purely for the satisfaction they get from belonging to them and affiliating with the other members. Bowling teams or groups of birdwatchers are like that. But even in these groups, some members are more important and more central to the group while others may have only peripheral or marginal importance. Those who are the most charismatic or entertaining, the more popular members, the ones with the best advice or the most esteem among their peers are the most central. Those who are less likable, popular, or sought-after have more marginal positions. Again the group has more power over its marginal members than over those who are the most central. *The more the group values a member, the less power it has over the person.*

Options Outside the Group

The other side of the coin is the value the individual consumer places on the group. When people have a lot of options outside the group or don't find belonging to the group especially rewarding, they don't value the group very much. But when "it's the only game in town," so to speak, or when they really get a lot of satisfaction from belonging to the group, they value it very highly. People who value the group are much more likely to conform to its norms and bow to any pressure the group exerts than would those who don't really value the group much. *The more the member values the group, the more power the group has over the person.*

The influence a group has on an individual member depends on both the value of the group to the member and the value of the member to the group. These relationships are shown in the matrix that follows.

Value of Group to Member	Value of Member to Group	
	High	Low
High	Low pressure High conformity Medium influence	High pressure High conformity High influence
Low	Low pressure Low conformity Low influence	High pressure Low conformity Medium influence

These relationships have a lot more than just academic interest to marketers of consumer goods. The marginal group members, at the upper right in the matrix, are very subject to group norms. They often have few other options, and the group is very important to them. Yet they don't have a lot to offer the group. These are precisely the people who are most sensitive to marketing appeals based on group norms. They can be approached in two ways. One is to convince them that the group norms require the purchase and use of the goods. The other is to persuade them that buying and using the goods will make them more valuable to the group. The ultimate approach is to combine the two, promoting the goods as both required by the group norms and also helping to contribute to the group.

> **Burger King recently promoted their premium hamburger with a series of TV commercials featuring friends, family, or coworkers talking about Herb, a fictitious character who had never tasted a Whopper. They didn't speak of this unseen character as though he was a complete nerd, just an ordinary guy with a bizarre trait—he'd never tasted this spectacular hamburger! The subconscious message is that you're pretty strange if you don't do what's *normal*, to eat and enjoy the product. This message hits strongly at marginal group members who can't afford to deviate much from group norms.**

Sometimes the consumers who are most free from group pressure are of more interest to marketers than those who are most constrained. These are the people in the lower left part of the matrix: those who the group values highly, even though they don't value the group very much. These are often the innovators who are willing to try new or different consumer products or services. Their opposite counterparts, the marginal people, can't afford to take many risks: What if the group doesn't like it? The people who are central to the group but don't value it a lot can take chances without having to worry about pressure or rejection.

Yet since these central group members are important to the group, the others are likely to follow their example. If they try something new and find it satisfactory and effective, the others may well follow suit. After all, these are the people who more often *set* the group norms, rather than having to follow the existing norms. Since they're likely to be innovators and also key influentials or opinion leaders, they are often the new product marketer's avenue to the group and everybody else in it. They can best be approached with appeals to their *independence* and *position*, rather than to conformity.

> The appeal in a magazine ad for General Motor's 1986 Oldsmobile illustrates the best approach to those who are relatively insensitive to group norms. The appeal borders on *independence* and there's no mention of the necessity to conform. Headline: "The category of personal luxury car is again a category of one." Lead copy: "The car that has defined personal luxury for a generation now redefines the category." Listen to the copy references: "outstanding"—"revolutionary"—"leading edge"—"inspired." End copy: "This car obeys but one basic rule: never, never be conventional." This approach isn't likely to be appealing to conformers, but more independent types may seek to match their self-image with that of the car.

How Group Norms Are Enforced

The group can use any one or a combination of four means to enforce norms and obtain conformity from members. In a nutshell, they are:

Authority. The group has a leadership function and the norms are followed because the group's authority is recognized as legitimate and proper.

Reward. The group has the power to provide or withhold rewards such as recognition, status, or affiliation, bestowed on the basis of conformity.

Sanction. The group has the power to punish nonconformity by assigning unpleasant roles, denigrating status, or establishing other penalties.

Threat.   The group obtains conformity by threatening the deviant member with temporary ejection or permanent expulsion from the group.

Authority.   Marketing appeals based on this means of norm enforcement just indicate to the consumer that the group has made "this" choice. It's what "everybody" in the group does. Magazine ads for Lever Bros'. Dove brand use the headline "Why are you still using soap when women from Scranton to Sacramento will tell you Dove is better?" There's no reference to what will or won't happen if the consumer doesn't do it too.

Reward.   Appeals in this category identify what social benefits consumers will receive if they buy and use the goods. The group rewards are described in the most vivid graphic terms possible. Hanes hosiery has consistently promoted their brand with the slogan "Gentlemen Prefer Hanes." The ads show one or more men casting admiring glances at the Hanes woman.

Sanction.   With this approach, the shoe is on the other foot— the appeal describes the terrible things that will happen if the product *isn't* bought and used. Such TV commercials usually picture embarrassment or humiliation in front of the group because of deviation. An original classic of this ilk was Procter & Gamble's "Was My Face Red" campaign for Crisco shortening. In these 1940s vintage radio commercials, homemakers described how they were embarrassed by serving tough piecrust. "Junior said in front of everybody, 'The pie's great, but why'd ya bake it on a *paper plate?*' Was My Face Red!"

Threat.   This is the ultimate fear weapon, a step beyond mere sanction. The punishment here is worse than mere loss of face, it's total rejection, isolation, and loneliness as a result of failing to buy and use a product that's required by the group. Procter & Gamble's Head & Shoulders shampoo was originally named for it's ability to protect both hair and apparel from dandruff flakes. Ads showed others in the group turning away, with disgusted looks on their faces, from the unfortunate nonuser with "unsightly dandruff."

Combinations.   Two or more approaches can be combined for even greater effect: The legitimate authority of the group may be portrayed, a reward from the group for conformity may be identified, and a punishment may also be cited for deviation.

CONSUMERS DEPEND ON REFERENCE GROUPS

We've talked a lot about the influence that groups exert on members, about the pressure they put on people to conform to group norms. This might give the impression that consumers routinely resist social influence from groups. But in fact, nothing could be further from the truth. Certainly there are situations where we may wish our groups' norms were different or that we didn't have to live by them. That's real freedom, but unfortunately the benefits of freedom always come with an unpleasant side-effect: *responsibility*. Certainly neither you nor we would voluntarily submit to group norms just to shirk the responsibility that goes with freedom. But perhaps we could candidly admit that almost everybody else does, including our consumers. So most people not only don't resist group influence, they go looking for it.

Three Functions for Reference Groups

Reference groups do three things for consumers: provide *information,* serve as means of *comparison*, and furnish *guidance*. A brief summary of the three functions follows:

Informative. This group provides *descriptive information* about the social and material world; it shows the consumer what exists and what alternatives are available.

Comparative. This group provides a social *standard or benchmark* for status assessment; it indicates how the person is doing when no objective standards exist.

Normative. This group provides the *norms and rules* governing attitudes and behavior; it tells a consumer what to do and what not to do in social situations.

Marketers use consumer reference groups in a couple of ways: They can actually provide the reference group in the promotion, using models or representatives, or they can identify groups in the consumers' social sphere that favor the purchase and use of the goods. The nature of the group influence, the required perceptions of the consumers, and the results of the influence when marketing appeals use each type of reference group are outlined and compared in the following list.

Informative Groups	Comparative Groups	Normative Groups
INFLUENCE DEPENDS ON THE GROUP'S:		
Degree of expertise, knowledgeability, or experience.	Comparability of status or condition with that of the person.	Power to bestow rewards or punishment on the consumer.
THE CONSUMER MUST SEE THE GROUP AS:		
A credible or believable source of information.	Providing an appropriate standard for judging status.	A potential source of positive or negative reinforcement.
THE GROUP'S INFLUENCE WILL LEAD TO:		
The acceptance and application of the information.	The recognition of individual status as superior or inferior.	The modification of beliefs, attitudes, or behavior patterns.

INFORMATIVE REFERENCE GROUPS

Consumers get a lot of information about products and services, brands and stores from advertising. But they know the information isn't very unbiased or objective; sponsor X says brand X is best, sponsor Y praises brand Y, and sponsor Z claims brand Z is superior to both. The amount of media information is also limited. It's usually confined to only a brief sketch. So consumers often turn to those around them, to *informative* reference groups, for information that is more credible and complete.

> **Colgate's Palmolive dishwashing liquid uses the character of Madge the manicurist, Procter & Gamble's Comet Cleanser uses Hazel the plumber, and Folger's Coffee uses Mrs. Olson to inform and instruct the model homemakers in their TV commercials about the benefits of the products. These personalities aren't used in the same way as clinic-jacketed pseudodoctors who explain analgesics and antacids. The three models mentioned here are surrogate informative referents; stand-ins who do not explain to the audience directly but inform the characters in the ads while the homemaker audience looks on.**

COMPARATIVE REFERENCE GROUPS

In many situations, consumers can't find an objective standard for gauging their status in some respect. In that case, social comparison is the only answer. They turn to a *comparative* reference group, as the cliche "keeping up with the Joneses" shows. Whether they feel a sense of satisfaction or see a need for improvement depends on who they use as a benchmark. So marketers can provide such a standard or suggest certain groups, who just happen to use their goods. In effect, they're telling the consumer "If you want to keep up, buy our brand!"

> **The lead copy line of a magazine ad for a GM 1985 Chevrolet reads "Even if you've never owned a Caprice, you've probably known someone who has." Similarly copy for a BMW magazine ad reads, in part, "From Greenwich, Connecticut to Greenwich, England, the staid sedans that once characterized 'the leisure class' are giving way to a far less leisurely class of automobile."**

Both car makers are identifying comparative reference groups for their prospective markets—one citing "family car" buyers, the other the young but affluent crowd. The implication inherent in both appeals is that the reader isn't doing so well if he or she hasn't attained the "right" level and doesn't drive the "right" car to go with it.

NORMATIVE REFERENCE GROUPS

Consumers use normative reference groups to decide what to do and what not to do. These groups provide guidance and direction that are often sought and welcomed by consumers. The norms and roles that groups provide were outlined earlier. These informative, comparative, and normative categories are based on the way consumers use the group, rather than on the nature of the group itself.

TV commercials for Almaden Vineyards Mountain Chablis point out San Francisco's proximity to California's wine country and identify San Franciscans as really knowing their wine. Then they provide a purchase norm by noting that this group drinks twice as much of this vintage as they do of two other leading brands combined. This TV spot also shows a wine merchant advising the vacationing couple to choose the advertised brand. Such normative influence is effective, especially since inexperienced buyers are uncomfortable about making their own choice.

Three Kinds of Reference Groups

Consumers refer to three different kinds of groups: *membership, aspirational,* and *symbolic* reference groups. Here's a sketch of how the three differ from one another:

Membership.   Groups to which consumers belong, interacting with others and sharing mutual influence.

Aspirational.   Groups to which consumers would like to belong or intend to join, so influence is unilateral.

Symbolic. Groups to which consumers neither belong nor intend joining, but whose norms exert influence.

Membership groups usually exert the strongest influence on the consumer's purchase and consumption patterns. But aspirational reference groups also exert strong influence, even stronger than membership groups, at times, but usually for a much shorter period of time. Consumers who anticipate joining a group and are striving to prepare sometimes engage in what's called *anticipatory overbuying.* As noted earlier, they may not have a clear picture of exactly what goods are required by the new situation, but they eagerly acquire the goods they associate with the new role and group, whether or not the image they have in their minds is accurate or erroneous. Finally, symbolic groups provide influence that is very pervasive, spread across many different kinds of products and services, and for long periods of time, although the influence is the least vigorous and potent. Famous individuals and celebrity groups may be symbolic referents for consumers, even though they may never have direct contact with such people.

REFERENCE GROUPS CUT BOTH WAYS

The direction of influence exerted by a reference group can be either *positive or negative.* With positive reference groups, the consumers accept the norms, attitudes, and actions of the group as a guide to their own. So they'll buy and use the same products, brands, or services and shop the same retail outlets. But with negative reference groups, the consumers reject the values, attitudes, and behavior patterns of the group and actively avoid emulating the (other) members of the group. Whether a reference group is positive or negative has nothing to do with the character of the group per se. Any given group might be a positive reference point for some consumers, a negative referent for others, and completely irrelevant for still other consumers.

Marketers can use either positive or negative reference

groups in their appeals, or both. Obviously, "the good guys" are the ones that use our brand, while it's the nerds, klutzes, and oafs, the trolls and mutants who use the "other" brand. As noted earlier, it's possible and often effective to mix them both in the same appeal, in a commercial playoff of the old "white hat–black hat" routine of B-grade western movies.

> **Television commercials for Miller Lite beer include several famous athletes playing and having fun together, while praising the qualities of the brand. Suddenly, among these likable folks, comedian Rodney Dangerfield appears, playing the fool, as always. Somehow he always manages to screw up the game or whatever else is happening. But Dangerfield is also relatively ignorant of the virtues of Lite beer, as well. The audience identifies with the famous sports figures (who prefer Lite) and psychologically disassociates from the (uninformed) comic character—scoring a one–two punch with positive and negative referents.**

THE BASES OF GROUP INFLUENCE

A social group has *power* to require or prohibit purchase and consumption of certain goods when the group is sufficiently attractive and the consumer values identification or association with the group. Some groups have *expertise* that's valuable to the consumer as a source of information and advice about consumer goods. When consumers try to assess their own potential satisfaction with some kind of goods, where individual reactions might differ sharply, the *similarity* of the group members to the consumer is important. At other times, consumers might want to identify with group members because they are *attractive* figures, worthy of being emulated, in the consumers' eyes. The different forms of influence outlined below can operate separately or in unison within the same marketing appeal.

> *Power.*   The group norms or role requirements may *require* the purchase and/or use of certain goods, subject to authority, reward, sanction, or threat.

Expertise. Group members or the group as a whole may have special expertise or be viewed by the consumer as experts, *advising* the individual on complex issues.

Similarity. The group or some of its members might be viewed as *representative* of the individual member, serving as a gauge for predicting personal reactions.

Attraction. The consumer may wish to identify with or *emulate* some or all of the group members out of respect, admiration, or adulation.

Celebrity Referents for Consumers

Marketers often use celebrities for reference group appeals, in one of six different ways: (1) they may *endorse* the product, (2) they may provide a *testimonial* for the goods, (3) they may be seen using the product, with its *placement* in a dramatic performance, (4) they may *dramatize* the use of the product, (5) they may *represent* the product or service as spokespeople, or (6) they may allow their name to be used as the *brand name* itself. Here's a brief sketch of the six kinds of celebrity relationships:

Endorsements. The celebrity, whether an expert on the goods or not, merely agrees to the use of his or her name and image in the promotion for the product or service.

Testimonials. The celebrity, usually an expert, has experience with the brand, product, or service, and attests to its value and worth, based on that experience.

Placements. The product or service is placed in a motion picture or television drama where it's either merely seen by the audience or used by a leading character.

Dramatizations. Celebrity actors or models take part in portrayal of product or service in use during a dramatic enactment specifically designed to show the goods.

Representatives. The celebrity agrees to become a spokesperson for the brand through multiple media over an extended time, until he or she is closely identified with it.

Identification. The celebrity independently, or in partnership with a producer, introduces his or her own brand, carrying the celebrity name as the brand name.

> *Endorsements: "Would I Lie? Trust Me on This."* Marketers look for endorsements from celebrities who have a very trustworthy appearance, image, and reputation. Danny Thomas, Roger Staubach, Art Linkletter, and Ed McMahon have all endorsed various forms and brands of insurance. They have one thing in common—they're all mature males with well-established reputations and an authoritative demeanor. But sometimes sheer popularity is enough, as when rock star Michael Jackson endorsed Pepsi Cola. But the ultimate coup has to be Pepsi convincing Geraldine Ferraro to endorse the brand.

> *Testimonials: "I Know 'Cause I've Been There!"* Comic actor Bill Cosby is famous for his humorous but sensitive portrayals of the kids in the neighborhood, back in the good old days. He was a natural for Jell-O puddings and desserts. Television ads showing the charismatic Cosby together with a lovable collection of preschool kids, urging moms everywhere to loosen up on the Jell-O for their youngsters, provided high-validity testimonials for the product's worth.

> *Placements: "If It's Good Enough for ET or 007 It's Good Enough for Me!"* When products are placed amidst the action in movies or TV shows, the mere association of the goods with the characters in the story provides a powerful reference group appeal. Even when the character isn't human! The classic case was ET, director Steven Spielberg's reptilian extra-terrestrial automaton, lured from his hiding place with Reese's Pieces candy or getting a little sloshed on Coors beer. James Bond, Ian Fleming's novel and movie superspy, has also lent his image to several consumer products. In 007's recent adventure, *A View to a Kill,* Bond saves himself from drowning by breathing air from the Michelin tire of a submerged car, and later jimmies a door lock with a

credit card clearly labeled with the name of the cataloger, "A Sharper Image." Such placements are likely to become even more popular in the near future, despite some objections from critics.

Dramatizations: "Between the Sheets with J.R." Cannon Sheets, no less! Dramatizations were used by Cannon Mills to sell sheets and towels with reference group appeals, using such celebrities as Larry Hagman, ("Dallas" bad-guy J.R. Ewing), Joan Collins from "Dynasty," the late master chef James Beard, actress–model Brooke Shields, and the dean of comedians, Bob Hope. These dramatizations were headlined "Two of the most famous names in America sleep—cook—bathe together," followed by portrayals of the stars using Cannon products.

Representation: "Don't Leave Home Without It!" Karl Malden, the Joe Average of the movie and TV screen, represents American Express Traveler's Cheques. He has routinely appeared on radio and television ads as well as in print media advertising over the past several years. So often and so long, in fact, that the association with AE has probably boosted his name and image recognition well beyond what it was when he started. Since this service is sold to average consumers in all walks of life, the use of this authoritative yet pleasant, nonthreatening personality to represent the service is a logical choice.

Identification: "Paul Newman's in the Kitchen Again." A rash of famous personalities have tried (often in vain) to capitalize on their celebrity and name recognition by independently or cooperatively introducing lines of consumer goods carrying their own name: Roy Rogers Roast Beef restaurants, Johnny Carson clothing for men, Arthur Treacher's fish and chips restaurants, [Rodney] Dangerfield's restaurant and lounge, and most recently [Paul] Newman's Own brand of "healthy" foods. Such efforts have often proved unsuccessful for a variety of reasons. Usually the celebrity name alone won't suffice, especially if the production and/or marketing efforts are insufficient or unpracticed. But there are notable exceptions: Newman's Own spaghetti sauce sells at about a $15 million a year clip, not to mention the salad dressing or gourmet popcorn, for another $10 million annually. This, without a penny's worth of paid advertising. The company depends on Newman's name and image on the label and his press coverage alone. Incidentally all profits go to charity, and the firm contributed about $7 million in the first three years of operation, starting in 1982.

Common Man—Common Woman

Celebrity status has its allure, and expertise has authority and credibility. But most reference group appeals use the "common man" or "common woman" approach, and successfully at that. Consumer goods of all types are shown in social settings, with people much like those in the audience using them successfully. Hundreds of typical TV mothers launder their typical TV children's clothes, right before your very eyes. Paunchy do-it-your-selfers build marvelous things with tools you can get right now by calling an 800 number. Bespectacled young husbands mull over investment plans and make the "right" decision while aproned wives look on with concern. Exuberant children destroy whole armies of toy enemies with their supercreatures while the kids on the other side of the TV screen cheer. With reference group appeals, everyone gets to "try it before they buy it."

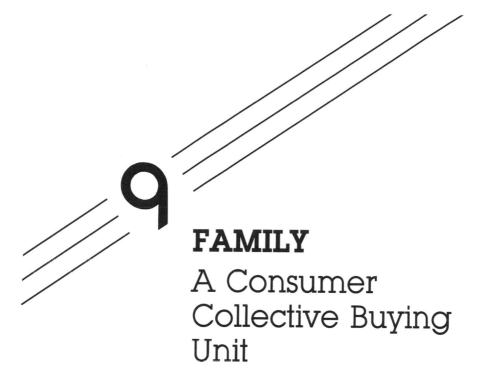

FAMILY
A Consumer Collective Buying Unit

"I make all the *important* decisions in my family," Mac told his buddies. "I decide what we should do about the national debt, Communism, the troubles in the Middle East. I let the ol' lady decide about unimportant stuff: where we'll live, when to get a new car, where the kids go to school, what kinda furniture, where to go on vacation . . . . All that little junk I don't wanna bother with."

Decision making and family buying often are specialized.

Only a small fraction of the purchase decisions by those living in a family, a household containing more than one person, are actually *individual* decisions. Even when they buy things that we typically see as personal products and services, the other members of the family ordinarily have a strong influence on the person making the decision. A household is almost always a single economic unit, a financial entity, as well as a social entity. Almost every adult family member has some degree of financial autonomy—some monetary independence and purely personal discretion about what to buy and use. But except for the very richest and the very poorest families in the society, the vast majority pool their income and disposable resources. As a result, individual income and personal preference (the ability and willingness to buy) are usually less significant to consumer marketers than are household income and family preference. Since the household, rather than the individual, is often the basic element of behavior in the marketplace, the family often emerges as the appropriate unit of analysis of gauging consumer markets.

JUST WHAT IS AN AMERICAN "FAMILY"?

The terms "family" and "household" aren't as clear-cut as we might first think. They can be a little ambiguous at times, and that causes problems when we study markets. Any time statistical data are listed in terms of families or households, it's always advisable to check carefully to see just how these units are defined. If their definitions and yours are different, you could be thinking of apples while they've been counting oranges. Sometimes that won't make too much difference, but at others it could lead to gross discrepancies, so take care.

"Family" Versus "Household"

The term "family" refers to a special social unit. A family consists of two or more people who are related by blood, marriage, or adoption, living in the same household. So all relatives in the same household are a family, according to the U.S. Department of Commerce. By contrast, a "household" consists of all those who occupy one living unit, whether or not they're related. There are over 60 million households in the United States. There are also "subfamilies," consisting of single parents or married couples (with or without minor children) living in a housing unit who are related to the male or female head of the household. So we have three rather different units to regard: *families,* kinfolk in one housing unit; *households,* including everybody in one housing unit, whether they're related or not; and *subfamilies,* married couples or single parents related to a head of household and living with them. So the total numbers and average incomes vary, depending on which unit of analysis we're using.

Four Kinds of Families

We can also talk about families in sociological rather than economic terms. We'll take a look at the different kinds of "families" to which consumers belong. Then we'll take a look at the functions families serve and also briefly examine the myths and realities of the American family structure.

FAMILY OF ORIENTATION OR PROCREATION

The family into which you were born is your family of *orientation.* It includes your parents and siblings. When sociologists speak of a person's *ordinal position* in the family, they're referring to whether the person was the first, second, third, and so forth, child of the family. The family that you form through marriage is your family of *procreation,* including your spouse and any children. So when we refer to a child's family here, we'll be talking about the family of orientation. But most of the time when we refer to consumers' families, it will mean their family of procreation, including their spouse and/or their children.

NUCLEAR OR EXTENDED FAMILY

The nucleus of the family consists of a husband and wife and perhaps one or more children, or else just a single parent and his or her child(ren). This kind of nuclear family is what's typical of our society, but certainly not of the whole world. With *extended* families, other relatives are living with the nuclear family members: a parent, perhaps, a grandchild, or a brother or cousin of one head of household. In our society, the children of the family are expected (in fact, more or less pressured) to leave the home when they reach their majority. Nor do heads of household much welcome a brother-in-law moving in more or less permanently, let alone more distant relatives. Even parents of household heads are often strongly encouraged either to live alone or to take up residence in a special care facility for the aging.

In many parts of the world, and especially in less developed economies, exactly the opposite is true: Extended families in one household are the rule rather than the exception. Even in several countries of Western Europe, it would be regarded as rather odd, indeed, if a single child of the family moved out and took up residence elsewhere, by himself or herself. Others would wonder what was wrong with the person or the family, just as we do if we learn of single adults living with their parents. And in much of Asia, young men, when they marry, bring their brides into the households of their families of orientation, so that many nuclear families may occupy a single residence and household. The strong tendency to maintain only a nuclear family within a household profoundly affects the nature and character of American society. Obviously it also has very fundamental effects on the way that families here behave in the marketplace, compared to what's typical elsewhere.

A host of companies and sometimes whole industries find that demand for their goods are completely dependent on or strongly affected by the rate of family formation and the creation of new households. It wouldn't seem too difficult to predict household

formation, since it's usually very closely tied to the age of the population, and we have good data on that from the decennial census. But both the cyclical fluctuations in the economy and the vacillations in social trends also play a major role.

New household formation was at a rate of about 1 million per year during the 1960s, but it leaped to a 1.7 million rate during the 1970s and experts predicted even better things for the 1980s. Unfortunately for many, that wasn't to be. During the economic slump of the early 1980s, the rate barely exceeded the 1 million of the 1960s. *American Demographics*, a Dow Jones & Company publication, expects things to improve during the second half of the decade, with a rate of about 1.3 million new households per year. Then it's back to the doldrums, with a mere 1 million a year again for the first half of the 1990s. According to their projections, there will be about 100 million households in 1995, and the preponderance will be middle-aged consumers.

Along with changes in household formation, changes in house ownership versus rental patterns confound the picture for some consumer marketers, especially those in the building industry itself. About 70 percent of new households formed in the 1970s were homeowners. That should change to about 72 percent or 75 percent in the last half of the 1980s, then zoom to about 83 percent during the first half of the 1990s. Condominiums and multi-family units enjoyed a day in the sunshine during the early 1980s recession, but only because of that. The choice of American new families remains the detached, one-family home, regardless of whether or not they can afford it within the economic climate of the times.

THE FUNCTIONS THE FAMILY SERVES

Two *cannot* live as cheaply as one, despite the old adage, nor, most certainly, can three or four! Yet few would deny that two or more people in a family can live a lot more cheaply than if they each took up individual residence. (Divorce and the separation of households are leading causes of personal bankruptcy in this country.) So one important function of the family is simply economy of resources. And that function is even more vital outside affluent societies such as ours. But the economic function of the family extends beyond mere financial benefits. Family formation allows individual members to specialize, improving performance, eliminating duplication of effort, and making life easier for all concerned.

Families provide their members with *emotional support,* and often this psychological function is more important than the economic one. Empathy, sharing, companionship, and defense and support in times of stress are all benefits family members routinely provide one another.

The socialization and training of children can best be accomplished in the family. Within this primary social grouping, children's personalities are shaped and formed, their values are developed, they're taught how to deal with the social world around them and given instruction and example about how to conduct themselves: how to speak, dress, behave, and a thousand little things that make each person a unique individual.

Last but perhaps not least, families are a way of building and sharing a complete *lifestyle;* a way of going, so to speak. Personal and family lifestyle aren't necessarily synonymous, but they're at least closely related. We'll discuss lifestyle more completely in a later chapter.

THE CHANGING STRUCTURE OF THE FAMILY

Earlier it was noted that the nuclear family is typical in the United States. The conventional stereotype is mom, dad, and a couple of kids. The traditional, diamond-shaped family structure over time is shown in Figure 2. But in fact the stereotypical picture is more myth than fact: fewer than one family in twenty fit the mold of a single-marriage, two-parent household including a couple of children of the marriage. In fact, there's a greater proportion of single-parent households than that today. This contemporary alternative is shown in the Figure 3.

Separations, divorces, and remarriages are frequent, but

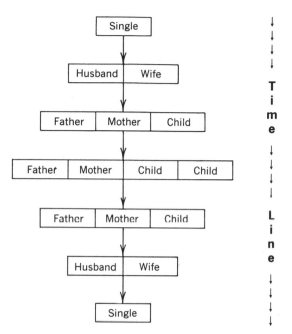

Figure 2. Traditional American family structure.

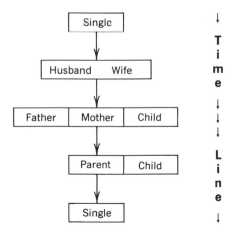

Figure 3. Contemporary alternative family structure.

other factors also enter in. Over 10 percent of American families have a female but no male head of household. A fairly substantial proportion of households are occupied by unmarried couples, although only a small fraction of them are parents. It's difficult to document the exact percentage, but there are a little over 4 percent of nonfamily households in the United States, not including single householders living alone. It's not uncommon for young couples to share a household for some time before marriage. In that case, it constitutes a distinct preliminary step in family formation.

A moment ago we spoke about how new *household* formation rates often vary separately from the age distribution of the population. Such deviations are largely due to economic conditions. But the average age at the time of *family* formation has also become older. Delays in marriage and parenthood beyond the traditional ages are more the result of social than of economic conditions. Young singles and childless young couples have very different purchase patterns from those later in the family life cycle, as we shall soon see.

> The stereotypical image of how an American family lives is as outmoded as the old image of family structure. Let's take eating, for example. Perhaps there never were many families like the one television viewers watched and admired on the Donna Reed Show, some thirty years ago. But some came pretty close. Mom, up early, hurrying around the kitchen in her prim housedress and apron—Dad and Junior sipping orange juice and debating how they wanted their eggs. That's an anachronistic sentimentality today.
>
> Gone are juice, coffee, eggs, toast, and conversation about the new day around the family breakfast table. Instead, consider a Croissan'wich, an Egg McMuffin, or a Breakfast Jack. (Burger King, McDonald's, and Jack-in-the-Box, respectively.) From 1977 to 1984, the number of people eating lunch in a restaurant rose less than 5 percent, and the number eating dinner out rose less than 25 percent. Growth in breakfast meals out during that period rose well over 50 percent, and the total breakfast tab is a

mere $10 billion—less than a tenth of the annual bill for all meals out. Some analysts attribute it to more working women, but that's only a part of the story.

Families once sat down together for meals, but "grazing" is becoming more popular today, even when eating at home. Junior wanders into the kitchen to grab a snack. Sis comes in later. Dad has a bite to eat when he gets home from work. Mom waits almost to bedtime. People eat smaller portions, eat more often, and nibble irregularly. The food processing companies that market groceries are fighting back against the fast-food outlets by modifying unit sizes, such as Stouffer's Lean Cuisine in one- or two-serving packages; similarly with archrival Campbell Soup Company's Le Menu frozen entrees.

Variety and speed of preparation are the buy-words for many of these food marketers. A *Good Housekeeping* ad for Campbell's Soup pictures no less than 30 red-and-white labeled cans, for a different variety every day of the month. To accommodate the grazing phenomenon, Campbell heavily promotes its cup-of-soup concept with TV commercials showing *one* parent and a child or one family member only, enjoying the quick-to-make hot soup.

The examples of marketers' adaptation to the changing American family are legion; these are but a few. It's interesting to note that the leaders of many of our social institutions—in politics, education, religion, the arts, and so forth—resist mightily the changes in families and lament the passing of "the good old days." By contrast, American business has responded with "lightning speed." It would seem that lethargy and nostalgia are luxuries marketers can ill afford in the hectic pace of competition.

COMMONALITIES AND DISTINCTIONS

Consumer goods are often marketed to families, rather than to individuals, but families aren't an homogeneous collection of buying units. For the marketer, the objective is to identify the main characteristics and modal patterns that typify different

kinds of families, then examine how they relate to the purchase and consumption of the goods. The brand, product, service, or store can then be targeted to certain kinds of families
and the appeals can be fitted to one kind of family's special
needs. For example, there are big differences between families
with working mothers and those where the female head of
household is exclusively a homemaker. Women in the former
category are usually sensitive to the role conflicts resulting from
dual careers as wife–mother–homemaker and working woman.
They welcome consumer products and services that help them
to be effective in both roles and reduce some of the conflict
between roles.

By contrast, women who are completely dedicated to homemaking (and there's still a substantial proportion of such families) have more time and energy to devote to the home and
family. They often tend to judge themselves and others by their
ability to maintain a very neat, well-kept home. They get a lot of
identity from their family roles, take greater pride in their
homes, and really get involved with housekeeping. At the same
time, they may feel a little bored or "locked in," so they like
some excitement, romance, and fantasy associated with the consumer goods they buy and use.

The women in these two categories have very different concerns and buying patterns, and they're sensitive to different
kinds of marketing appeals: For working wives and mothers,
speed, ease, convenience, and proficiency are the buy-words
for appliances and household goods. Their counterparts, who
are exclusively homemakers, respond more to power, effectiveness, novelty, "fun," and excitement. It's hard to split the difference! Often marketing appeals that try to ride the fence between these two kinds of families and types of orientations fall
flat among both groups. Marketers who try to be everything to
everybody sometimes end up being nothing to nobody. A better
course of action for consumer marketers might be to segment
families by type and focus on a specific target group for a specific product or service, brand or store.

FAMILY ROLES AND INTERACTIONS

The family roles that different members play and the way they interact with one another affect what consumer goods the family buys and uses. Earlier, in Chapter 7 where social roles were discussed, we identified nine purchase- and consumption-related roles. We also looked at social influence and interactions in Chapter 8. Now it's time to consider these things again, relating them directly to the family as a consumer buying unit.

Family Purchase and Consumption Roles

The nine roles directly related to buying and using consumer goods identified earlier are outlined on the following page. Let's take a closer look at what each one involves and who typically plays each role within the family.

THE INFORMATION FILTER

Family members who play this role affect behavior in the marketplace because they regulate and control the information about what's available and what's desirable. Which family member plays the role for any given product or service depends on two things: *expertise* and *interest*. For example, men are usually more knowledgeable or expert concerning mechanical or electrical things. They also typically have more interest in such things. So the man of the house is often the one who plays the role of information filter for the purchase of such goods as cars, major appliances, home repairs, and the like. He may not make the ultimate choice or implement the decision, but he can affect the choice significantly because he's the one who knows what's available, what's good, and what's not. But don't think it's always an adult who plays the filter role. Children pay far more attention than adults to advertisements and commercials about such things as their toys and playthings, while mom or dad usually makes the decision and buy the product. In such cases, it's the child who has the interest and expertise. This and

Name of Role	Type of Purchase- or Consumption-Related Behavior
Filter	Regulates the flow of consumer goods information
Influencer	Helps shape other people's evaluations of goods
Decider	Makes the actual purchase or consumption decision
Buyer	Implements the decision and purchases the goods
Preparer	Converts the goods to a form that can be consumed
Consumer	Actually uses or consumes the products or services
Monitor	Regulates or controls consumption by other people
Maintainer	Services or repairs goods so they're ready to use
Disposer	Discards goods that are no longer wanted or needed

the other roles differ among family members, depending on what kind of goods are being considered.

> **Young children are heavy consumers of ready-to-eat breakfast food cereal, and they're often more informed about the flavor and characteristics of the different brands. Even though mom makes the actual purchase at the checkout stand, cereal marketers often advertise directly to the kids with TV ads during children's programming.**

THE INFLUENCERS OF PURCHASE DECISIONS

One family member will often influence another concerning a purchase of consumer goods. Influence is most likely to result because the influencer is sharing in the consumption of the goods. But that doesn't necessarily have to be the case. Marketers sometimes encourage one family member to influence another, even though the influencer isn't really involved in buying or using the product or service.

> Procter & Gamble advertised Scope brand mouthwash with television ads that showed one family member telling another to get rid of "medicine breath" and use pleasant-scented Scope. Similarly, Armour-Dial's ads for Dial soup use the slogan "Aren't you glad you use Dial? Don't you wish everyone did?" The last sentence is designed more to encourage influence among family members than to win sales directly by a single user.

THE PURCHASE DECISION MAKERS

The decider is the one who makes the final choice about whether or not to buy, what to buy, and when. But it isn't always the "one" family member, since some decisions are made individually while others are made jointly among two or more members of the family. Which family member or members make the decision depends on a variety of factors, not the least of which is the relative power of individual family members. In some families, roles are very specialized: she decides these things, he makes the decision about those, and the kids make the choices about other goods. In other families, with less role differentiation, joint decision making is more common. We'll look at the most important determinants of which kind of decision process families typically use in a moment.

> Men have traditionally been regarded as the decision makers for the purchase of the "family" car, while women were viewed as only influencers of the decision. But economic changes that lead to a high proportion of two-car families, changes in typical family structure and composition, and social chances resulting in shifting feminine sex role prescriptions have all resulted in a greater proportion of feminine car purchase decision makers. Recognizing the trend in the late 1970s, GM began promoting Cadillac to women with ads in magazines such as *Town & Country* and

Vogue. Buick also courted women car buyers with ads in such highly selective media as *Cosmopolitan, Ms.,* and *Working Woman,* to avoid alienating males.

THE PREPARER OF THE PRODUCT

While many consumer products are ready-made and need little if any preparation, many products families buy do need a substantial amount of preparation before they're ready to be consumed. While there are many others, food products are probably the most notable. The role of preparer is often specialized within the family. One member is the cook, another may be the chief mechanic in charge of unpacking and assembling appliances and hardware devices, and so forth. When preparation of a particular kind of product is usually elaborate, time consuming, and/or requires special skills, the simplicity and ease of preparation of a particular brand is often a major selling point. As noted several times earlier, the family spends less time together today than formerly, and since both heads of household are often in the workforce, preparation tasks often fall to the children or to those unaccustomed to such work. With less and less time for preparation of products, families today often place a premium on things that are quick and easy to prepare.

> One *Parents Magazine* ad for General Mills Bisquick brand of baking mix features the slogan "You've got it made with Bisquick." The ad is accompanied by a five-sheet, half-page insert containing "Dinnertime recipes made in under 15 minutes," which the busy cook can tear out and retain, to encourage use of the product. Preparation time, "5 min. to prepare," for instance, is noted in bold red print on each recipe. Even the brand name itself implies quick preparation of biscuits and quick breads.

THE ULTIMATE CONSUMER OF THE GOODS

In the contemporary American family, consumption is far more often an *individual* role than it once was. In the past, family members ate common meals and children were expected to eat the same foods as their parents. (How could we ever forget?)

But joint consumption by most or all family members extended far beyond the kitchen. Children shared the same playthings and siblings accompanied one another to recreation and entertainment. Today each child is more likely to share and belong to a *peer* group. There was once a "family" car; today, the two-car garage is often the norm and there's his and hers. When homes included a single bathroom, it and many of the toiletry items it contained were jointly used by family members. But more and more homes today have two or more bathrooms, individually assigned to bedroom occupants. So even consumption of toiletries often becomes individualized by family member, each with different preferences and consumption rates.

Irish Spring toilet soap is for men; Dove is for the ladies; it's Ivory for the baby; and the toddler crowd enjoys a bath with Mr. Bubble. It often works that way, but not always. Secret brand deodorant is a feminine product, promoted as "pH-balanced" for a woman's special body chemistry. It's also billed as "Strong enough for a man." But since men eschew feminine products, it's not likely to be a big seller to the male market. By contrast, women usually do readily accept masculine gender brands. The name and promotion of Right Guard brand deodorant was heavily slanted to the male market. Yet Gillette found that women often used the same deodorant spray as their husbands, since there was no body contact with the applicator. Thus they encouraged joint consumption by depicting couples who shared a single container asking, "Hey! Who's got my Right Guard" and getting into friendly squabbles about possession of the precious can.

THE MONITOR OF CONSUMPTION

One adult in the family rarely regulates or controls the consumption of another, although it does happen occasionally. For instance, the chief cook may attempt to regulate the fat, cholesterol, or sugar intake of other adults and children of the family, or one spouse may try to limit the other's consumption of alcoholic beverages. But most commonly, parents monitor and control the consumption of their children, including everything from their diet to their TV viewing or record purchases. The family car and credit card purchases of gasoline are certainly not always at young Junior's or Sis's disposal. This monitor role and the way it's performed have dual impacts on the individual family member-consumers who are regulated; both indirect and direct effects. The indirect effects have to do with what children learn to value and prefer and what they learn to avoid. While you might question it, based on personal experience as a parent, children do actually learn about consumption from their parents and family, and often carry the lessons forward to adult life (except for a brief, rebellious suspension during adolescence). In the direct sense, monitoring governs or attenuates what the kids will consume, when, and how often. So even though a marketer wins the preference of the child consumer, that may not be sufficient. It may also be necessary to convince mom or dad, or both.

> Parents have become increasingly concerned about a healthy diet for the family, and especially for their children. Healthy food is in and sugary foods with "empty" calories are out! So are the companies that market them. Hershey Foods Corp. meets the problem head on. With ads in *Parents Magazine*, among others, they showed young "Messy Marvin" polishing off a glass of chocolate milk, and the headline, "How to make milk disappear." This ad for Hershey's Syrup isn't aimed at the Marvins and Mabels of the juvenile set, it's aimed directly at Mom the Monitor.

> Smucker's approaches the problem a little more obliquely. They modified their preserves (which they then have to call "spreads"). With ads in such media as *Better Homes and Gardens* ("The Idea Magazine for American Families"), Smucker's used the headline "The great taste of Smucker's and only $\frac{1}{2}$ the sugar, $\frac{1}{2}$ the calories." Again, aimed directly at monitoring moms, the copy says "You'll be glad to serve your family Smucker's great family of Low Sugar Spreads." The consumers don't have to be sold, but the monitors do!

THE MAINTAINERS OF THE GOODS

The consumer goods maintenance role is important because it's usually very specialized within the family and often involves goods of substantial value. The maintenance requirements are often key factors in the choice of consumer durables—homes, cars, appliances, equipment, and the like. Even more importantly, the maintenance of consumer products may involve significant purchases of other products and services to facilitate the maintenance or repair. Such maintenance-related buying ranges from the obvious home and car upkeep items to more obscure products and services such as the purchase of a sonic cleaner for jewelry or replacement batteries for a child's toy.

Services for upkeep and repair are also important, from clothes cleaning, shirt laundering or shoe repairs to furnace, air conditioner, or major appliance repair services to the processing of a casualty insurance claim. Many retail service businesses listed in the Yellow Pages are sought by those in the family who perform the maintainer role. Maintenance is sometimes so lucrative for marketers that it warrants selling the original product at near or below cost, such as when safety razors were provided almost free in order to secure the sale of blades, or when cameras are sold well below what the market might bear, just to facilitate the sale of film. In other instances, upkeep and repair are so costly to consumers there's a real advantage in providing them with "disposable" products: flashlights, cigarette lighters, or aluminum foil baking pans are examples.

Meet "Mr. Goodwrench," the GM service repair technician (that's a garage mechanic, if you haven't guessed) who always insists on "GM quality service parts." With ads in such male-oriented magazines as *Popular Mechanics*, GM fights the competition, the independent repair parts suppliers and independent auto repair facilities as well. Many auto parts cut across several makes of GM vehicles, so they introduced the Goodwrench brand to capture Chevrolet, Pontiac, Oldsmobile, Buick, Cadillac, and GMC truck owners in one "swell foop"! Meanwhile, the Mr. Goodwrench character represents an "all-brand" GM repair

facility: "No one knows your GM car better than Mr. Goodwrench. No one."

THE DISPOSER OF OBSOLETE PRODUCTS

The consumers' garages, basements, attics, closets, and cup-
boards will only hold just so much obsolete or unused goods.
After that, something's got to go! The family members who play
the disposer role perform that function. In some ways, choosing
what to discard and what to retain is similar to an original purchase. It takes judgment and some authority within the family,
too. Otherwise the disposer gets the "What ever happened to
my _____ ?" routine, followed by an indignant, "How dare
you throw out my good old _____ ?" But without disposal,
there wouldn't be room for new goods, so marketers may encourage it.

Who Plays What Family Role

Any one consumption-related role isn't necessarily played by
the same family member from one family to the next, from one
time to the next, or from one kind of goods to the next. But,
then, neither are these role assignments completely random or
chaotic. So we can detect some fairly consistent patterns among
certain consumer groups and for particular product classes. For
instance, men often play the dominant roles regarding purchase
of things outside the house and for things electrical or mechanical. On the other hand, the interior of the home, the furnishings
and appliances, as well as food and clothing, are often the woman's domain. In some families, these important roles are often
performed jointly by the male and female heads of household;
in others there's a great deal of specialization, mostly independent choices, and very little crossover between the two sexes.
While it sometimes depends on the particular interaction patterns for a given family, much also rests on the characteristics of
the family.

Social Class. As we'll see in Chapter 10, midscale families tend to make more joint decisions and to share consumption-related roles more than either those further downscale or further upscale.

Role Specificity. The more specific the role assignments are and the more rigidly the prescriptions are followed for other kinds of roles, the less consumption-related role sharing and joint decision making there will be.

Family Life Cycle. As we'll see in Chapter 12, younger families make more joint decisions, but those later in the family life cycle have had more time to specialize roles and they tend more toward autonomous decisions.

Product Importance. There tends to be more consumption-related role-sharing and more frequent joint decisions for products and services that are very important to the family than for those of lesser importance.

Purchase Urgency. Role-sharing and joint decision making take time for interaction and deliberation by multiple family members, so role specialization and autonomous decisions are more common for urgent purchases.

Perceived Risk. The more risky a purchase seems to be, the more likely family members will be to share consumption-related roles and make a joint decision about whether or not to buy the product.

Family Decision-Making Conflict

Who dominates when a husband and wife are in conflict over a purchase decision? That depends on each family's interaction patterns, as we'll see in a moment, but we can reach one very important generalization: The woman is far more dominant within the contemporary American family than she was traditionally! While women were the purchasing agents and made the majority of buying decisions for the family of the past, they often operated on authority borrowed from or delegated by the male head of household. Those days are gone forever. Today's woman enjoys far more autonomy than ever before, partly as a result of the feminist movement, but perhaps more importantly because of the economic independence working women have today.

WHEN PUSH COMES TO SHOVE

When the irresistible force meets the immovable object, the outcome of the struggle depends on the relative power of the husband and wife. And as noted in Chapter 8, power and influence depend in large measure on the value the respective rivals place on the decision and on the relationship or the family, itself. The following family power matrix is only a variant of the more general diagram shown earlier for all social groups.

When the decision is very important to both heads of household, that leads to something of a power balance. Since they're both very involved, there's likely to be a joint decision—an accommodation or compromise between them. By contrast, when *neither* attaches much importance to the purchase, there's also a power balance, but instead of mutual influence and a joint decision, there's likely to be an independent choice by the one most involved. In the other two cases, the one that places the most value or importance on the buying decision is likely to dominate and the other spouse to conform.

Value to the Husband	Value to the Wife	
	High	Low
High	Power balance Mutual influence	Husband dominant Wife conforming
Low	Wife dominant Husband conforming	Power balance Independent choice

MARKETING TO AMERICAN FAMILIES

Family economics and sociology are subjects that completely occupy heavier tomes than this. So we can't document the contemporary American family situation very thoroughly here. But we can offer some brief insights and generalizations in summary form before we turn to social class.

Families Are Buying Units. Families, rather than individuals, are often the appropriate unit of analysis for assessing markets and focusing marketing appeals.

Families Are Functional. Family formation allows the members to live more economically, but families also provide several noneconomic benefits to members.

Families Are Dynamic. Old images and stereotypes die hard, but consumer marketers must recognize changing family conditions to market to them effectively.

Families Provide Roles. Family members specialize, serving different consumption-related roles, and marketers have to satisfy different family role requirements.

Families Contain Conflicts. When different family members have different preferences, things are usually reconciled in favor of the one who most values the decision.

Clearly the family will require some careful study by many consumer goods marketers. There are a couple of effective approaches: macro and micro. One is to analyze the most relevant statistics on American families. The other is to investigate how the product or service is purchased and used by and within the family. Usually both are necessary and effective.

10

SOCIAL CLASS
A Place on the
Public Ladder

The Great, Absolutely Infallible Living Room Test

Downscale Indicators	*Upscale Indicators*
TV in living room	TV in den or bedroom
Religious pictures	Abstract oil paintings
Floral print drapes	Plain, solid curtains
Print wallpaper walls	White or off-white rooms
Bowling trophies	Crystal, porcelain art
Plastic furniture	Hardwood furniture
Bare by necessity	Minimalist by design
Doilies, slipcovers	Tapestry wall hangings

Marketing managers often feel their customers will like what they like. But this *self-reference criterion* is usually wrong. Executives are seldom in the same social class as those in the target market. What's more, there isn't much interaction between people in different classes, and when there is it's usually short, distant, and formal. So people in one social class don't have much of a chance to get to know people in another.

THE DISTINCTIONS AMONG SOCIAL CLASSES

Social class distinctions are vital to consumer goods marketers. Social classes differ not only in their power, prestige, and wealth, but also in their *values, attitudes, lifestyles,* and *behavior patterns.* People in different classes buy different goods, they differ in what they're able and willing to pay, they buy things from different outlets, and they're exposed to different media. What one class welcomes, another may totally reject. As a result, social class is very often the basis for segmenting markets and picking target segments.

The social class differences outlined here are only trends or tendencies. There's some overlap, lots of individual differences, and no sharp, clear lines between classes. It's just as foolish to assume people of different classes will *always* behave differently as it is to assume they *never* do. There are no iron-clad rules, only intelligent insight and educated guesswork. But we can identify modal patterns of thought and action that are typical of each social class.

THE THINGS THAT DETERMINE SOCIAL CLASS

A person's social class is easier to recognize intuitively than it is to describe mechanically. Social class isn't a single variable; it's a combination. People sometimes think that income is synonymous with social class, but it's only part of the story. At least three separate social class determinants should be considered: *education, occupation,* and *income.* Marketers can use census data for these three variables to get a picture of the social class composition of their markets. But as many as seven social class indicators can be used:

Income.   The annual earnings of the consumer or combined income of the family or household.

Wealth.   Net worth of the individual or the family, whether accumulated or inherited.

Education.   Years of formal education, technical training, and degrees or credentials earned.

Occupation.   Blue-collar or white-collar and specific job or position of both heads of household.

Family.   The prestige or status of the family in the eyes of the community and at large.

Dwelling.   The type, value, and maintenance of the home as well as ownership or nonownership.

Neighborhood.   The condition of the immediate surroundings, property values, and status of neighbors.

SOCIAL CLASS DIFFERENCES

Marketers usually work with only two or three categories of social class: *blue-collar* and *white-collar,* or *working, middle,* and *upper-middle* classes. We'll just refer to *upscale* and *downscale* consumers here. But these are mainstream groups, not those at the very top or bottom of the hierarchy. To provide a mental picture of how upscale and downscale consumers differ, we'll look at sixteen different aspects of daily life.

Use of Time

DAILY PATTERNS

Time patterns differ sharply by social class. Upscalers are an hour or so later than downscalers in just about everything they do throughout the day. Blue-collar workers get up in the morning over an hour before their white-collar counterparts. They start work, have lunch, finish work, eat dinner, and retire for the night at an earlier hour. A typical factory starts work at about seven or seven-thirty in the morning, while the average store or office starts business around nine o'clock or later. These differences affect the traffic patterns on the streets and in the stores and restaurants. They influence exposure to radio and television programs and preference for morning versus evening newspapers. The audience for late-night programming are mostly upscalers, and they prefer the morning to the evening newspaper.

TIME HORIZON

Time horizon is determined by how far a person can see into the future and plan or anticipate events. Upscalers' time horizon extends from many months to several years into the future. Downscalers are more immediate. A longer time horizon allows upscalers to plan for the future: to set goals, develop their expectations, anticipate potential trouble, and cope with it in advance. They can maintain their efforts over an extended period of time in pursuit of an important objective. Working class consumers with a shorter time horizon aren't likely to maintain a weight-loss diet or exercise program, or maybe even get treatment for physical disorders at an early stage.

> Those who can least afford to pay higher prices shop more often at convenience stores, rather than supermarkets. They don't look ahead, plan menus, and make out a grocery list for the week, so they buy food as they need it, day by day. Since they're "only going to pick up a few things for dinner," they go to the quick-stop around the corner, rather than to the supermarket, and pay more.

Degree of Abstraction

LANGUAGE AND SYMBOLS

Middle class people use more subtle and complex forms of expression than working class consumers. Simile and analogy are meaningful to upscalers but often lost on downscalers. Metaphorical expressions can be taken literally by downscalers. Abstract symbols and poetic phrases are far more understandable and attractive to the upscale consumer. The same abstract expressions that provoke curiosity and intrigue among upscalers may cause downscalers to "tune out" very quickly. Downscalers prefer graphic language and simple grammar.

CONCRETE VERSUS INTANGIBLE

Downscalers prefer tangible goods, as opposed to intangible services. Upscalers are the main consumers of intangibles. They buy experiences, while downscale consumers want durable, physical objects to show for their money. Upscalers are willing to buy such intangibles as life and casualty insurance and air travel and resort visits. Downscalers put their money into vehicles, appliances, or sports equipment.

> **Ads and sales pitches for motor homes often point out to downscalers: "All you have to show for all that money you spent on vacation last year is a handful of hotel receipts." Upscalers might "pencil it out" and discover that the tangible vehicle is more expensive to own and use for a short time each year than it would be to buy intangible hotel accommodations. But when downscale consumers spend money they often want "something to show for it."**

Modes of Emotionality

HOSTILITY AND RESENTMENT

Downscalers more freely express hostility and aggression, while upscalers are reluctant to express anger or resentment openly. They shy away from physical expressions of rage or aggression. Among downscalers, hostile feelings are more prevalent and more likely to be "acted out" through gesture or even direct, physical violence. Upscalers are less defensive and aggressive. They see physical violence as a last resort and interpret recourse to verbal abuse and violence as signs of social and intellectual inadequacy.

SENTIMENT AND ATTACHMENT

Downscalers don't readily express sentiment and attachment. By contrast, upscalers feel more free to express love, sentiment, and attachment, both publicly and privately. Downscalers interpret displays of caring and attachment as weakness, while upscalers perceive them as positive and ennobling.

> Television ads for Miller Lite beer, directed to working class men, show camaraderie and fellowship among the male characters, but in reverse: The men are shown kidding and joshing with one another in fained hostility. The open respect among men often shown in Michelob or Budweiser ads for upscale, male audiences might embarrass working class males.

Perceptions of Risk

DIFFERENTIAL AWARENESS

Downscalers see the world as risky and perhaps dangerous. They don't feel adequate to cope with loss or adversity, they're risk-averse, and they use avoidance to maintain security. Upscalers feel risk implies both danger and opportunity; the degree of negative risk is proportional to the rate of positive return. While downscalers see risk "at almost every turn," upscalers view risk as less prevalent—certainly not ever-present in their lives.

> Working class consumers tend to be more strongly loyal to well-advertised national brands than are middle class shoppers. Downscalers often prefer small neighborhood stores where they

are known by the staff. Upscalers feel competent to evaluate the goods themselves. Comfortable with anonymity, they tend to prefer the larger department stores, supermarkets, and shopping malls.

REACTIONS TO LOSS

Predetermination and fatalism are typical of downscalers when faced with a significant loss. Upscalers blame themselves for not avoiding the negative consequences. By contrast, downscalers attribute failures and losses to external causes: to fate, luck, chance, or some other external factor. They're more free from guilt, but upscalers use loss as negative feedback, taking corrective action to avoid future mistakes.

Family Interactions

ROLES AND RELATIONSHIPS

Downscalers adhere to the traditional sex roles. They make sharp distinctions between the roles and responsibilities of husband and wife. She handles the cooking, clothes, children, and inside of the home; he has the car, garage, yard, and anything mechanical or electrical. He makes the major decisions and there's less joint decision making and less shopping together. Upscalers have some of the same patterns, but they're not as pronounced; there's more sharing of responsibility and joint decision making, and spouses more often shop together.

> **Ford Motors designed a promotional effort to reach the female car market. Using broadcast, print, and direct mail advertising, they promised that women who visited a dealership would get special attention and whatever information and help they needed to make a choice. Dealer sales programs featured prizes and inducements for women who visited for a test drive. The target audience was middle and upper-middle class women only, since working class women seldom make the purchase decision for mechanical goods such as automobiles.**

AUTHORITY AND DISCIPLINE

Children play a major role in "child-centered" upscale families. Discipline might be administered by either parent and they ordinarily deprive the child of some reward. Working class fathers are the main disciplinarians and punishment ranges from ridicule or verbal abuse to actual physical measures. Downscalers depend more on authority and less on reason. In a confrontation between a student and a teacher, upscale parents are loyal to their kids while downscalers feel the child is wrong and the authority figure is right. Downscalers may "rule" their kids, but upscalers see them more as equals, as miniature adults.

EXPECTATIONS FOR CHILDREN

Working class parents stress obedience and want submissive, well-mannered children; their children have to be polite and respectful to others, especially adults. Their expectations are encapsulated by the Scout Code: trustworthy, loyal, helpful, friendly, courteous, kind, obedient, cheerful, thrifty, brave, clean, and reverent. By contrast, upscale parents want their children to be cooperative, loving, sharing, happy, and self-controlled. They encourage creativity, admire precocity, and want their children to be eager to learn. They reward delay of gratification and urge their children to plan, analyze, think, and speak in abstract terms.

Community Involvement

AFFILIATION AND ALIENATION

Upscalers identify and participate more closely with the external community. Downscalers don't think they have much influence or control over the external community, including the neighborhood, workplace, political jurisdictions, and religious institutions. Sometimes feeling powerless and left out, they often think the world is controlled by a power elite, for good or for ill. They identify with their heros and condemn the villains.

Upscalers don't usually believe in power conspiracies in Wall Street, Madison Avenue, Detroit, or Washington.

> **Small discount retailers sometimes claim they've "cut out the middle man," for huge savings. Downscalers often believe wholesalers or manufacturers have power to take advantage of their position, "gouging" customers. They are more likely than upscalers to believe certain retailers are "on their side" while others are against them. Upscalers are skeptical of bizarre, maverick stores, but downscalers identify with them and believe they've "beat the system."**

MOBILITY AND INTERACTION

Upscalers symbolize their social standing with their clothing, personal appearance, home, cars, and other socially visible products and services. Their orientation toward achievement creates more interest in upward social mobility and they see it as a viable possibility. Social striving takes the form of selective affiliation, as well as the more obvious financial avenues. Downscalers are concerned more with *maintaining* than with *improving* social status, so they affiliate with family and friends at their own social level. They see attempts at upward social mobility as pretentious and regard such efforts as "putting on airs," as affectations.

Family Dwelling

LOCATION AND ENVIRONMENT

The home has a more singular purpose for downscalers than for upscalers. For upscalers, their home is their single most important status symbol, and they'll invest heavily in its symbolic value. While downscalers buy only the house and its proximity to work, school, and church, upscalers buy and pay dearly for "the neighborhood" as well as the house itself.

> **The price difference between identical houses on identical lots in different neighborhoods is the "premium" upscalers pay for the social status obtained from the location.**

INSIDE VERSUS OUTSIDE

Because the outside of the house is more socially visible than the inside, upscalers devote a larger part of their home expenditures to the lawn, shrubs, landscaping, and facilities such as a patio, spa, pool, or tennis court. Downscale homeowners spend little on external property. They may do little more than cut the grass and keep the house painted. When they do get into gardening, they usually prefer "flower beds" to shrubs and greenery, and they may surround them with painted bricks or stones and include hand-cut and painted figurines or cheap statuary.

Home and Furnishings

FURNITURE AND DECOR

Upscalers see both functional and symbolic value in their furniture. Keenly aware of configurations, their furniture has to be well coordinated. They prefer simple designs and solid, subdued colors. Downscale furniture buyers pay less attention to coordination, and if they do seek it, they may buy inexpensive, ready-matched suites of furniture for an entire room. They like bold colors and contrasts and they value prints and patterns over solid colors or uniform textures. They won't sacrifice comfort or durability for elegance of appearance.

> Interior walls and windows, lighting and accessories reflect the social class of the home's occupants. Upscale social strivers have homes with white walls and textured fabric drapes in plain, solid colors. Prints, paintings, tapestry, or hanging sculpture may decorate the walls. The lighting is indirect and well integrated. New purchases for the home are judged mostly by the way they'll "fit in."

> By contrast, downscale homemakers paint walls in various colors or use wallpaper. Print curtains and patterned drapes are popular. Rooms are more "busy" with accessories. Religious pictures and icons, figurines and knick-knacks, family photographs, and handcraft items decorate the rooms. Diplomas, trophies, and awards may be displayed. Furniture and accessory purchases are

often spontaneous and items are judged for their individual appeal, without much consideration for the surroundings.

HOUSEHOLD APPLIANCES

Convenience, simplicity, and reliability are the hallmarks of upscale appliances. Power, complexity, and "labor-saving" features are characteristic of downscale appliances. Working class people may symbolize their status with the common household appliances they own, "displaying" them where they're visible. By contrast, upscalers take appliances for granted and they don't see much social meaning in them, so they hide appliances out of sight. They like the appliances to match in both brand and design.

> Both Black & Decker and the GE appliance division, recently acquired by Black & Decker, offer "Spacemaker" countertop appliances that are closely matched and coordinated, and designed to fit under the kitchen cupboard, rather than on the countertop itself. The GE series even includes a TV–AM/FM receiver and an AM/FM radio/cassette recorder in their Spacemaker Kitchen Entertainment Series. These products are geared largely to the middle class homemaker, and so they're designed for inconspicuousness rather than prominence in the kitchen.

> It's interesting to note that the Black & Decker ads in such media as *Home* magazine used headlines that are plays on words to emphasize that the under-cupboard line is above the countertop: "Pie in the sky" for the oven, "Help from above" for the mixer, "It also opens up space" for the can opener, and "Great coffee comes from high altitudes" for the coffee maker. More abstract middle class readers may be amused by such wording, but many more concrete working class homemakers are likely to miss the pun.

Clothing and Jewelry

JEWELRY AND APPAREL

Clothing and jewelry reflect the self-concept of upscale consumers. They're conscious of style and the fashion cycle and they're more willing to sacrifice comfort for appearance. Downscalers think first of durability and comfort in clothes. They pay less attention to coordination and often ignore obsolescence because of changing fashions, keeping their garments until they're worn out. Upscalers like simplicity and "quiet elegance" in clothing and jewelry. Their working class counterparts prefer more bold colors and patterns, sharp contrasts, and more strikingly obvious decoration.

> The use of artificial versus natural materials corresponds closely with social class: the higher the social status, the greater the preference for natural fabrics. Working class people like manmade fabrics that are easy-care and wrinkle-free—nylon, rayon, polyester, and "permanent-press" fabrics. The lower echelons of the white-collar ranks are characterized by their polyester knit suits. At a higher level, wool or cotton blends are popular. But only natural fabrics—wool, cotton, silk, and linen—are completely acceptable for the high end of the spectrum, even for undergarments. At the uppermost levels, a rumpled appearance is vastly preferable to looking shiny and wrinkle-free.

PERSONAL APPEARANCE

Downscalers regard the purchase of a new garment or accessory as a luxury that they usually buy for a specific occasion. They economize on the use of personal care services, preferring to do it themselves or have a friend or relative help where possible. Upscalers view the products and services required for personal care and appearance as necessities, and spend a much larger proportion of their income on them. They may treat their wardrobe and jewelry purchases more as "investments" than as expenses.

Physical Care and Treatment

BODILY ATTITUDES

Working class consumers identify with their physical self. Both more pride and more shame are associated with the body, but they take it as it is and don't see it as very manageable. Upscalers see their body more as a "residence" than as "themselves." Their identity and self-perceptions are associated with their mind and personality. They view the body as manipulable and they have a sense of accomplishment or guilt regarding what they are and aren't able to do with their physique. Upscale people are keenly aware of performance, but downscalers more often focus on their physical proportions, and especially those associated with sexuality.

> While downscalers identify closely with their physical self, they don't feel they have much control over what they are physically. They attribute physical conditions such as obesity to their genetic endowment, so they're likely either to accept it or sporadically indulge in "fad" diets. Some working class men are devoted to "pumping iron" for muscle building, but neither sex provides a good market for products and services geared to general long-term physical fitness. Upscalers comprise the market for many services that provide *social reinforcement* for progress: Jazzercise, Family Fitness Centers, Weight Watchers, Nautilus Gyms, and the like. These people are less concerned with what their body is than with what they can do with it. Performance is what counts!

MEDICAL CARE AND TREATMENT

Upscalers are more likely to seek preventive medical care such as annual physical examinations or prenatal care and testing during pregnancy. They sometimes monitor their own blood pressure or watch their cholesterol count. They often take medication with religious regularity and observe dietary and exercise requirements carefully. Downscalers often delay remedial care if they're ill or injured, until it is absolutely necessary. They place more responsibility on physicians and health care providers and less on themselves. They sometimes fail to continue with treatment or medication when discomfort has diminished.

Dietary Habits and Attitudes

QUANTITY AND DIVERSITY

Downscalers eat more often and serve more food than up-scalers. They judge the quantity and taste more than they do quality and nutritional value. Upscalers put more emphasis on light foods such as salads or fresh fruits and vegetables. They eat a more varied diet, enjoy the novelty and diversity of ethnic foods, and willingly try the new food products and services. Downscalers are "meat and potatoes" people, preferring the familiar and traditional to the exotic or unusual. They rely heavily on fast foods—hamburgers, pizza, fried chicken—and they eat candy or sweets between meals on a regular basis. Upscalers are more likely to limit their intake of sugar and salt, or avoid what they call "junk food." They show a preference for natural foods over those that are highly processed or things that contain artificial additives or chemical preservatives.

UPSCALE PRODUCTS AND BRANDS

Stouffer, Lean Cuisine, Le Menu frozen entrees
Hain, Health Valley canned and packaged health foods
Dannon yogurt, Haagen-Dazs ice cream
Local, out-of-the-way ethnic restaurants

DOWNSCALE PRODUCTS AND BRANDS

Banquet, Swanson frozen TV dinners
Hamburger Helper, Kraft Macaroni and Cheese casseroles
Jell-O Pudding Pops, Baskin-Robbins ice cream
McDonald's, Burger King, Jack-in-the-Box hamburgers

GROCERY SHOPPING AND BUYING

Upscalers often "watch their diet," plan their menu for days ahead, and shop at supermarkets or even health food stores. They keep an ample stock of a wide variety of foods, replenishing as needed. Downscalers tend to purchase and prepare food on a day-to-day basis, shopping more often, buying smaller unit sizes, and getting less on any one visit to the store. They like convenience stores or small, ma-and-pa stores that are closer and quicker for frequent visits, where they'll be recognized by the clerks.

> Supermarket chains such as Safeway, Winn-Dixie, Jewel, and Piggly Wiggly serve the whole socioeconomic spectrum, rather than targeting one level. But they modify their merchandising policy by store, according to the social class of the local neighborhood. Compared to stores in downscale areas, upscale stores provide greater depth of selection, fewer generic brands, more novelty items, and more fresh versus processed foods.

PREPARING AND SERVING MEALS

While cooking is usually the sole responsibility of downscale family women, upscale men often share in these tasks. Downscale families put "plenty of good, solid food" on the table. They don't pay much attention to the combinations served in a single meal. They serve everything for the meal simultaneously and eat it from a single plate. Upscale cooks limit the quantity, emphasizing the type and quality of food. They often consider not only the combination of flavors and aromas, but also the blend of colors and textures. Some upscalers see food as a symbolic expression of their self-image and view food preparation as creative or inventive. Routine upscale meals can be almost ceremonial or ritualistic, but that happens only on holidays and special occasions in downscale families, who are more pragmatic. They ordinarily see cooking as a required task or chore and place less emphasis on tableware and decor.

> Innovative kitchen appliances such as food processors and microwave ovens were adopted first by upscalers long before they were accepted among downscalers. A few years ago, Cuisinart popularized the food processor among upscalers so successfully that the term "Cuisinart Culture" came to designate a specific lifestyle. But these appliances weren't purchased to simplify food preparation so much as to allow creation of more complex

cuisine—a typical middle class motive. By contrast, novel kitchen gadgets and devices sold by direct advertising on TV and by pitchmen and women with in-store demonstrations sell well to the working class cook. Their motives for buying all those Gensu knives, Moulee choppers, and Teflon-coated cookware are to save time and work rather than to create exotic or unusual gourmet dishes.

Recreation and Entertainment

CHOICE OF ALTERNATIVES

While upscalers find recreation in activity and participation, downscale recreation is much more likely to involve only watching and listening. The games and sports preferred by upscalers and downscalers differ markedly. Golf, tennis, skiing, and sailing are upscale activities, while bowling, hunting, fishing, and water skiing are downscale recreations. Upscalers use air travel and frequent hotels and resorts in unfamiliar cities or countries, while downscalers use "RVs" and go camping or stay with friends or relatives when traveling.

SERVICE AND EQUIPMENT

Upscalers may spend freely on music lessons or coaching from a golf or tennis pro. Downscalers lean toward spectatorship in sports and entertainment. They develop strong loyalty to local sports teams or popular music groups. These superstars are their personal heros. The bars, taverns, pool halls, and bowling alleys play the same role for downscalers as do the cocktail lounges, health, racket, and country clubs for the upscalers. Upper-middle class buyers want the most advanced, technically superior sports equipment, to improve their performance. Downscalers seek speed and power instead. They're the ones who own jet-skis, snowmobiles, power boats, motorcycles, off-road vehicles—motorized toys.

Famous athletes, the popular sports heros, are paid large sums to endorse or represent sporting goods targeted to downscalers. By

contrast, advertisements for athletic equipment for upscale men may feature models who represent typical weekend athletes. The product is shown in a social setting and the appeal is to improve performance.

Work and Leisure

OCCUPATIONAL ATTITUDES

Upscalers usually focus more on achievement or accomplishment than on security or maintenance of the status quo. Downscalers are more likely to worry about being fired or laid off than about missing a promotion. They don't expect to enjoy their work or take much pride in it. By contrast, the occupations of upscalers are often the single most important source of their personal identification. They expect to get much more from the job than just a salary. Downscalers accept authority on the job and expect to be supervised closely by "the boss." They often hold those high in the organization in awe. Upscalers want autonomy from "the person to whom they report." They're vitally concerned with their status within the organization and the symbols that indicate it.

> Often the primary source of personal identification for professional men and women lies in their occupation—their work! These men and women are excellent prospects for a wide variety of work-related goods: briefcases; calculators and computers; luxury writing instruments; business clothing; books, manuals, and courses; trade magazines and journals; travel services and accommodations; and many, many more. By contrast, working class people often don't want to think about their job, *even when they're at work*, let alone when they're not.

WORK/LEISURE TRADE-OFF

Upscale workers spend more time at their work than downscale people, they do it voluntarily, and they expect to be rewarded for it. Their salary represents their performance, not just their time. The blue-collar workers want regular wages for normal hours and overtime rates for anything beyond that. People in high-status occupations "take their work home with them," both literally and figuratively, but working class people rarely if ever do.

> **Downscalers like recreation that takes a lot of time but costs very little. Upscalers value their free time highly. Taking time for leisure activity means they have to forgo the income they might have earned, incurring "opportunity costs." The cost of the recreational and leisure products and services they use is disproportionately low. So they spend freely on expensive leisure products and services. At the highest levels the price elasticity of demand for leisure goods may be very low. Some even *prefer* higher priced goods over less expensive things. If so, the demand curve for the goods takes on a positive rather than negative slope—demand and sales volume will increase rather than decrease as price goes up.**

PURCHASE AND CONSUMPTION

The upscaler and downscaler sketches just presented show profound differences between them, extending into almost every aspect of daily life. They have dramatic effects on the way they behave in the marketplace.

Financial Practices

SAVINGS AND INVESTMENT

Upscalers and downscalers differ both in what they have and in how they handle it. Upscalers, with their longer time horizon and achievement orientation, save more than their downscale counterparts. They may regularly save part of their income. They're concerned about the liquidity of funds and the rate of return they'll receive. Downscale people often save only to accumulate money for a specific purchase, so they may not be concerned about the rate of interest they receive. They may hold short-term savings in cash, rather than in the bank.

CREDIT AND BORROWING

Credit is used more by upscalers than by downscalers because credit is more available to them. But upscalers use credit for different reasons than downscalers. They often carry half a dozen credit cards and use them often for large and small purchases, for convenience, rather than funding for a purchase. So they usually pay the entire balance each month. Downscalers who have credit cards more often use these accounts as a form of installment credit to fund their purchases.

Media Exposure

BROADCAST MEDIA AND CONTENT

Downscalers depend more on broadcasting for news and sports and they're devoted to TV for entertainment. Daytime TV audiences contain mostly downscale viewers, but the late-night audience is largely upscale. Public affairs programs and public broadcasting attract an upscale audience. So do nature shows and special dramatic programs and series. The game shows, soap operas, and sitcoms reflect the tastes of the downscalers, who also enjoy crime and action-adventure shows. At the lower end, wrestling and roller derby are popular. Upscale radio listeners are interested in news and sports (particularly during drive-time). They prefer FM to AM radio and they like easy listening music, mainstream jazz, soft rock, and perhaps light classics. Downscalers like hard rock, country-western, pop ballads, and nostalgia such as big band music. Upscale listeners welcome instrumental music while downscalers prefer vocals.

PRINT MEDIA AND CONTENT

Upscale readers tend toward the morning daily newspaper while downscalers prefer the evening edition. Upscalers like news in depth, the editorial section, financial news, and "the columns." Downscalers lean toward front-page news and picture content, sports and home sections, comic strips, advice columns and minifeatures such as astrological forecasts. General readership magazines are designed for a specific social class. *Town & Country, New Yorker,* and *Architectural Digest* are at the upper extremes. Just below are *Vogue, Fortune,* and *Home & Garden.* News magazines like *Time* and *Newsweek,* women's magazines such as *Glamour, Redbook,* and *Savvy,* and sophisticated men's magazines such as *Playboy* and *Penthouse* are read mostly by those in the upper-middle range. In the lower-middle range are *Good Housekeeping, Ladies' Home Journal, Reader's Digest, People,* and *Sports Illustrated. True Confessions, True Romance, Hustler, Mechanics Illustrated, Road and Track,* movie and fan magazines, and weekly tabloids such as *The National Enquirer* are at the lower extreme.

Shopping and Buying

PLANNED OR IMPULSE BUYING

Upscalers anticipate their needs and plan many of their purchases. For consumables such as groceries and household supplies, they keep shopping lists, buy them on regular shopping trips, and regularly replace them in their inventory. Downscalers are likely to buy goods as they're needed, on an immediate basis, and they engage in impulse buying more often than do upscalers. Prepurchase deliberation is greater among upscalers who get large amounts of their product information from media well before buying. Downscalers often get product information from relatives or friends, or wait until purchase is imminent and rely on advice and suggestions from sales people. So "word-of-mouth" advertising is more important for working than for middle class consumers.

RETAIL OUTLET SELECTION

Upscalers usually prefer department and specialty stores in shopping centers for their larger purchases and for fashion goods. Downscale shoppers may be intimated by these stores, preferring the smaller neighborhood stores instead. They do buy a wide range of goods from large discount stores, but upscalers shop them only for the well-known, national brands and rarely buy fashion goods at such outlets.

RISK REDUCTION AND LOYALTY FACTORS

While upscale buyers tend to judge products on their own merits, downscalers are more likely to avoid perceived risk by purchasing national brands, so they are strongly brand-loyal. They also develop loyalties to a few stores and depend heavily on them and their salespeople. If they're unfamiliar with the brands, they're likely to equate price with quality, automatically assuming "you get what you pay for." Upscalers are more willing to take some risks regarding products and stores, trying new outlets, brands, and product offerings.

THE TOTAL PICTURE

It would be impossible for us to identify all of the differences between upscale and downscale consumers, and there's really no need to do so. The ones we discussed here are outlined in Table 4. They were selected because they're important and indicative. Many of the most important aspects of personal mentality and daily life were identified, but there are many others that also influence purchase and consumption of products and services. The more familiar you become with these social class differences, the better able you'll be to recognize others that might be important to consumer acceptance of your product or brand, store or service.

Because of all the important differences among social classes, it's usually impossible to design a single, uniform product or service offering, distribution or delivery mechanism, advertising or promotional program, and pricing policy that would be equally appropriate to those at many different places on the social spectrum. But tailoring the marketing mix to the particular values, attitudes, and behavior patterns of a single market segment at one level leads to markedly greater consumer acceptance.

Table 4. Contrasting Class Orientations

	Upscale Consumers	Downscale Consumers
The Use of Time	Late daily schedule Longer time horizon	Early daily schedule Shorter time horizon
Degree of Abstraction	Abstract, complex Intangible goods	Simple, concrete Tangible goods
Modes of Emotionality	Little hostility Express sentiment	Open aggression Eschew sentiment
Perceptions of Risk	See little risk Loss is feedback	World is risky Externally blame
Family Interactions	Few sex roles Precocious children	Many sex roles Obedient children
Community Involvement	Often participate Upwardly mobile	Lacking potency Maintain position
Family Dwelling	Home symbolic Outside important	Proximity important Inside important
Home Furnishings	Coordinated furniture Reliable appliances	Durable furniture Labor-saving devices
Clothing and Appearance	Fashionable clothes Services necessary	Practical clothes Services luxuries
Physical Care and Treatment	Body a residence Self-reliance	Identify with body Experts responsible
Dietary Habits and Attitudes	Judge quality Cooking creative	Judge quantity Cooking a chore
Recreation and Entertainment	Active participation Technical goods	Spectatorship Powerful equipment
Work and Leisure	Seek achievement Paid for performance	Want security Paid for time
Financial Practices	Routinely invest Credit a convenience	Save for purchases Credit for purchases
Media Exposure	Informative programs Current events	Entertainment only Games, amusement
Shopping and Buying	Planned buying Judged on merits	Impulse buying Brand loyalty

The distinctions among the various groups of consumers that have traditionally been used to delineate market segments, such as age, sex, or geographic location, are becoming less and less important, and the trend toward homogeneity across those dimensions is likely to continue. By contrast, the distinctions between social classes are increasing in number and importance to marketers. Social class will become an even more important means for segmenting markets in the future because the working class and the middle class in this society are on fairly divergent paths.

CULTURE
The Dictatorship
of Normality

Every culture has its own distinctive strong and weak points. If you were in charge of arranging an international conference, would you ask: The Italians to organize it? The British to bring the food? The Germans to furnish the entertainment? The French to provide the hospitality? The Americans to watch the budget? You don't have to be a cultural anthropologist to do better than that!

The influence of the culture on consumers is very pervasive and profound, but at the same time, it's almost completely *invisible*. Someone once noted that "If you wanted to know about the nature of water, the last creature you should ask is a fish." How, indeed, could one understand or explain "wet" if one had never experienced "dry"? The cultural values of our society are like that. Society's values, mores, and norms are more or less invisible to us because we're so completely immersed in the culture from which they spring.

AN INVISIBLE HAND GUIDES CONSUMERS

One of the most peculiar characteristics of cultural influence is the fact that it seems to us to be the "natural" way to think, feel, or behave. Even though the way of going is arbitrary, it appears not only to be the *right* way, but also the *only* way to go. In the following pages, we'll identify both *our* way of doing things, and also some *alternative* ways that other societies and cultures do them. We can best identify and understand our culture by examining the *contrasts* between what we do and what others have elected to do.

Probably one of the first things you'll discover is that our way seems to be proper and correct, while *their* way seems to be improper, ineffective, awkward, or even immoral! But if we could get into the shoes of someone from another culture, we'd quickly find out that their way of doing things seemed right and the norms of this culture would look all wrong. So it's important to keep in mind that *cultural* dictates are merely ways some society has devised to cope with common human problems and aspirations. They're often arbitrary, and the only reason they work well is because the vast majority of the people in the society understand the dictates and agree on them.

We know of almost two hundred different definitions of culture. There's not much agreement among anthropologists concerning exactly what culture includes and doesn't include. On the other hand, we all have a pretty good intuitive understanding of what culture means. I might not be able to describe an elephant very well, but I sure recognize one when I see it. All we need to do to identify culture is note a few of its main features.

What Culture Includes

Culture is complex, but it's an integrated whole: the various threads are all woven together into a fairly seamless fabric. Culture includes knowledge—facts and techniques that are shared by society. But it also includes a whole series of beliefs and assumptions about the social, material, and spiritual world. There's also an aesthetic or artistic component to culture; it defines, in large measure, what we regard as beautiful and as ugly, as well as the symbols we'll use to represent the physical features of the world and the rituals and ceremonies we'll observe to celebrate life. And culture is highly normative as well. It includes the society's morals, folkways, mores, laws, and customs: what we can do, must do, and can't do.

Dynamism and Continuity

Before we really explore American cultural values, we should note a couple of other features about culture itself: it's both stable and dynamic, and it's a means of communication from one generation to the next. Culture won't change overnight, but it won't stay exactly the same from one century or even one decade to the next. Sometimes change occurs gradually, and on a few occasions, culture might seem to veer off in a different direction very rapidly. It's often because of cultural change that there seems to be a more or less perpetual "generation gap" between the youth and the senior members of society. The more rapid the change, the wider the gap.

But culture is always stable enough to be the vehicle for passing what we know and how we live from one generation to the next. If it weren't fairly enduring, each new generation would have to start all over again, right from page one, back in the cave.

AMERICAN CULTURAL VALUES

Culture teaches people what's valuable and what's valueless. We discussed individual values much earlier, but these cultural values are more comprehensive because most people in the society share them. That means that the consumer products and services we market have to be fairly compatible with these values or a large proportion of the buying public will reject them. We'll look first at personal values, then identify social values and environmental values that the culture dictates.

Personal Values of the Culture

Our culture tells us what a person should be and should value. We could identify many different personal values, but we'll just deal with six of them that have a major impact on how people behave in the marketplace.

PERSONAL VALUES

Ours	Others
Activity	Passivity
Industrious	Leisurely
Materialistic	Spiritualistic
Postponement	Gratification
Seriousness	Humorousness
Abstinence	Sensuality

THE ACTIVE AMERICAN

You've probably seen the little sign people sometimes tack up that says "Don't Just Sit There—*DO* Something." That pretty much says it all about our active orientation. Starting right from kindergarten, children are taught to stay busy. Unfortunately, both in school and later at work, people are rewarded more for activity and effort than for performance and results. One of the first things that foreign visitors notice is the way that Americans always seem to be in a hurry. A student who had just arrived from Asia had an interesting observation. He said when he saw all the traffic moving so rapidly during the morning rush, he figured it was because many were a little late for work. But then, to his great surprise, he found that they drove just as madly during the evening rush, even though they were just on their way home and didn't have a deadline. "Why are they in such a hurry, just to get home?" he asked. Frankly I was stumped. How would you explain it? It's just the way we are?

> **Spiegel's cataloging operation recently shifted its merchandising policy from economy to fashion, targeting upscale, 21- to 54-year-old career women who are pressed for time. Their motive for buying by catalog is to avoid the demands on their time when shopping at retail stores.**

THE INDUSTRIOUS AMERICAN

Hard work is part of the Protestant work ethic. Consumers are a little skeptical about goods that promise effortless results or that eliminate the need for hard work. On the other hand, they do readily accept many labor-saving devices. This presents a bit of a contradiction, but it can be explained: Marketers usually provide consumers with a rationale for buying labor-saving products or leisure goods. We tell them the device will let them devote their time and effort to some other activity. It's not important whether they actually do or not. What's important is that they have an acceptable way out of the bind concerning hard work. Similarly, leisure goods are sold not so much on the basis of comfort and ease, but rather on the need for "self-caring," for looking after one's health. The acceptable rationale in this case is simply that if they stay healthy and fit, they can work more, but if they don't, that might disable them.

> Beatrice uses magazine ads to promote the "Soup Starter" line of "Homemade soup mix" with the headline "Soup from a can is okay for lunch . . . but dinner calls for something more." They note that "you add your own fresh beef or chicken." The appeal is based on the homemaker's distrust of things that are too easy. With this product, they save time but still contribute some effort.

THE MATERIALISTIC AMERICAN

Materialism is as much a part of the Protestant work ethic as hard work. This cultural concept says that one's worth can be measured in dollars and cents (income and wealth) or by material possessions (what one owns and displays). We Americans pay lip service to inherent human dignity, but it extends only to the most basic human rights. As a matter of practical fact, people don't think very much of people who are poor, those who don't have much. We assume that it's their fault, despite arguments to the contrary. By the same token, we admire the wealthy among us, often regardless of how they got that way. Even notorious thieves are an object of fascination, simply because they have money or property. Some social critics contend that we're moving away from our materialistic orientation, but this seems doubtful. If there's no equation between "standard of living" and "quality of life," the majority of Americans still seem to act as though the two are the same.

> Status symbols such as automobiles are commonly promoted as indicating the owner's worth. For instance, GM used magazine ads for the Pontiac Grand Am showing the car on a dock by an impressive power boat. The headline: "So no one has to ask you how you're doing lately."

THE DELAY OF GRATIFICATION

This culture has traditionally stressed the necessity to postpone gratification over extended periods of time. It allows us to pursue things like formal education over many years, before we finally begin to receive the benefits of our efforts. But there are some indications that suggest we're changing toward a more immediate orientation regarding gratification. In fact, the extensive use of personal credit suggests that many consumers have learned to obtain gratification and postpone effort. Buy now—pay later appeals are very potent. Consumers more often do that rather than save for months to make a large purchase.

> **The number of MasterCard and Visa charge cards held by American consumers is estimated at about 125 million. The average cardholder has seven different bank cards.**

THE ABSTAINING AMERICAN

Hedonistic we're not! Things that are openly sensual are distrusted in this culture. Consumers buy such products only with the proper rationale. It has to be good for them or they must have earned it or some such reason. But appeals that frankly state "this feels great" are likely to fall on deaf ears. The song lyrics "this feels so good it must be wrong" are more descriptive of this culture. Don't think this runs in the face of the "me generation." It doesn't. Self-centeredness and self-interest are one thing—hedonism and sensuality are another.

> **Clinique cosmetics for both men and women find acceptance where others fail, because of the medical connotations of the brand name, the scentless products, the clinical appeals, and the austere, almost generic packaging.**

THE SERIOUS AMERICAN

We usually equate levity with frivolity; humor is antithetical to "serious purpose." The fool of the medieval court was often a skilled satirist and a valued advisor to the king; he kept things in perspective, even if he did slay a few sacred cows along the way. A comic today is little more than an object of amusement. Humorous or comic appeals to consumers usually get their attention, but they often fall short of selling the goods.

> **In the 1970s, Alka-Seltzer used a series of extremely humorous TV commercials that were so notable they made the expression**

"Try it . . . you'll like it!" a common cliche. The spots got every-one's attention and big laughs, but apparently didn't sell the product. The company abandoned the routine in favor of a less humorous approach.

Social Values of the Culture

The cultural values identified previously relate to individual consumers and their personal self-image. Other cultural values focus more on the individual within the social context. They specify what one should and shouldn't value with regard to social interaction. There are many more than just these eight, but these are the ones that seem to have the strongest influence on how and why consumers buy. We'll take a brief look at each one and comment on the likelihood of change, if any.

SOCIAL VALUES

Ours	Others
Casual	Formal
Romantic	Practical
Competitive	Cooperative
Individualism	Collectivism
Youth-oriented	Seniority-oriented
Child-centered	Adult-centered
Dichotomous	Continuous
Performance	Position

THE CASUAL SOCIETY

We don't much stand on ceremony in this culture, in our speech, dress, or manner of behavior. Social interactions even among strangers are much more likely to be casual than formal. We simply say "Hi" more often than "Good day." Whether it's a waiter talking to a restaurant patron, a patient speaking to a physician, or a sales clerk dealing with a customer, the conversation is likely to be friendly and casual. This is why people from more formal societies often regard Americans as crass and boorish. We don't put much importance on observation of the social niceties and recognition or position. In fact, we often see them as pretentious.

> Sales representatives are more credible and effective when they wear fairly formal business attire, regardless of how their clients dress. But they should speak to their customers in a friendly, casual manner, rather than with a formal approach. The only precaution is to avoid being overly *familiar* with clients.

THE ROMANTIC AMERICAN

We strongly believe that "love conquers all," despite all evidence to the contrary. Our good, hard, practical mentality dissolves into a pile of mush at the first glimpse of a romantic symbol or image. While those in other cultures find it difficult, if not impossible, to see anything remotely romantic about a bar of soap or a frozen dinner, Americans see all kinds of romantic possibilities, especially with a little help from the marketer.

> Sales of such products as greeting cards, boxed candy, and flowers are clustered around major holidays. St. Valentine's Day has become a major sales event for everyone from Whitman's to Fanny Farmer or See's candy stores to Russell Stover to Godiva chocolates, largely because of intense promotion. Hallmark has even attempted to *initiate* a holiday, Grandparent's Day, and gain its acceptance among the romantic, love-oriented American public.

THE COMPETITIVE SOCIETY

Americans benchmark their performance by comparison with others. We're strivers who think in terms of winning and losing. We call successful people "real winners" and less accomplished people "losers." We see rivalry and competition all around us, and when it isn't personified, it's at least symbolic. Many consumer products we buy are nothing more than trophies that symbolize our success in the "game of life."

> BMW appeals to prospective car and motorcycle buyers with magazine ads headlined "Winning isn't everything, but the trophies do have a certain appeal." The lead copy line adds emphasis: "Possession of an extraordinary inner drive is what marks some individuals as destined to succeed."

THE INDIVIDUALISTIC SOCIETY

In this culture, *collectivism* is a bad word. To Americans, it conjures up Orwellian images of sacrificing individual freedom and submitting to control. *Individualism,* on the other hand, we see as synonymous with virtuous self-reliance, independence, and personal freedom. It's a moot point whether or not this individualistic orientation is practiced only in the breach—the point is that consumers think in terms of individualism and don't respond well to appeals to conformity. Even the most conservative, staid belonger likes to think of himself or herself as an independent thinker and doer who just happens to agree with the consensus.

> Magazine ads for Halsa Swedish Botanical Shampoos and Conditioners feature five different formulas for different colors and types of hair. The same formula would serve the vast majority of the market, but multiple choice lets the buyers indulge their sense of individual identity.

THE YOUTH-ORIENTED SOCIETY

An elderly professional woman of Chinese descent once told me a story about her attitude toward aging and how it contrasted with ours. At an afternoon coffee gathering with several other ladies, one of them snidely commented that since she was the oldest, she could go first. She recognized very clearly that it was intended as a snub; but it isn't an insult to an elderly Chinese matron. To her, it was still a sign of respect and admiration to have someone openly recognize her seniority. Despite her conscious recognition of the insult, she always liked that woman after the incident. Americans are the same way, but in reverse. We associate youth with vigor and attractiveness.

Within the appropriate age-role limits, the younger the image of the product, the better chance it has for acceptance.

> Charles of the Ritz named a moisturizing skin conditioner "Age-Zone Controller" to emphasize the youth appeal. The illustration of the model in the magazine ad is captioned in part, "I've discovered that it's easier to face the world when I like what I see in the mirror." The ad copy concludes, "Look in the mirror in two weeks. And smile at a younger-looking you."

THE CHILD-CENTERED SOCIETY

The focus not only of family life, but of social life, as well, is often on the child. Juvenile concerns are just that in many other cultures. But we often think of children as not only innocent and naive, but also as rather fragile and sensitive. While many other cultures regard their children as robust little creatures, we tend to pamper our kids and to be exceedingly concerned about their well-being. We're not nearly as interested in imposing demands on our children as we are in meeting theirs.

> "The quality of *The First Years* . . . so much depends on it" reads the headline of a *Parents Magazine* ad for The First Years brand of over 200 "thoughtfully-designed, mother-tested" products. The ad copy refers to the company's "Mothers' Council" under the guidance of a physician who also heads a children's hospital child development center. Such marketing appeals both depend on and also intensify the child-centeredness of American parents.

THE DICHOTOMOUS PERSPECTIVE

Americans are better at recognizing black and white than distinguishing among shades of gray. We don't like small gradations or continuities. Instead we like to deal with good and bad, right and wrong, young and old, expensive and cheap, friend and foe: We live in a binary world. This "switch" mentality—on or off—can hurt marketers who communicate with consumers in a more continuous idiom. Often it's best to express product features and characteristics in simple, dichotomous terms, especially for less educated, downscale markets.

> **Magazine ads for Procter & Gamble's relatively new and high-ly successful Liquid Tide laundry detergent feature a simple, dichotomous comparison of two socks, under the headline "Toe to toe." The ad states, "Liquid Tide beats the socks off other liquids," rather than presenting a lengthy discussion of product effectiveness in many different situations. The au-dience is allowed to generalize from only a single, two-way comparison.**

THE PERFORMANCE ORIENTATION

Americans judge their peers mostly on the basis of their perfor-mance, rather than on the historical social position of the fam-ily. In fact, social position itself is largely determined by the performance and contribution of the individual and the family of the immediate past. Except for the very top echelons of the society, one's ascent on the social ladder isn't very limited by one's initial station in life. This is different from many other cultures, where something of a social caste system remains. The opportunities for upward social mobility here make strivers sensitive to marketing appeals for goods that will help their performance and consequently assist them to obtain higher status.

> **Corum watches are promoted with a headline that says it in a single phrase: "Achievement has its own rewards."**

The most important cultural consideration for marketing and promotion is to avoid appeals that are *contrary* to cultural val-ues and dictates. The appeal need not be geared specifically to one particular cultural value or norm, but it *must not violate any* of the major cultural value orientations.

Material Values of the Culture

The cultural values outlined previously relate to the social environment. The six that follow are related more to the material environment.

MATERIAL VALUES

Ours	Others
Order	Disorder
Optimism	Fatalism
Conquest	Integration
Progress	Stability
Change	Tradition
Risk	Security

THE ORDERLY AMERICAN

Compared to most other cultures, Americans are extremely neat and orderly about virtually everything. We impose geometric symmetry on just about everything to which we put our hands. If "cleanliness is next to Godliness," we are a holy people indeed! Our penchant for cleanliness is graphically expressed in our language: If we're angry with some fellow, we might call him an SOB. But if we're *really* angry, then he's a *dirty* SOB, which is, of course, vastly worse! We also extend our need for orderliness on the natural environment. Visitors from abroad sometimes gain the impression that we would level and pave the entire nation if we but could. Americans, more than just about anyone else, enthusiastically welcome and even seek out products that promise cleanliness and orderliness.

THE OPTIMISTIC AMERICAN

This culture puts value on control and acceptance of responsibility, but we also expect the results to be *positive*. We firmly believe that things will work out for the best, even during the darkest hour. Americans rarely see things as predetermined; destiny plays a very small part in our lives, and when it's even mentioned, there's often the underlying assumption that we can control it toward the good. This inherent optimism, coupled with our sense of responsibility, makes American consumers very susceptible to marketing appeals that are positive and up-lifting.

THE CONQUERING AMERICAN

Americans compete not only with others in the social world, but also with nature, itself. We turn our competitive inclinations toward the material world, seeking to conquer and overcome the environment. Nature is often (unfortunately, *too* often) something to be tamed and brought under human bondage and control. The recent ecological and environmental movement has only just begun to affect this cultural value, but there's a long way to go. Most Americans still take an adversarial posture toward the material things and seek to master the material world.

THE PROGRESSIVE AMERICAN

In this culture, life is not a random walk. We see almost every-thing as going someplace with a specific destination. Americans automatically expect improvement, growth, and progress. "More" is synonymous with "better." We seldom see the mate-rial world as splayed out on a horizontal plane; rather we see it in a hierarchical format, or at least on an incline. And the direc-tion the world is taking is up, not down. So there's a certain stubborn insatiability about the American consumer that cre-ates a perpetual need not only for more, but for *new.*

THE DYNAMIC AMERICAN

Our cultural values toward change go hand-in-hand with those of progress. New and dynamic things are valued far more than the traditional and the conventional. Many societies put a great deal of trust in the tried-and-true, regarding new solutions with skepticism. By contrast, we often find the old ways a bit boring and tiring, while we greet new and different options with a good deal of trust and enthusiasm. If there's one American buy-word, it's NEW.

THE RISK-TAKING AMERICAN

The American consumer is typically a risk taker. This society frowns on those who place too much value on security and refuse to take risks. People are expected to "give it a shot," even though the outcome may be uncertain. When things go badly, we usually don't feel that we shouldn't have taken a chance. Instead we take comfort in the fact that we gave it a good try. "Hindsight is always 20/20" someone mutters, and then we go on to take another chance. Because of the American consumers' willingness to take risks, along with their belief in progress and change, the rate of new product introduction (and acceptance) is astronomical.

Order, change, conquest, progress, performance, optimism, risk—they all revolve around Americans' fascination with material goods, with property! These values mean a high-velocity change rate for consumer goods. This means the marketers' assessments of their *products' life cycle* is very important: introduction, growth, maturity, decline, withdrawal. But making those assessments isn't so easy; it requires careful study and hard-headed judgments.

After microcomputers were invented, computer industry analysts jumped from the position that *nobody* would want a home computer to the belief that *everybody* would eventually have one. Both views proved to be mistaken. But in the meantime, firms from the relatively inexperienced Texas Instruments to the very experienced IBM first jumped into the fray, then found it necessary to withdraw. While Americans are innovative and readily accept such new products, there are limits. A more careful analysis of the product's *function* within the home and the *needs and value preceptions* could have avoided many ill-fated ventures.

Even when there's ready acceptance of an innovation, it doesn't guarantee a durable market. Because of the cultural values identified here, Americans are also rather capricious about moving into (*and out of*) new products and services. The video arcade game craze is a case in point: Large manufacturers such as Atari committed huge sums to obtain volume production, while hundreds of small entrepreneurs opened entertainment arcades. But the fad proved to be short-lived, and expenditures have dwindled. Home video game consoles and cartridges followed a similar, transient ascent and decline. The product life cycle took more the shape of a peaked mountain than a plateau. The American consumer—here today, gone tomorrow!

TRENDS OF CHANGE IN CULTURAL VALUES

Cultural values are fairly durable, and they won't change overnight. They're so resistant to change it would be virtually impossible for one company or even for an entire industry to cause any appreciable change in the values of the society. So marketers have to take cultural values as they are and work with them, not against them. But this doesn't imply that cultural values are constant over many decades or centuries. Important political, technical, economic, and social changes often result in shifting cultural values. For instance, women were drawn into the work force in large numbers for political reasons during World War II. As the trend continues, women enjoy greater economic freedom. This, in turn, has affected cultural values regarding the family. Discoveries and inventions such as oral contraceptives and computers are technical changes that become reflected in social norms and eventually in the cultural values of the society as a whole.

The more rapid the rate of change in these various aspects of life, the more quickly cultural values are shifted and modified to accommodate the new situation. So American cultural values are probably changing more rapidly than at any time in the history of the world. And as these values change, so, too, must companies change their marketing to consumers. Often the flux in cultural values creates both jeopardies and opportunities for consumer marketers; some get hurt, others are benefited. Jeopardy and opportunity: two good reasons to stay abreast of cultural change.

Trends in the Sixties and Seventies

Pollster Daniel Yankelovich and his organization have monitored American sociocultural trends over time for many years. In the mid-May 1971 issue of *Marketing News*, Yankelovich outlined 31 different trends in five categories. They're briefly synopsized in Table 5. Many of them proved to be very durable and persistent, and their effects are more obvious today than when they were first reported. Some others were only short-lived and can't be seen today. Only very few actually turned out to be contrary to the direction of change in cultural values today. Many of the problems experienced by tradition-bound companies today have their origins in these cultural changes. Those who were able to adapt benefited; those who ignored the trends or refused to conform to them suffered for it.

Cultural Trends in the Eighties

SRI International conducted a three-year, $1 million study of cultural values in the 1980s, sponsored by sixty American companies. The results were reported by Arnold Mitchell in *Changing Values and Lifestyles* in 1981. A list of the thirteen trends Mitchell identified follows. Notice that several of them are closely related to some of the cultural trends detected by Yankelovich a decade earlier. It's also interesting to note that the individual changes are often related to one another. For instance, the shift from quanity to quality is compatible with a

Table 5. Direction of Change in the Early 1970s

Psychology of Affluence
Greater emphasis on improving physical appearance
Greater expression of individuality through consumption
More concern for health, well-being, diet, and exercise
New status symbols that deemphasize material possessions
Greater interest in social and cultural self-expression
Greater concern for expressions of personal creativity
More demands for challenging, meaningful occupations

Antifunctional Trends
Restoration of romance, mystery, and adventure in living
Reactions against sameness, quest for novelty and change
Enhancement of beauty in people's daily surroundings
Move toward sensory experience and sensual gratification
New concerns with mysticism and spiritual experience
Introspection and a greater need for self-understanding

Reactions Against Complexity Trends
Simplification and rejection of excessive complexity
Rejection of the artificial and a return to the natural
Emphasis on ethnic identification and differentiation
Increased involvement in the immediate community
Greater reliance on technology than on tradition
Shifting away from bigness and needs for growth in size

Trends Away from Puritan Values
Growing tendency to put personal pleasure before duty
Deemphasis of gender stereotyping and sex roles
Emphasis on the present, not living for the future
Relaxation of sexual prohibitions, especially for women
More acceptance of stimulants and psychoactive drugs
Shift from self-improvement to greater self-acceptance
Shift from institutional to personalized religious beliefs

Trends Related to Child-Centeredness
Shift from regimentation toward tolerance of disorder
More challenges, less acceptance of conventional authority
Increased rejection of hypocrisy, sham, and exaggeration
Shift from women's homemaking to external career pursuits
Renewed interest in familial pursuits and satisfactions

shift from abundance to sufficiency and a change from extravagance to frugality. This close correspondence between the individual categories of change suggests that there are only a very few, fundamental underlying changes in the core culture and the thinking of a majority of those in the society.

DIRECTION OF CHANGE
IN THE EARLY 1980s

From	Toward
Extravagance	Frugality
Quantity	Quality
Complexity	Simplicity
Abundance	Sufficiency
Waste	Conservation
Pretense	Authenticity
Impressive	Meaningful
Fads	Fashion
Formality	Flexibility
Traditional	Experimental
Collective	Individual
Mechanical	Personal
Efficient	Pleasing

Two Common Denominators of Change

While there's no single thread that binds all the cultural changes expected in the late 1980s and early 1990s, we can identify two underlying forces that are distinct but related to one another: awareness of institutional limitations and awareness of material limitations. We'll take a look at the genesis of each, then see how these forces affect marketing programs.

A CRISIS OF FAITH

The great depression of the 1930s ended an ear of almost complete confidence in America. It gave birth to a crisis of faith in social institutions that spawned the fraternal movement—individuals turning away from institutions and toward one another at the peer level. In close parallel, the Vietnam War also ended the era of complacency and trust in institutions that preceded it. For many, the "military-industrial complex" became an onerous thing, and belief in other social institutions—church, education, the legal system, law enforcement, corporate America, and the like—also sagged. But this time, instead of turning toward one another in fraternal embrace, Americans turned to themselves, turned inward and individualistic. This shift in orientation is reflected in the last five or six changes identified in the preceding list. But the others listed earlier can be attributed to another set of underlying forces.

THE PSYCHOLOGY OF SHORTAGE

Since the beginning of the century, conservationists have been telling us that the Earth's resources are limited and that we'd run out if we extrapolated current consumption rates into the future. Mostly their warnings fell on deaf ears; they were summarily classified as doomsayers, and we went on our happy way, until 1974. Then, as we all sat in our cars in the lines at the gas pumps, such warnings began to take on new meaning: *It was just possible that they might be right!* But Americans became concerned about far more than just oil shortages. They got alarmed about everything from the population explosion to endangered species of wildlife to air, water, and solid waste pollution to the danger of nuclear holocaust. That was the beginning of a shift from a psychology of unlimited growth (more is better) to a psychology of shortage (less is better). This is the dominant thread that ties together the items on the first half of the aforementioned list.

Both the forces of personalization and limitation have profound effects on consumers' actions in the marketplace. Not everyone, but many are looking for different products and services; they respond differently to costs and prices; they're sensitive to different promotional appeals; and they seek different modes of distribution. We'll conclude with some suggestions for modification of the marketing mix to accommodate these very broad underlying cultural trends.

MODIFICATIONS TO THE PRODUCT OR SERVICE

Given the emphasis on personalization and individuation, identical, mass-produced consumer goods will find increased resistance in the marketplace. The trends call for a broader choice of customized or individualized goods.

THE PRODUCT OR SERVICE

Simplify the product and/or consider downsizing units
Individualize the product line and/or offer more options
Improve the efficiency and/or effectiveness of the goods
Increase durability and/or avoid disposable products
Reduce packaging and/or make packaging readily disposable
Eliminate unnecessary frills and/or improve functionality
Create products and services that help consumers conserve

PRICE POLICY AND ADMINISTRATION

Consumers are increasingly aware of perceived price/value ratios and less likely to assume that the price automatically reflects the value of the product or service. Nor are they as willing to pay for anything about the goods they regard as unnecessary. Both price flexibility and correspondence with functional value are important.

THE PRICING OF THE GOODS

Price according to the consumers' perceived benefits
Higher prices must reflect greater inherent value

Use special sales, coupons, and so on, to be price-flexible

Don't assume a high price will imply high value to consumers

Consider externalizing some costs, passing tasks to consumers
(they assemble it, add some ingredients, finish it, etc.)

Provide various levels of quality and price for each line

PROMOTIONAL CAMPAIGN GUIDELINES

Mass marketed goods are progressively losing their markets to more specialized products and services that are promoted with more specialized appeals in more selective media. There's also greater need than ever before for careful product positioning.

THE ADVERTISING AND PROMOTION

Put the emphasis on quality, functionality, and effectiveness

Use promotion to differentiate the product; make it unique

Position the goods, relative to others, in the consumers' minds

Avoid the hard sell; depend on more informative ad content

Limit the use of hype, exaggeration, puffing, and superlatives

Consider comparative advertising based on superior quality

Choose high-involvement media that are also highly selective

DISTRIBUTION STRATEGY AND OUTLETS

The development of technology for transporting, storing, handling, and displaying consumer goods has proceeded hand-in-hand with the need for more adroit distribution to the buyers. With greater individualization and self-indulgence, there's a market in January for fresh blueberries from Australia, and also the means for providing them; there is a large demand for Washington apples and a small demand for Kiwi fruit from New Zealand, as well. Consumers are increasingly willing to pay for effective distribution and helpful retail services, but less and less willing to pay for fancy frills and expensive but meaningless symbols.

DISTRIBUTION CHANNELS AND OUTLETS

Rationalize and realign the channels of distribution

Try smaller outlets or "unitize" shops within large stores

Consider direct marketing or direct-response advertising

Seek outlets that reduce consumer search and shopping time (superstores, high-service outlets, demonstrations, etc.)

Externalize distribution costs with warehouse or factory stores

Stress in-store personal selling and quality after-service

There are some real benefits to those who latch onto a cultural trend and ride it successfully. As you've noticed, a genuine cultural trend is enduring and it provides a solid base for many years. But culture has an even more important meaning for marketers: You can't violate cultural dictates—run against cultural norms and values—and market consumer goods successfully. Marketing programs and appeals need not necessarily be based on a particular cultural feature or trend, but they certainly can't contradict any of them.

12

LIFE STAGES
Steps on the Stairway of Life

Phase	The Buy-Words that Work the Best
Teens	This is what you need in order to belong.
Twenties	This is what your friends expect of you.
Thirties	This is for a good, solid person like you.
Forties	This is what the pros and experts buy.
Fifties	This is something to judge for yourself.
Sixties+	This is very effective and economical.

Time works its way on all of us. Much of what we are is the result of the maturation process. Time and experience invariably etch their marks on both our physical and our psychological selves. So people of different ages are not only perceived differently by others, but they also see themselves differently. In this chapter we'll consider some of those changes—the ones that are fairly common to everyone of a certain age. We'll look at both the *individual* phases of life and at the stages in the *family* life cycle.

HOW CONSUMERS CHANGE OVER TIME

People change in two different ways: gradually and suddenly. Some changes take place very slowly and continuously over the days, weeks, months, and years. The shifting values and attitudes creep so slowly it's like watching the hands of a clock; they seem to be stable and the only way you can tell they're changing is by comparing them over a broad span of time. But there are also dramatic episodes of life that produce more radical changes, almost at once: a marriage, the birth of one's first child, a midlife career change, the sudden and unexpected loss of a loved one, or retirement. When this kind of change occurs, the person might find that one day everything is as usual, and the next day things have been irrevocably altered forever. That kind of radical change can have a profound effect on the individual consumer's life.

Your wardrobe might be a good metaphor for looking at the two kinds of change over time. You may have built your wardrobe by slowly acquiring one or two garments at a time to fit the seasons and the demands of your business and social life. This gradual process may continue for months or even for a few years. But sooner or later, some dramatic change will probably come along. Maybe a new job or some new affiliation requires very different clothes from those you've collected. During a short period, you might engage in "the great closet purge," as you reluctantly discard many old, familiar garments. At the same time, you might engage in a flurry of shopping, trying new styles and colors. Then, when you're satisfied, you may return to another stable period. Life is much like that. People build a "life structure" that's satisfactory for awhile, with only minor changes. Then something causes a radical shift and they re-build and start over.

The changes consumers experience don't always happen at the same time or in the same way for everyone, but there's some commonality; people are more similar than they are different. There are some very identifiable trends and some useful lessons we can draw from them. But it's important to note that these are only trends, and while the patterns identified in the next section are typical, there are always some deviations and exceptions.

MARKETING TO JUVENILES AND ADOLESCENTS

The younger the child consumer, the more likely there will be parental involvement in the purchase and/or consumption of the goods. Infants' needs are met entirely by parental choices and purchases, but as children in this society mature, they play a more and more important part in the procurement and consumption of the things they need and want. And it starts quite early, indeed. Children of only 3 or 4 years of age often have strong preferences about the kinds of toys they want, the types of food they'll eat, and even their modes of dress.

The Preteen Consumer Set

There's a great deal of parental determination or influence on consumption by juveniles. Mom or dad may play the role of information filter, decision maker, buyer, preparer, and/or maintainer of many of the child's consumer goods. But there's a wide range of children's products and services that require marketing to both the children and the parents, ranging from toys and clothes to foods and snacks, from music or dance lessons to schools or summer camps. For such goods, the marketer has to win the hearts and minds of the children as well as the approval and assistance of the adult parents.

> **Del Monte promotes their Fruit Street brand of juice-based beverages for children with a dual approach. Television commercials during prime viewing time for children (Saturday and Sunday mornings) promote the drink to the children with the slogan "It's so much fun you can taste it." Meanwhile, in print ads directed to parents, "Del Monte proposes a juice truce," noting that children want sweet drinks while mothers are concerned about nutrition: Fruit Street satisfies both, since it's 50 percent juice and has no artificial coloring, flavoring, or preservatives.**

THE KIDS' CAPRICIOUS CHOICES

Fads and fancies sweep through the juvenile market like wildfire. While children are often sophisticated consumers at an early age, they also exhibit the childish frivolity that drives the marketers of juvenile goods crazy while it pleases and amuses the rest of us. But it's amazing how closely their tastes and preferences reflect the cultural trends of adults. Marketers of children's goods who are keenly aware of contemporary social trends in the adult world sometimes benefit greatly from that knowledge.

> **One of the ten modern social trends identified by John Naisbitt in his recent best-selling book *Megatrends* is that of "high tech/ high touch." He notes that the high rate of mechanization of consumer goods must often be offset by intensification of the "softer" side: greater prevalence of "touchy-feely" products and services. Long-time toy maker Tonka Corp. translated awareness of this double-track trend into marketing success by creating two diametrically opposed toy lines: On the high-touch side, their cuddly Pound Puppies show promise of acquiring the popularity of the highly successful predecessor in the kids' arms, the Cab-**

bage Patch dolls. Even the most macho ten-year-old boy seems to find something precious about the stuffed toy canine waif. But if they tire of such sentimentality, Tonka has another fascination for them—the GoBots, colorful, hard plastic fighting robot characters so complex and intricate only a child could figure out how to transform them from vertical figures to miniature vehicles on wheels.

THE PERSONIFICATION OF TOYS

Children are *personalizing* consumers. Highly imaginative and creative, they project human (and superhuman) characteristics onto practically anything remotely resembling animate beings. No wonder, then, that they're so fascinated with animated cartoons. Recognizing their proclivity for personalization and their devotion to animation, toy marketers have capitalized on the combination.

> Toy characters can become cartoon characters to increase their popularity among children. Not only Tonka's GoBots, but also Mattel's Masters of the Universe and Hasbro's Transformers and G.I. Joes became television cartoon characters to amuse the children's viewing audience. In the process, the shows become 30-minute, rather than 30-second commercials for the products.

> It can also go the other way, as well—movie and television characters can become toys: Coleco licensed Rambo for dolls, while movie Ewoks and robots such as Star Wars' C3PO and R2D2 are stars of Lucasfilm's "Ewok/Droids Adventure Hour," a Saturday morning TV show full of characters licensed by toy marketers.

> This successful marketing strategy for children sometimes arouses the ire of social critics, concerned about what it's doing to children's minds. But condemnation of the practice of converting products to animated characters and vice versa appears inappropriate and prohibition seems unlikely. On the other hand, it would behoove the marketers to regulate the content of the cartoon shows themselves to protect both their juvenile audience and their reputation within society.

Table 6. Spending Patterns for Teens 16 to 19

Boys		Girls	
Income (Percent)		Income (Percent)	
Earnings	59.2%	Earnings	59.6%
Allowance	40.8	Allowance	40.4
Total	100.0	Total	100.0
Expenditures (Percent)		Expenditures (Percent)	
Movies, entertainment	16.7	Clothing	24.4
Gasoline, car	15.9	Cosmetics, fragrances	18.8
Clothing	15.2	Gasoline, car	8.1
Food, snacks	12.3	Movies, entertainment	7.9
Personal grooming	6.5	Food, snacks	7.1
Hobbies	3.7	Hair Care	4.4
Coin-operated games	3.6	Jewelry	3.8
Books, paperbacks	1.8	Records	2.7
Magazines	1.8	Books, paperbacks	2.0
Records	1.7	School supplies	1.6
School supplies	1.5	Magazines	1.3
Cigarettes	0.4	Coin-operated games	0.5
		Cigarettes	0.5
Total	81.0	Total	83.0
Savings	19.0	Savings	17.0

Source: Rand Youth Poll, Teenage Economic Power, 1983.

The Teenage Consumer Market

The last baby boomer just recently turned twenty! Teenagers
are fewer, yet those who market to them have good reason to
rejoice—they're spending more than ever before. On the low
side, estimates are about $30 billion, and they range all the way
to a high of about $50 billion, with another $10 billion or so
going into teenagers' savings. But these spending power figures
represent more than just increased affluence on the part of
teens (See Table 6.) They're also playing a larger role in the
economic life of the family and assuming more individual responsibility and independence as well.

In the early 1980s, one teen in five lived in a father-absent home, and only three out of four lived in a two-parent household. But even in a two-parent family, teens are more self-reliant today than a decade or two ago. While once their food was prepared for them, their clothes were purchased and maintained by mother, and they were chauffeured about in the family car, today, it's all or mostly up to them. They're often expected to make their own decisions and to take care of many of their own food, clothing, and transportation needs. Consequently, more marketers are promoting directly to them with such selective media as *Seventeen* or *TeenAge* magazine.

A very high proportion of teen spending power is strictly discretionary. So even though their total disposable income is relatively small, compared to adults, they have far more latitude in their choices in the marketplace. As a result, they're also more responsive to promotional appeals.

> **The soft drink giants, Coca-Cola and Pepsi Cola, haven't abandoned baby boomers, but they have shifted their focus sharply away from that maturing crowd toward teenagers. Teens from 15 to 18 consume more soft drinks per capita than any other group, according to Business Trend Analysts. Seven out of ten drink at least one soft drink every three days. In 1984, Pepsi boosted their brand share by nearly a point over the previous year by promoting their brand as the choice of the new generation, with teen superstar Michael Jackson's help. Coke responded by modifying the brand to a sweeter, less carbonated formula, thought to be more preferable to teens. In a lightning response, Pepsi soon had a 15-year-old in their TV spots, making the switch to Pepsi Cola. The battle for the teen market continues while the baby boomers look on.**

THE STAGES OF ADULT LIFE

There was a time when developmental psychology was synonymous with "child" psychology—not so today. We know now that adult consumers go through a process of growth and change as they mature. The phases of adult life don't necessarily correspond to age decades, but there's enough commonality to make that breakdown meaningful. So we'll identify the typical patterns for consumers in their twenties, thirties, forties, and so forth, mostly because these periods are easy to understand and recall.

Consumers in Their Twenties

This is a time of search and conformity for young people, who are fully aware of the fact that they're setting the course for later life. For the first time, many of the decisions they make will have an impact on their life beyond the next few days, weeks, or months. They have a strong concern for what's "right" and "wrong," what they "should" and "shouldn't" do, according to social norms. Sensitivity to group and societal norms is the ear-

Factor	Typical Condition in Their Twenties
Family Status	Young single, early married, or young child.
Occupational Status	Ending formal education, starting a career.
Social Conditions	Many casual friends, many changes with marriage.
Principal Concerns	Popularity with peers, getting a good start.
Major Decisions	What career to pursue, with whom to mate?
Dominant Needs	Independence, sexuality, exhibition, diversion.
Value Emphasis	Social, intellectual, then economic, political.
Appeal Sensitivity	To their own peers, as a reference group.

mark of people at this stage. Marketing to this segment often relies heavily on appeals to conformity, citing group or social norms, without reference to experts who are authority figures. The norms are based on relevant reference groups, rather than on individual authority.

General Motors promotes their Celebrity Eurosport, "Today's Chevrolet," with print ads strongly appealing to young adults beginning their careers. Listen to the copy verse, under the headline, *Corporate Blue:*

Imagine a color
in all its hues
what some call success
is just chasing the blues.

Well, the day has dawned
and the sun's getting hot
your heart says go
don't ever stop.

It's how you move
it's what you see
you know where you're going
where you want to be.

If you start right now
you can light the fuse
pull out all the stops
we're gonna chase the blues.

Sun on the left
sea on the right
got the good life ahead
and the car in flight.

Point it down the road
there's no time to lose
in your heart you know
how to chase the blues.

The copy of this *Cosmopolitan* magazine ad (jointly sponsored by designer Anne Klein II, whose clothes the model wears) is rife with double meanings relevant to consumers in their twenties, concerned with conflicts between independence and responsibility, peer pressure and personal values.

Consumers in Their Thirties

This is a time of solidification and commitment. Even those highly committed to experimentation and change often feel a strong pull toward greater stability, mostly in the spheres of family and vocation. Those who married early have either survived the "seven year itch" or uncoupled from their original partner. Those who postponed the process of pairing and family creation are likely to feel that "this is the time" and maybe that it's "now or never." This stage may contain a strong sense of frustration for many. It's a time of great aspirations and few resources. New parents often approach that role very seriously. Minor mishaps at home or at work can be fanned into major catastrophes with terrible consequences.

There's often a pull toward traditional values and conventional lifestyles, defined by societal norms rather than peer

Factor	Typical Condition in Their Thirties
Family Status	Married couple only or with young children.
Occupational Status	Career path identified, now settling in.
Social Conditions	Attention to family and job limits contacts.
Principal Concerns	To become sure and stable at home and at work.
Major Decisions	Whether or not to have any (more) children.
Dominant Needs	Achievement, nurturance, security, recognition.
Value Emphasis	Economic, social, then intellectual, aesthetic.
Appeal Sensitivity	Acceptance and approval from society at large.

groups. This a time to "put down roots" and solidify tastes and preferences—to start "the long pull" toward complete maturity and eventual seniority and authority. Personal anxiety can be a problem, but they may feel that agitation and discontent are signs of instability or failure. But this stage is also filled with energy, enthusiasm, a high level of idealism, and often fruitful dedication to both personal and social principles and causes.

> By contrast to the auto promotion just mentioned for those in their twenties, Chrysler Corp. promotes the Dodge Lancer in magazine ads with the headline "We hid a sports car inside." One of several of a new breed of cars, the Lancer combines the practical aspects of a family sedan with the performance of a sports car. The copy deals with "First, the fun." Then, "As for practicality . . . ." Both the conception of such cars and their promotion are geared to drivers in their thirties, meeting their compulsion to conform without relinguishing some youthful abandon.

Consumers in Their Forties

This is often a period of uncertainty and discontent, when people turn inward toward their own desires. Caught in the bind between durable commitments and strong desires for personal satisfaction, many experience a midlife crisis. The route divides into two paths at that fork in the road: Those choosing conformity and conventionality find a smooth, straight, well-paved, clearly marked, and often exceedingly boring path. Those who choose personal gratification over convention are on an unmapped, narrow, twisting, rocky road that's also exciting, exhilarating, and novel.

Positive marketing appeals to youth and vigor are effective, but negative (fear) appeals to prevention of aging may backfire. One way or the other, most of these consumers resolve their contentions with society: Conventionalists reluctantly conform and self-satisfiers reject social norms, so appeals to conformity are ill-advised. People of this age are more comfortable with self-indulgence—they feel they've earned it—and more hospitable to luxury as opposed to utility. Appeals based on personal

Factor	Typical Condition in Their Forties
Family Status	Full nest of children, often separation, divorce.
Occupational Status	In the long pull or mid-life career change.
Social Conditions	Well-established affiliations and routines.
Principal Concerns	Coping with boredom and maintaining momentum.
Major Decisions	Whether or not to change marriage or career?
Dominant Needs	Diversion, consistency, nurturance, sexuality.
Value Emphasis	Economic, aesthetic, then social, intellectual.
Appeal Sensitivity	To respected, well-recognized authority figures.

values and self-determination work well compared to those based on family or job necessity.

> With two-page ads in such magazines as *Ladies' Home Journal* and *Good Housekeeping,* famous TV actress Linda Evans introduces Clairol's New Ultress gel hair colorant to middle-aged homemakers with the slogan, "You could be the best you've ever been . . . ." Whether in a stable state or in transition, women of this age group are responsive to *credible* (but not exaggerated) glamour appeals, especially those portraying an authority figure as well-recognized, glamorous, and admired as this one.

Consumers in Their Fifties

This time is of fruition and attainment of authority, when consumers really come into their own. Accepting the impossibility of their impossible dreams, they abandon them, but they're compensated by the realization of maturity and recognition while health and energy are yet barely on the wane. Cynicism is held at bay as they take command of their social and material world. Long experience in many roles has demonstrated both their capabilities and their limitations. Declining health may be acknowledged as inevitable, but it's not imminent, it's still well beyond the horizon. Recognition of competence and authority arrive simultaneously at home and at work. In family life, elders pass the mantle of authority to the next generation. On the job, their seniority and experience gain the respect of peers, subordinates, and superiors. Consumers' attitudes are in part a function of the external social situation, so these interactions have a significant effect on their attitudes and values, and they learn to see themselves as "having arrived." Even though they may realize they haven't reached the lofty position they once aspired to and probably never will, the daily satisfactions and rewards of seniority are an effective balm for the disappointment.

Factor	Typical Condition in Their Fifties
Family Status	Children departed or departing, few demands.
Occupational Status	Well-established, assuming command posture.
Social Conditions	More time for and devotion to outside interests.
Principal Concerns	Solidification of position, preparing to retire.
Major Decisions	Which commitments to maintain or to terminate?
Dominant Needs	Achievement, dominance, recognition, stimulation.
Value Emphasis	Political, aesthetic, then economic, religious.
Appeal Sensitivity	To the self as the most competent judge.

Rather than basing marketing appeals on authority or conformity, it's more effective to present the facts and tell these
consumers, "You be the judge." They feel they're competent to
evaluate and choose for themselves. They would rather set the
standards themselves than bow to social norms. Nor are they
likely to take the word of what they see as *another* authority.
They respond well to consumer goods that assist them in the
process of personalization and individuation. With fewer fears
and uncertainties than others, they're relatively unresponsive
to marketing appeals based on fear or those offering reassur-
ance.

> **Magazine ads for German-made Merkur XR4Ti, imported by
> Ford's Lincoln-Mercury division, illustrate very well how facts
> are presented to mature consumers who prefer to judge for them-
> selves. Superimposed on the low-angle photo of the car, a 6
> column, 20 row table has a detailed comparison of the Merkur
> with the BMW 318i, Saab 9000 Turbo, Audi 4000S Quattro, and
> Volvo Turbo. The headline for the car notes that "Its objective is
> not to compete with the (others), but frankly, to surpass them."**

Consumers Sixty and Beyond

Because many consumers, and especially males, tend to retire
during their sixties, there are some significant differences at
this stage between the time before and after retirement. Generally this is an era of gratification and fulfillment. Despite the
prevalent (and erroneous) assumption that "old" people are
largely tired, poor, and sick, these consumers are mostly occupied with the harvest of their life's work. Only a small minority
are destitute, in ill health, and experiencing hard times. In the
main, consumers in this age bracket are well-off from most
points of view.

Often people this age relinguish much of their authority and
responsibility but retain positions of influence, becoming the
"power behind the scenes." They may provide advice and
counsel to their juniors at work and at home. While their dependence on others may increase, they rarely become submissive,

and many become more assertive or even openly aggressive. With the feeling that they've been there and back already, they sense that they have little to gain by conformity and observance of the social niceties and little to lose by their protagonism, expression of judgment, or exceptional candor. Often practical, down-to-earth, and unpretentious, they are their own people and they know it.

This market for consumer goods seeks products and services that are safe, reliable, practical, and perhaps traditional. Marketers shouldn't rely on fear appeals. They contain too much threat for those very aware of danger and limitation. Nor do appeals to conformity or to authority have great potential for this market. Instead, they find clean, simple, straightforward presentations of product or service value most appealing. They also have fewer psychological prohibitions against self-indulgent luxury.

Factor	Typical Condition in Their Sixties+
Family Status	Empty nest, maybe sole survivor, grandparenting.
Occupational Status	Preparing to retire, retired, part-time work.
Social Conditions	Strong affiliations with their age cohort group.
Principal Concerns	Economic security and finding social purpose.
Major Decisions	What to down-grade and how much to change?
Dominant Needs	Security, independence, affiliation, succorance.
Value Emphasis	Religious, social, then aesthetic political.
Appeal Sensitivity	To functional utility and economy of the goods.

> Print ads for Lindsay's Know It All brand water conditioning appliance sport the headline "Smart Buy." With this brand, says the copy, "What you need is what you get. No more, no less." The tag lines is "Quality water at a price you can afford." Both the product itself and the promotion are appropriate to consumers of any age, but especially for the more mature, who neither shy away from a little luxury such as soft water, nor willingly spend more than they must to get it.

Remember that these descriptions are only tendencies and there's no ironclad boundary between consumers of adjacent age cohort groups. There's some overlap and some who are exceptions to the modal patterns identified here.

In Chapter 1 we identified fifteen collateral need categories and in Chapter 3 we outlined six core consumer values. The emphasis consumers place on these different needs and values depends on their personality and situation, but it also hinges on their stage in the life cycle. Table 7 outlines the most typical need and value emphases across the decades of adult consumer life and identifies the dominant appeal sensitivity of each.

THE FAMILY LIFE CYCLE

The *family life cycle* concept is similar in some respects to the *life stage concept,* but the unit of analysis is the family, rather than the individual. Use by marketers of the family life cycle, rather than age, is based on a couple of assumptions: that family status has an important effect on purchase patterns and that the stage in the family life cycle no longer corresponds closely to the age of the consumers in the society. Both of them seem to be pretty well substantiated, as noted in Chapter 9, on the family.

The Basis for Family Life Cycle

The family life cycle phases listed in Table 8 are based on four demographic variables: age, marital status, employment of the adults in the family, and the age of the youngest child. About

Table 7. Need and Value Emphasis by Age Group

	Twenties	Thirties	Forties	Fifties	Sixties+
Needs					
Achievement	Medium	High	Medium	High	Low
Independence	High	Low	Low	Medium	High
Exhibition	High	Low	Low	Low	Low
Recognition	Medium	High	Medium	High	Low
Dominance	Low	Medium	High	High	Medium
Affiliation	Medium	High	Medium	Medium	High
Nurturance	Low	High	High	Medium	Medium
Succorance	Low	Low	Low	Low	High
Sexuality	High	Medium	High	Medium	Medium
Stimulation	High	Low	Medium	High	Medium
Diversion	High	Medium	High	Low	Low
Novelty	High	Low	Low	Low	Low
Understanding	Medium	Medium	High	High	Medium
Consistency	Low	Medium	High	Medium	High
Security	Low	High	Medium	Low	High
Values					
Intellectual	High	Medium	Medium	Low	Low
Economic	Medium	High	High	Medium	Low
Aesthetic	Low	Medium	High	High	Medium
Social	High	High	Medium	Low	High
Political	Medium	Low	Low	High	Medium
Religious	Low	Low	Low	Medium	High
Sensitivity	Peers	Society	Authority	Self	Utility

Table 8. Family Life Cycle Stages

Phase	Eldest Adult	Marital Status	Employment Status	Youngest Child	Approximate Percentage
1	Young	Unmarried	Any	None	11%
2	Young	Married	Any	None	4
3	Any	Unmarried	Any	Preschool	4
4	Any	Married	Any	Preschool	27
5	Any	Unmarried	Any	Elementary	1
6	Any	Married	Any	Elementary	16
7	Any	Unmarried	Any	Adolescent	1
8	Any	Married	Any	Adolescent	18
9	Elderly	Married	Employed	None	6
10	Elderly	Unmarried	Employed	None	8
11	Elderly	Married	Retired	None	3
12	Elderly	Unmarried	Retired	None	1

four out of five families fall neatly into one of these twelve phases, while the others don't fit well because of multiple-family households or other atypical circumstances that defy classification into a practical, simple scheme.

The Family Life Cycle Stages

Attitudes, lifestyles, and consumption patterns all differ markedly and consistently from one phase of the family life cycle to the next. In some cases, differences in consumers' family life cycle stage are far more important than differences in their life stage by age. That's because both earning power and financial burdens vary from one stage of the family life cycle to the next. So consumers at different stages not only buy different family-related products and services, but they also evaluate other, more personal or individual goods differently. Table 9 identifies each of the twelve phases of the family life cycle and lists the major financial conditions and purchase patterns that are typical of each stage.

> The family car is the quintessential example of a consumer product that must fit the stage of the family life cycle very closely. While housing needs change markedly from one stage to the next, consumers don't change their dwelling as often as they trade cars. With both wear and obsolescence, people usually trade cars every few years, so they can choose one that corresponds closely to their family situation. Their family life cycle stage is often the appropriate unit of analysis for assessing the market for automobiles.

> The buyer's family life cycle stage affects several aspects of the purchase decision: a new or used car, an expensive or an economical model, a large or a small vehicle, one car for the family or two or more, and the kinds of features and options included on the car. What's more, family life cycle stage and the transition from one stage to the next materially affect how often buyers trade.

Table 9. Earning and Spending by Family Life Cycle Stage

Phase of Cycle	Financial Condition	Typical Purchase Patterns
Phase 1 Young, unmarried, childless	Both income and expenses are limited, there's little saving, free spending, beginning use of credit, and little financial stress.	Apparel, fashion goods, personal care products and services, recreational goods, things related to mating and dating, *basic* necessities and supplies for the home, cheap transportation, education, (shared) apartment rent.
Phase 2 Young, married, childless	Resources adequate (two incomes), little financial burden, free spending, use of credit, low saving, little stress.	Consumer durables, major appliances and furniture, audio and video home entertainment goods, air travel, restaurant meals, spectator entertainment, vacations, apparel, and personal care products.
Phase 3 Unmarried, preschool children	Income strictly limited (unmarried new parent), cautious spending, credit not readily available, no savings, high financial stress.	If home-sharing, food and housing expenses shared and dependent on FLC phase of others. If nesting, buying patterns similar to next phase, appliances, furniture, childcare products and services including daycare.
Phase 4 Married, preschool children	Income limited if not both working, few liquid assets, careful spending and credit, little saving, distress and discontent.	Purchase and furnishing of first home, durables, especially large and small appliances, child-care products and services, life and casualty insurance, transportation and utilities.
Phase 5 Unmarried, gradeschool children	Income limited, careful spending, credit used if available, little saving, high financial stress, substantial discontent.	Rent or mortgage payment, economical appliances and furniture, food, clothing, education, transportation expenses for child, limited personal spending, housekeeping and/or child-care costs, low-cost recreation.

Table 9. (*Continued*)

Phase of Cycle	Financial Condition	Typical Purchase Patterns
Phase 6 Married, gradeschool children	Income improved, the man's income increases, the woman may return to workforce, saving increases, and there's less financial stress.	Large quantity "family size" purchases and larger unit sizes, home-related durables, new cars, education-related expenses, vacation and recreation spending increases, car travel is high.
Phase 7 Unmarried, adolescent children	Conditions vary widely, there may be stress or crisis after divorce, credit may be unavailable but the situation is often temporary	Similar to following phase if there's little financial stress, buying limited to necessities with financial deprivation, immediate needs take precedence, especially for teenage children.
Phase 8 Married, adolescent children	Peak earning power, often dual incomes, children may work, moderate saving, credit for large purchases, some investment.	Furniture and appliance replacements with better quality, optional appliances and equipment, larger luxury or recreational items, additional cars, boats, RVs, elective medical services, college costs for children.
Phase 9 Elderly, married, childless, employed	Most favorable financial position, low burdens, high contentment, saving and investment high, assistance to children.	Home ownership at peak level, much spending on personal interests, recreation and travel high, adult education, avocational goods and services, luxury home improvements and cars, art objects if affluent.
Phase 10 Elderly, unmarried, childless, employed	Very adequate resources, often survivor insurance benefits, high income from job seniority, few burdens, retirement saving and/or investment.	New, downsized housing, furniture and appliances, vacation, travel and recreational goods and services, spending on personal interests, gifts for family and friends, medical care with age.

Table 9. (*Continued*)

Phase of Cycle	Financial Condition	Typical Purchase Patterns
Phase 11 Elderly, married, childless, retired	Income sharply diminished, expenses reduced, fixed income from accumulated assets, planned spending, no use of credit.	Downsized housing, often with relocation to better climate, perhaps retirement community, downsized home furnishings, medical expenses, health and personal care products, many leisure expenditures, gifts for others.
Phase 12 Elderly, unmarried, childless, retired	Low, fixed income, substantial assets including spouse life insurance benefits, little stress, careful planned spending, no need of credit.	Medical services and health care products, high recreational spending with ample leisure, contributions to children and grandchildren, downsized housing and household durables, seldom relocation.

Each of the American big-three auto makers covers the entire range of family life cycles with their various divisions and the many models of each brand. Given the number of alternatives any one dealer offers, they can serve virtually anyone who visits the showroom, from the young, single buyer to the elderly, retired widow. But some foreign car makers are more closely confined to only a few stages of the family life cycle.

Sweden's Volvo and West Germany's BMW are both closely associated with yuppie baby boomers, while Mercedes-Benz has little promise for young, growing families on a tight budget. Both Japan's Mazda and Honda were pretty closely associated with a narrow range of family life cycles during the 1970s. With the introduction of the popular RX-7 and Prelude, respectively, both companies broadened their market from the "full-nest" categories to include youthful and senior singles and couples.

Marketing to particular stages of the family life cycle usually requires more than merely differential promotional appeals and/or retail outlets. It's often necessary to create or modify product or service characteristics and/or pricing strategies to fit specific stages of the family life cycle. For instance, Volkswagen vans once had the larger full-nest categories pretty much to itself. But the decline in the popularity of the air-cooled engine led to changes in the marketplace that opened a niche for competitive car makers.

As baby boomers moved into the full-nest categories in force, several car makers introduced stylish minivans, the contemporary family life cycle counterpart to it's predecessor, the family station wagon. With more women in the work force and more two-earner families, the two-car garage became the norm. Many full-nest families now elect to own a conventional sedan or even a sports car, as well as a minivan with ample room for the entire family on trips. Those car makers who first perceived the trends accurately and moved quickly to create a product for that market obviously benefited more than those who came later.

WHAT FACTORS COUNT AND WHEN

Both the phases of the individual consumer's life cycle and the stages of the family life cycle are based on the *maturation process.* That means they're related to the *passage of time* during a consumer's life, but *not* closely associated with the *history* of any given era. In other words, both of these cyclical concepts suggest what consumers will do in the market place when they reach a particular stage, regardless of whether they reach it in the 1960s, 1970s, 1980s, 1990s, or beyond.

Maturation Effects on Consumers

Consumers at a later stage of life have more financial resources and spending power than those at earlier stages; this was true in the past, and probably always will be, aside from current economic conditions. Similarly, full-nest families need larger cars and houses than do singles or couples, regardless of the current state of car production, home-building technology, or energy availability. The maturation effects of life stage and family life cycle are fairly durable with the passage of time. But that's not to say that they're completely independent of history. People at different phases and stages are differentially sensitive to historical events, and they have differential impact on various groups. For example, the social and political events of the Vietnam era had dramatically more impact on those in the early phases of adult life at that time than on those who were either young children or those who were more mature. Similarly, the great depression shaped and influenced the values of those who are now senior members of our society, but that era has little meaning for those who came later.

Historical Effects on Consumers

We're all, in some ways, products of our unique personal histories. Those of us born into a particular era have our individual experiences, but we also share many experiences and influences that are directly related to the times. In Chapter 11, we discussed some of the more important social trends that are peculiar to this era, that reflect conditions at this particular time in history. We'll also consider similar historical factors in the following chapters on consumer lifestyles and on demographic trends and conditions. Maturation and history interactively affect consumers' choices.

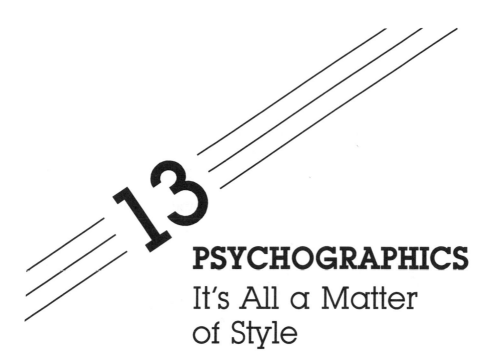

PSYCHOGRAPHICS
It's All a Matter of Style

He's an engineer living in an urban, high-rise condo, he wears Brooks Brothers clothes, listens to jazz, likes minimalism, fancies fine wine, and dates a lot.

She's a small-town librarian, dresses neatly but simply, visits her parents on Sunday, doesn't drink, has few friends and two cats, and likes classical music.

What kind of car does each of these people drive?

Any one person's or family's purchase and use of consumer goods aren't disorderly or chaotic; they're *patterned*. Consumers don't take a random walk through the marketplace, they shop and buy deliberately, according to a fairly coherent set of criteria. That's because life isn't merely a stochastic process—it's usually planned and anticipated. Of course, much of what we do and much of what we buy and use is routine or habitual. But even then, there's usually a set of strategies and tactics that go into building the routine in the first place. The consumer's life isn't usually tightly regimented and rigid, but it's fairly well integrated and consistent. While there's room for acting on the spur-of-the-moment, for indulging in an impulse purchase from time to time, the general rule is to stick pretty close to the basic plan.

PSYCHOGRAPHICS: THE PROFILING OF LIFESTYLES

A consumer's lifestyle includes all of the patterned behavior the person exhibits in daily life—at work and at play, in the home and outside, alone or with family or friends, day or night, during weekdays or weekends. Our lifestyle includes what we eat and drink, where we live, what we have in our homes, what we wear, how we take care of ourselves, and even such things as our religious preferences or sexual practices.

Psychographics versus Demographics

Demographic variables such as age, sex, education, occupation, income, or family life cycle explain people's choices in the marketplace. It's pretty easy to understand why young mothers buy a lot of disposable diapers while elderly singles don't. On the other hand, demographic status certainly doesn't explain everything. Why do some young mothers choose disposable diapers while others still use washable cloth diapers? And why do some of them always buy one brand while others strongly prefer another, and a few use a generic product while still others buy whatever is cheaper or on special sale? Often such differences result from different lifestyle patterns.

There's often a *tendency* for consumers in certain demographic categories to adopt, and especially to reject a certain kind of lifestyle. You won't find too many septuagenarians pursuing a "swinging singles" lifestyle. On the other hand, there's ordinarily no one-to-one correspondence between a given lifestyle pattern and a particular demographic segment. Some demographic categories include several different lifestyles, and some lifestyle patterns cut across a broad range of demographic categories.

Lifestyle or psychographic analysis is important to marketers because it tells them not only about a consumer group's characteristics, but also about their activities, their interests, and their opinions (see Table 10). It fleshes out the skeleton and gives them a vivid picture of consumers of a certain type.

Activities, Interests, and Opinions

To identify lifestyle patterns, marketers often conduct research to measure and compare people's activities, interests, and opinions; what they usually do or how they behave; what interests, intrigues or fascinates them; and what they believe or assume about the world around them. Table 10 lists some of the variables used in each category. In this chapter we not only look at a couple of the most popular psychographic analysis services marketers use, but also at some examples of lifestyle analysis for specific kinds of consumer goods. All of these breakdowns and classification systems are based primarily on activities, interests, and opinions, and secondarily on demographic characteristics.

Table 10. Typical Psychographic Variables

Activities	Interests	Opinions
Work	Family	Themselves
Hobbies	Home	Social issues
Social events	Job	Politics
Vacation	Community	Business
Entertainment	Recreation	Economics
Club membership	Fashion	Education
Community	Food	Products
Shopping	Media	Future
Sports	Achievements	Culture

Source: Joseph T. Plumber, "The Concept and Application of Life Style Segmentation," *Journal of Marketing,* January 1974, pp. 33–37.

MONITORING LIFESTYLE TRENDS

We identified some of the contemporary sociocultural trends in Chapter 12. These changes in cultural values lead to different lifestyle patterns. But everyone in the society doesn't shift to a new orientation simultaneously. In fact, some shift almost instantly while others never do change, and most are someplace in between these extremes. So as the trends run through the society, those who adapt to them pursue one kind of lifestyle while others who don't readily adapt follow another lifestyle pattern.

Focus on Social Trends

The firm of Yankelovich, Skelly and White has conducted annual "Monitor" surveys of a probability sample of 2500 adult Americans since 1970. About 120 business firms and other organizations currently participate and sponsor the Yankelovich Monitor service, at an initial cost of about $2,500 for the first year and less for subsequent participation. The Yankelovich Monitor tracks over 40 different social trends over time, including new ones and dropping those that are no longer vital as it becomes appropriate.

The trend toward *personalization* is an example of the trends the Yankelovich Monitor includes. This is the trend toward personalizing consumer goods that we mentioned earlier in connection with changing cultural values. In the survey, this trend is measured with such items as:

1. The importance of choosing and using "products that reveal their style and personality"
2. The degree they accept nonconformity in lifestyle and appearance even when there are social penalties
3. The perceived need to add "one's own personal touch" to consumer products and services
4. The value they place on being different from others and showing it, rather than "fitting in"

Aside from just tracking relevant social trends, the Yankelovich Monitor also provides insight into market segments based on consumer lifestyle. Based on the patterns of response to social trends from different segments of consumers, they've identified six basic lifestyle and consumption patterns in two broad categories:

Successful Adapters	Traditional Values
New autonomous	Traditionals
Gamesmen	American dreamers
Scramblers	Aimless

Simplifiers and Nonsimplifiers

When we discussed cultural values, one of the two basic themes that underlies shifts in several important social values was the psychology of shortage: the ways we cope with realization that the world's resources are limited. While many in the society have come to that realization, many others have not. For those who have, that awareness and insight have created a different set of value premises, social characteristics, and consumption patterns. Taken together, those changes define a distinctly different lifestyle pattern from those who retain the older, more traditional concept of a virtually unlimited world. Take a look at Table 11 which contrasts the simplifier and the nonsimplifier lifestyle patterns. Then let's see how marketers respond to consumers of each type.

> McDonald's recently introduced a new package for a hamburger sandwich with lettuce and tomato they call the McDLT. The package consists of a compartmentalized styrofoam tray, so that one section holds half the open-faced sandwich with the hot meat and the other holds the half with the chilled vegetables. It avoids the "soggy lettuce and runny tomato syndrome" effectively, but it is a rather more elaborate, complex package and they do stress the "technical" aspects of the new pack.

> One of McDonald's rivals, Foodmaker's Jack-In-The-Box chain, quickly moved to an indirectly comparative advertising program for their competing paper-packaged hamburgers and sandwiches. In their radio and television commercials they talk about the bland, tasteless nature of competitive products. With the comment that you might as well eat the package, the actor actually *bites into a styrofoam box*, then audibly spits it out.

> The Jack-In-The-Box campaign is addressed to people who value a simplifier lifestyle. They imply that the products of competitors such as McDonald's are highly processed, while theirs are freshly made-to-order, though they don't state it directly. They also hit subtly but hard at the elaborate plastic packaging. Simplifiers who are concerned with economy, with "overpackaging," with solid waste pollution, and with nonbiodegradable waste are likely to respond to this type of unconscious influence.

Table 11. Two Contrasting Lifestyles

Simplifier	Nonsimplifier
Value Premises	
Pychospiritual growth	Material growth
People within nature	People over nature
Enlightened self-interest	Competitive self-interest
Cooperative individualism	Rugged individualism
Rational and intuitive	Rationalism exclusively
Social Characteristics	
Smaller, simpler living	Larger, complex living
Reduction of complexity	Growth of complexity
Appropriate technology	Space-age technology
Identity from introspection	Identity from consumption
Greater local determination	Centralization of regulation
Emerging global institutions	Sovereignty of nation-states
Integrated work roles	Specialized work roles
Secular–spiritual balance	Secular dedication only
Durable, unique products	Mass-produced obsolescence
Global resources limited	Global resources unlimited
Cultural diversity	Cultural homogeneity
More relaxed existence	High-pressure existence
Consumption Patterns	
Conservation impetus	Consumption impetus
Quality of life	Standard of living
Smaller is better	Big is beautiful
Preference for quality	Preference for quantity
Essential products	Luxury products
Small, personal outlets	Large, impersonal outlets

Adapted from: Avraham Shama, "How Marketers Can Cater to 'Voluntary Simplicity' Segment," *Marketing News*, March 21, 1980, p. 3.

NINE VALS™ LIFESTYLE PATTERNS

Another psychographic analysis system popular among marketers was devised and initiated in 1980 by Arnold Mitchell and the firm of SRI International. The name of this service is VALS,

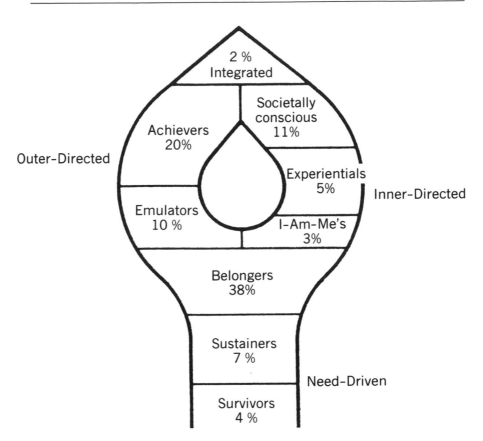

Figure 4. The VALS™ Typology. (Adapted From: Arnold Mitchell, *The Nine American Lifestyles: Who We Are and Where We Are Going,* New York: Macmillan, 1983 and the Values and Lifestyles (VALS™) Program, SRI International, Menlo Park, California.

an acronym for *Values and Lifestyles.* Unlike the empirically based Yankelovich Monitor program, the VALS system begins with a conceptual framework rooted in an understanding of both social classes and psychological maturation.

The VALS model, shown in Figure 4 and described in Table 12, has a dual rather than a single path from low to high socio-economic levels. The *outer-directed* consumers are more traditional types while the *inner-directed* categories represent more contemporary, innovative lifestyles. It's interesting to note that

Table 12. Characteristics of VALS™ Categories

VALS™ Name	Psychographic Pattern	Demographic Pattern
Integrateds	Cosmopolitan, psychologically mature, self-actualizing, and tolerant, they have a very good sense of proportion.	Mostly middle-aged or older, with excellent incomes and educations, a variety of different occupations and residential locations.

Inner-Directed

VALS™ Name	Psychographic Pattern	Demographic Pattern
Societally Conscious	Sensitive to social needs and concerned with their own inner growth, they're downsizers and simplifiers who prefer simple living.	Excellent incomes and educations, young to middle-aged, often in professional or technical vocations, various locations.
Experientials	Active, artistic, and participative, they seek and value experience for its own sake, and they're person-centered.	Young, good educations and fairly good incomes, many in technical or professional jobs, urban or suburban residents.
I-Am-Mes	Impulsive, dramatic, and defiantly individualistic, they're volatile, sometimes bombastic, and often experimental.	Nearly all young and mostly single, many from affluent families, often students or new at their jobs, tempo rary residents.

Outer-Directed

VALS™ Name	Psychographic Pattern	Demographic Pattern
Achievers	Materialistic, conventionally successful, efficient, comfortable, and accomplished, they have recognition and provide leadership.	Largely suburban dwellers, excellent educations and incomes, often leaders in business, government, or other institutions.
Emulators	Ambitious, status-conscious, competitive, and striving, they're upward-mobile, given to conspicuousness and display.	Mostly young, average educations, fairly good incomes, often with clerical, craft or machine operator jobs.

Table 12. (Continued)

VALS™ Name	Psychographic Pattern	Demographic Pattern
Belongers	Risk-averse, conforming conventionalists, they're traditional, formal, and nostalgic, and they avoid experimentation and innovation.	Blue-collar families, often retired, middle to low incomes, average or less educations, living outside metropolitan areas.
	Need-Driven	
Sustainers	Insecure, dependent, compulsive, and concerned with security and safety, they may be street-wise and determined.	Both city- and country-dwellers with very low incomes, little education, often sporadically employed or unemployed.
Survivors	Alienated, distrustful social misfits, they're fearful, conservative, and engaged in a struggle for their very survival.	Often elderly, little or no education, perhaps illiterate, street people or slum-dwellers living day-to-day in abject poverty.

Adapted from: Arnold Mitchell, *The Nine American Lifestyles: Who We Are and Where We Are Going,* New York: Macmillan, 1983 and the Values and Lifestyles (VALS™) Program, SRI International, Menlo Park, California.

while psychological maturity ascends from the lower to the higher levels of the model, *inner-directedness* represents more mature psychological development than does its counterpart. Yet the two groups are at approximately the same socioeconomic level of development, necessitating dual vertical paths.

Need-Driven Lifestyles

The *survivors* and *sustainers* at the lowest level of the VALS model have a lot in common. Both are poor, and their lifestyles are dictated largely by poverty and necessity, rather than as matters of choice. The thing that distinguishes the two groups is more psychological than economic: *Survivors* have given up and dropped out of the race; *sustainers* have not, they still have hope, and they're still trying desperately to hang in there. So there's little opportunity or probability that *survivors* will move up. On the other hand, sustainers at best are striving to gain entry into the *belonger* group, and at worst, they could slip into despair and survivorship.

The Belonger Lifestyle

The largest single lifestyle group in the VALS model is the *belonger* category, representing over a third of the population. *Belongers* aren't upwardly mobile; they're content just where they are, thank you! They often live in smaller communities and rural areas, and they see themselves as the "salt of the earth" and the "backbone of America." Traditional, hard-working folks, they don't much like innovation and change. They don't have a lot of money, though they can afford a few simple luxuries. They really don't need or want much more. They adhere very closely to traditional American values and conventional ways of thinking, including emphasis on the work ethic and suspicion of highly pleasurable things. In the main, they're conformists who would like to return to "the good ol' days" when one knew what was what and didn't have to cope so much with change. They often feel the world is moving too fast, and they don't value "techie" things. Nor are they especially concerned about resource limitations and downsizing.

> Since *belongers* are neither very affluent nor very sophisticated, many marketers assume that there isn't much to be made of this market, despite its size. Wrong! Witness the brilliant success of Family Dollar, a chain of nearly a thousand stores concentrated in the southeast but moving elsewhere fast. The stores are located in belonger heartland (over half in communities of fewer than 15,000 people) and the typical customer's family income is about $7,500 under the national median. The company's site location specialists look for oil spots because these people drive old, leaky cars. Nor are the stores very large by comparison with

a Wal-Mart or K mart; none exceed 8000 square feet and they carry only about 5000 items. Most of the merchandise is priced under $17 and the average sale is only about $6. That's a lot of trips to obtain the typical store sales volume. Store personnel become so well acquainted with their clientele that they notice a stranger.

Leon Levine, the chain's founder and chief executive officer, knows *belongers*. He came from that stock (though with holdings valued at over $140 million today, he's hardly still typical). When he plunked down $6,000 of his own money 25 years ago to start his first store, he wanted to keep it small and simple, like the ma-and-pa clothing store in rural North Carolina his mother managed and where he gained his first retail experience in his teens.

Family Dollar knows its niche among the belongers and thrives there as a result. With nearly a 7 percent return on sales of over $375 million in a recent year, the chain puts most other discounters to shame. And that's not atypical—the compound annual growth rate in sales over a 10-year span was over 20 percent per year; 32 percent for earnings. The traditional *belonger* values of hard work and frugality are reflected in the firms balance sheet as well. Expansion and improvement will be financed with *cash;* they have no debt!

Outer-Directed Lifestyles

The outer-directed track of the VALS model contains two lifestyle groups of substantial size: *emulators* and *achievers*. Of the two paths, this has more traditional types while the other has more contemporary lifestyles.

THE EMULATORS

This is a fairly young group, and mostly male. They're strivers, as opposed to the *belongers* who are content, if not complacent. *Emulators* cue very heavily off of the values of others around them. They try hard to copy *achievers,* who are more affluent and successful. But they often pick up on only the most obvious symbols and signals of achievement. Actually they don't really comprehend the essence of the more accomplished lifestyle of *achievers*. They want very much to distance themselves from *belongers*, from which families many came. But their dearest hope is to advance up the socioeconomic ladder, to take their place among the *achievers* they try so stridently to emulate.

> Emulators are extremely susceptible to promotional appeals that tell them in no uncertain terms what they must buy and use—not to *become* successful, but because they *are* successful. In other words, the appeal shouldn't be pitched toward *moving up*, but to *being there*. These are cooperators and conformers; they respond well to consensus appeals that use attractive, successful *achiever* models.
>
> Advertising in *Ms.* magazine, Anheuser-Busch promotes Michelob Light beer showing a full-time model and part-time business (coed) student. "Who says you can't have it all?" reads the headline. "My friends think I've got this glamorous life," the model is quoted. The tag line asks, "Why should *you* settle for anything less?" One's brand of beer has essentially nothing to do with one's academic or professional life, but *emulators* won't know that!

THE ACHIEVERS

These are the people who have lived by the rules and built the system. Now they control it and enjoy the benefits—they're largely a happy crowd, but not at all "laid-back." *Achievers* are a diverse group but they share many characteristics: they're self-reliant, hardworking, gifted, and successful. They're very outer-directed, taking most of their guidance from social norms and their peers. They tend to be friendly, comfortable, conservative, and affluent. This consumer segment accounts for nearly a quarter of the population: they're the one in four or five who are "in charge"—the managers, executives, physicians, attorneys, and other professionals. They're also bishops and pastors of large congregations, more accomplished artists and entertainers, professors and school principals, politicians, scientists, ranking military officers, and leaders in many other organizations and institutions. *Achievers* are often self-made; most weren't born to *achiever* families but "came up through the ranks" from the *belonger* lifestyles of their parents.

> Achievers are fans of the latest technology, and they're often innovative and optimistic—they usually feel that products and services are progressively improving. Quasar promotes their television receiver with two-page ads in *Fortune* magazine, showing the "techie" looking instrument over a completely stark background. The copy, in its entirety, is this: "Imagine television that escapes the extraneous. Television as a video window. Quasar did. And created Delta. Television infinitely close to art." Quasar uses the logo tag "Out of our minds, into your hands." Notice the high-tech vocabulary and the emphasis on innovative thrust. *Achievers* value such toys—they've earned them—they can afford them. So they buy many.

Inner-Directed Lifestyles

Inner-directed consumers represent a more mature stage of psychological development than the outer-directed. They're far less sensitive to external norms and role prescriptions; more sensitive to their own inner voice, tastes, preferences, values, and experience. The three lifestyles in this VALS trajectory—*I-am-me's, experientials,* and *societally conscious*—share several common characteristics: They're innovative and supportive of modern trends. They're more socially liberal and progressive than *emulators* and *achievers,* and they're not as materialistic. Money means less to them—they're more concerned with social movements and causes. They're a fairly impassioned group, self-expressive, individualistic, and concerned with people. In total, they account for about a fifth of the entire population.

THE I-AM-ME'S

This lifestyle is more transient than the others. It's just a passing phase (usually no more than a few years, at most) between the outer-directed belonger family of origin and the inner-directed orientation of mature adult life. These are mostly young people blatantly rejecting traditional values to break free of the mold—sometimes rambunctiously, sometimes floundering a bit. They feel their way in a life of ups and downs, ecstasy and tragedy. They conform closely to the rule of nonconformity. Self-individuation and social individuation are the dominant motives.

> **Sire records rock star Madonna epitomizes not only the tastes of an *I-am-me* lifestyle, but also the people in this group themselves. Neither her image nor her music have ever been accused of consistency or conventionality. While *belonger* parents look on in horror at this strikingly misnomered collection of contradictions, their *I-am-me* offspring share one opinion about Madonna—she is DIFFERENT!**

THE EXPERIENTIALS

This lifestyle is precisely what the name implies: a quest for direct, vivid experience. *Experientials* are fundamentally independent and self-reliant. They're very given to experiment, to try new things, if only to have done it. These consumers, more than any others, are guided by their own standards, values, and preferences. They take little notice or concern over what others do or would like them to do. A fairly young, well-educated group, *experientials* account for about one consumer out of fifteen. They lean toward technical and professional occupations and they're characterized by their liberality and progressive attitudes. They tend to be happy and well-adjusted, though they're neither as affluent as *achievers*, nor as much in command. On the other hand, they're confident of their own control. While they don't put much faith in institutions, they are pretty trusting of individuals. They take great satisfaction in a sense of growth, personal accomplishment, and experiential fulfillment.

> **Experientials comprise the bulk of the market for hardcore health foods and self-improvement programs of every kind. They also consume tons of brie and gallons of wine, but by the liter,**

not the gallon. They smoke occasionally (but never tobacco). While *achievers* populate the playing fields or stand in line for the ski lift, *experientials* might be found on a cross-country ski trail with a small group of friends. Their innovative bent makes them an ideal target for new recreational products and services. With a preference toward noncompetitive athletics, they're heavily represented among buyers of exercise equipment. Some can discuss the pros and cons of brand names such as "The Lean Machine" or "Total Gym" or "Polaris" or "Body Mate" or "Nautilus" or "DP Pro" or "Universal" or "Amerec" as enthusiastically as teenage boys talking cars.

THE SOCIETALLY CONSCIOUS

The inner-directed consumers with this lifestyle are the counterpart to the outer-directed *achievers*. Those of this ilk are mature, successful, and influential in their communities. There's a good deal of variation in the kinds of societal trends, issues, and events that concern the *societally conscious*, but they also share several common beliefs and values. These consumers feel very strongly that we should all live in harmony with nature, rather than try to subjugate or subdue it. They also value the nonmaterial aspects of life more highly than just material well-being. Rather than a more nationalistic view, they see this as one, small, fragile, interdependent world. They feel it's each person's task to make a contribution; we should each strive to leave the earth better than we found it.

The inner-directed *societally conscious* are guided more by their own inner values and standards than by social norms or peer pressure. They're psychologically mature, fairly sophisticated, and work effectively with the political system. Because of their involvement and maturity, they often enjoy positions of influence within their various communities and associations. This is a very well-educated group. Over a third have attended graduate school and well over half are in technical or professional occupations.

The *societally conscious* buyer is a "downsizer," less concerned about symbols and frills than about the essential worth of the product or service. They're less likely to be health food addicts than they are devoted to *healthy* foods. These are the buyers of high-fiber breakfast food cereals, granola bars rather than candy, and conventional foods that are naturally natural: raisins, prunes, fresh fruits and vegetables, unsweetened juices, and the like. Food processors have responded by removing preservatives, dyes, and additives that aren't really required. They also include special ingredients for better health and nutrition such as using low-cholesterol vegetable oils in place of animal fat or allowing fiber to remain, rather than removing it during processing.

Several supermarket chains have begun to display bulk food containers from which the grocery shoppers can help themselves, packaging and price-marking their own dry food. Such merchandising is popular with the *societally conscious,* who abhor elaborate packaging and don't appreciate the symbolic value of a national brand name.

The Integrated Lifestyle

Only about two out of a hundred consumers live an *integrated* lifestyle. They are at the highest level of the hierarchy of needs, pursuing self-actualization or self-fulfillment. The *integrated* lifestyle consists of a balance between the industry of the *achievers* and the social awareness of the *societally conscious.* Members of this group enter from either of those two lifestyles. They're a mature, sophisticated group, neither highly conservative nor extremely liberal. They represent the epitome of growth and accomplishment, often holding positions of *fundamental* responsibility rather than titular positions within their communities.

Marketers can use the VALS model in a variety of ways: to segment consumer markets and identify target groups, to design products and services, to choose a distribution strategy, or to form promotional appeals and select effective media. The overriding objective is to obtain a good, close match between the goods to be marketed and the lifestyle of the consumers.

SPECIALIZED LIFESTYLE PROFILING

The generalized lifestyle profiles such as those of the Yanke-lovich Monitor or SRI International's VALS model are applicable to many products and services. But marketers aren't restricted to these broad models. Individual psychographic studies can be used to identify lifestyle patterns that apply very directly and immediately to purchase and consumption of specific kinds of products. In the remainder of this chapter we'll look at three such specialized psychographic models and the lifestyle patterns they identify.

Food Consumption Lifestyles

Table 13 describes four lifestyle patterns based on the way people select and consume food products. Notice that the motivation and the criteria each group uses for evaluating and choosing groceries differ sharply from one another. These psychographic groups are differentially sensitive to promotional appeals, but they also want rather different products. So a few of the foods typically purchased by each group are also listed.

Clothing Buyer Lifestyles

The eight wearing apparel lifestyles outlined in Table 14 are divided into two groups: those who see their clothing as an investment that will pay some sort of dividends and those who view clothes merely as a utilitarian necessity of life. Within those two broad categories, apparel buyers also differ in their sensitivity to price and in their tastes for novel versus conservative clothes. The different psychographic groups not only want different products, but they're likely to shop at different outlets.

Car and Driver Lifestyles

Table 15 breaks the United States auto market into seven distinctive lifestyle profiles, based on a nationwide survey of

Table 13. Four Food Consumption Lifestyles

The Hedonists: About 20 percent of consumers want the good life. Pleasant things are important to them. They're looking for good-tasting food that's convenient and not too expensive. They don't worry about sugar, salt, fat and cholesterol. They don't count calories and they're not very concerned about the preservatives or additives in their food. They drink quite a bit of beer and soft drinks, and they chew gum and often snack on candy. They use margarine and they like presweetened cereal. [Pillsbury's Haagen-Dazs ice cream, Sara Lee frozen croissants, Procter & Gamble's Duncan Hines soft cookies, Pepperidge Farm bakery goods, Le Menu frozen entrees.]

The Avoiders: Another 20 percent are very concerned about good nutrition and too many calories. They avoid sugar and sweets, and they're careful not to eat processed foods that have many additives or preservatives in them. They stay away from fat and cholesterol. They're major consumers of wine, fruit juices, and decaffeinated coffee. They use unsalted butter and corn oil margarine, and they like nutritionally fortified cereal, yogurt, and sugar-free foods and beverages. [Hansen natural soft drinks, Quaker Rice Cakes, Hain natural soups, El Molino flours, Health Valley canned and packaged foods, Frito Lay no-salt chips.]

The Dieters: Some 35 percent are concerned about fat and calories. They avoid cholesterol, salt, and sugar, but they do like convenience foods. They aren't especially conscious of either taste or nutritional value and they don't avoid foods just because they have preservatives or artificial ingredients. What food doesn't contain is more important than what it does. They consume more diet soft drinks, iced tea, and diet margarine than others. They also like sugar-free candy and gum. [Stouffer's Lean Cuisine entrees, Weight Watchers entrees and desserts, Mrs. Paul's Light entrees, Carnation Slender liquid meals, NutraSweet sweetener.]

The Moderates: The remaining 25 percent are average in every respect. In all the different food and beverage categories they have close to median consumption rates. They don't lean toward any one kind of food or depend on a single criterion to judge food. They're not especially concerned about avoidance. They seek balance among taste, convenience, and a reasonably moderate intake of fat, cholesterol, sugar, salt, food additives and preservatives. [Sunkist fruit rolls, Quaker Oats Aunt Jemima breakfasts, Ralston Purina Chex snack mix, Bird's Eye frozen vegetables, Foster Farms chicken, Louis Rich turkey.]

Adapted from: Edward M. Tauber, "Research on Food Consumption Values Finds Four Market Segments; 'Good Taste' Still Tops," *Marketing News*, May 15, 1981, p. 17.

Table 14. Eight Wearing Apparel Lifestyles

	Investment Buyer	Utility Buyer
	Clothes Horse	**Daddy's Dollars**
Regular price Conservative taste	Buyers of either sex and any occupation, but especially those in sales occupations. Apparel spending for this group is very high.	Students and other young people of both sexes, under 25 with various incomes. Apparel spending is only moderate for this group.
	Executive	**Trendy Saver**
Regular price Novelty taste	More men than women, with management, technical, or professional occupations and high incomes. Spending for apparel is very high.	Mostly women students, homemakers, or clerical workers from 18 to 45 from various income groups. This group's apparel spending is low.
	Savvy Shopper	**Reluctant**
Bargain shopper Novelty taste	Mostly clerical women and homemakers over 25 with $20,000+ incomes. Apparel spending is fairly high and they shop more often than others.	Mostly men of all ages and with various incomes, but often blue-collar workers or retirees. Shopping is infrequent and apparel spending is low.
	Sensible	**Make-Do**
Bargain buyer Conservative taste	Mostly homemakers or clerical women over 35 with less than $30,000 incomes. Apparel spending for this group is very low.	The middle-aged of both sexes with families and moderate incomes, often with skilled trades. Apparel spending for the group is very low.

Adapted from: Rebecca C. Quarles, "Shopping Centers Use Fashion Lifestyle Research to Make Marketing Decisions," *Marketing News.* January 22, 1982, p. 18.

Table 15. Seven Cars for Seven Lifestyles

Car Lovers: About 30 percent of car buyers are in a love affair with their cars, but it's typically a short-time affair. They trade often and switch models frequently. The main evaluation criterion is style. They see the car as a reflection of their own lifestyle. They like their cars to be personalized and unique. [Cadillac Eldorado, Mercury Cougar, Pontiac Fiero, BMW 318i, Honda Prelude.]

Practical Folks: Some 18 percent of car buyers are very sensible folks who want good value and reliability above everything else. Style and roadability take a back seat to more practical considerations. They trade cars when it's financially expedient; when they can make a good deal and they're in a position to do so. [Chevrolet Impala, Ford Escort, Plymouth Reliant, Nissan Sentra, Honda Civic.]

Technical Types: About 13 percent of car buyers go for the high-tech features. They like fancy wheels, turbochargers, and special features "on the cutting edge" of technology. Engineering design, rather than aesthetics, plays the major role in evaluation. These consumers want more in their cars than most others. [Chevrolet Camaro Z28, Chrysler Laser, Ford Thunderbird, Honda Civic CRX, Porsche 944.]

Road Runners: Approximately 12 percent put the greatest emphasis on the driving experience, itself. They're quite knowledgeable and drive their cars very hard. They may choose a two-seater and they'll pay top dollar for their cars. The biggest consideration when making a choice is the handling and roadability of the car. [Audi 5000, Chevrolet Corvette, Mazda RX-7, Porsche 911, Porsche 928.]

Biggie Backers: Another 12 percent of car buyers want the luxury and comfort of a "full-sized" sedan. They want interiors as plush as their living rooms and they could care less about either the price or the gasoline consumption. They usually stick to the same make, the one they idealized as a kid. [Buick Electra, Oldsmobile 88 or 98, Mercury Grand Marquis, Chrysler Fifth Avenue.]

Fancy Firsts: About 10 percent of buyers go for whatever is new and unusual in a car, and they want to be the first to own one. They read about and study each new model and visit showrooms during introductions. They're not loyal to any one model or maker, and their trading is limited only by their budget. [Ford Thunderbird, Chrysler Laser, Honda Civic CRX, Nissan Pulsar, Toyota Supra.]

Only Utilities: Only 5 percent of buyers treat cars as transportation appliances and nothing more. These highly educated types don't get emotional about a car. They trade only when they have to and they aren't influenced by advertising or hype. The plainer the better; they want no frills. [Chevrolet Chevette, Ford Escort, Plymouth Horizon, Nissan Sentra, Honda Accord, VW Rabbit.]

Adapted from: "Our Autos, Ourselves," *Consumer Reports*, June 1985, p. 375.

10,000 respondents conducted in 1985 by the Opinion Survey Center of Toledo, Ohio. For each group, their cars play different roles in their pattern of living, from a central feature to a mere appliance.

THE PATTERNS OF CONSUMERS' DAILY LIVES

Marketers are prone to look closely at the specific need their product or service fulfills for the buyer, and rightly so. But we have to be careful not to take too narrow a focus; we shouldn't put on blinders that limit our scope of vision. While consumers may want something to meet a given need, that something has to fit into the total picture of things. It has to be compatible with all of their attitudes, beliefs, assumptions, habits, and the like. In other words, it has to fit into the whole lifestyle they've adopted. Almost no consumer goods are confined to only one tiny aspect of life, with no relationship to the broader whole.

The psychographic patterns of consumers help to determine what kinds of products and services they'll buy and use, and what they'll reject. Lifestyle configurations partly determine what features or attributes some form of consumer goods should have to be acceptable. So they help with product or service planning, creation, and modification. Consumers with different lifestyles tend to shop at different stores and depend more heavily on some types of retail outlets than others. Psychographic analysis also helps to identify the optimum distribution strategy. Consumer's psychographic conditions also imply certain attitudes toward price and condition perceptions of value. Analysis of consumer lifestyles can contribute to the marketer's choice of a pricing strategy. The lifestyle of consumers in the target audience also affects most aspects of promotion, including appeal strategy and the choice of advertising media. With promotion, consumer goods can be positioned according to the lifestyles of potential buyers. So psychographic analysis is helpful both for targeting a market and for managing the marketing program.

DEMOGRAPHICS
It's Just the Way We Are

Women buy their own cars while men shop for groceries, and nobody seems to act their age. American families are unstable and the quantity of education grows while quality has slipped. Some blue-collar jobs pay better than white-collar and the lab coat set does better still. The wealthy shop warehouse stores while modest incomes stretch for luxury cars. Consumer markets in a state of flux require *more* demographic analysis by marketers, not less!

Demographic variables measure the most basic, the most fundamental characteristics of consumers. Demographic characteristics are by far the most common variables for segmenting consumer markets and picking target segments. Purchase and consumption patterns usually vary markedly from one demographic category to the next. What's more, there's ample demographic data about markets, both from the census and from other sources, on which to base target marketing analysis.

SIX BASIC DEMOGRAPHIC VARIABLES

There are more demographic variables, but we'll consider just six of the most important ones to marketers: the *age, sex, family status, education, occupation,* and *income* of consumers. For some marketers, their consumers' ethnicity, religion, dwelling, and location are also important. We should note, too, that marketers often consider the combinations that compose demographic patterns, as well as the nature of each individual variable.

THE AGE OF CONSUMERS IN THE MARKET

The consumers' age obviously affects what they buy and use, as noted from the discussion of life stages in Chapter 12. The age of consumers affects their behavior in the marketplace in three important ways: First, some goods are appropriate only to consumers of a certain age because they have special needs. Second, tastes, preferences, and age role prescriptions differ from one age cohort to the next. Third, disposable income and spending power vary from one stage of life to another, as noted earlier. Marketers often base their plans on not only the current age distribution, but also the *trends* in age, since they can readily be predicted accurately.

The Shrinking Youth Market

The teen market in America is shrinking rapidly as the baby boomers mature. The size of the teenage cohort will diminish by about 20 percent during the decade of the 1980s. But more teenagers are employed now and their spending power as a group is growing faster than their numbers are decreasing. While the two forces counteract one another in some respects, that doesn't mean they equal out as far as marketers are concerned. Because today, there are fewer teens but on the average, each has more to spend. So for teen consumer goods with stable consumption rates per individual, the market is shrinking. But for discretionary goods where individual consumption isn't so limited, the market is actually growing in potential volume, even though the number of prospective buyers is dropping.

> Some cosmetics, such as skin creams, are consumed by individuals at fairly stable rates—any one person can only use just so much of it. Noxell Corp., makers of Noxzema skin cream and Cover Girl makeup, traditionally appealed to the teen market. But as baby boomers aged, Noxell went with them, appealing now to an older crowd, broadening rather than retaining their narrow place on the age spectrum. Similarly, Clearasil, a long-time Richardson-Vicks product, now comes in both adult and teen versions, in an attempt to retain their more brand-loyal baby boom buyers in the face of a smaller new group of teenagers.

> By contrast to goods with fixed per capita consumption rates, marketers of teen clothes, entertainment, travel, and recorded music find little stress on their markets from the diminishing numbers. The more affluent teens of today have higher per capita consumption rates of such discretionary goods, allowing their marketers to continue their focus on the same segment of the age spectrum.

The Aging Baby Boomers

The baby boom ran from 1946 to 1964, and those born during that period comprise a third of the entire United States population. Because of its astounding size and gigantic buying power, marketers of consumer goods naturally rivet their attention on the baby boom generation. But an homogeneous lot, they're not! As the baby boom generation moves through the institutions of society like a pig in a python, it first stretches them almost to the breaking point, then leaves behind a legacy of excess capacity. Those at the lead are squeezed for space among their numerous cohorts, but those who came later in the boom find plenty of room in many situations. Consequently, the early and late segments have rather different mentalities.

The state of the economy today and in the recent past, together with the radical fluctuations in the cost of energy and real estate, have created something of a crisis of expectations among later members of the baby boom generation. Many find that despite better educations, higher grade occupations, and more of the family in the work force, they aren't able to fare as well as their parents before them. They often seek to obtain the same traditional mix of consumer products and services, but satisfy themselves, by necessity, with smaller or cheaper goods.

> The first new car early baby boomers a decade or more ago purchased was typically a fuel-efficient subcompact import. Widespread disenchantment with Detroit left United States auto makers out in the cold. The American auto industry responded with their own lines of economical compacts and subcompacts to match their foreign adversaries. But as the baby boomers matured and became more affluent, they shifted their preference from economy and practicality to individuality and self-expression—values grown from the very press of that age cohort's population. Volvos, Saabs, Audis, and BMWs replaced the Volkswagens, Toyotas, and Datsuns in their garages.

> Not to be overcome in the struggle for the baby boom market, United States car makers recently brought forth an entire array of new models tailored to boomer tastes, needs, and budgets: Chrysler's LeBaron GTS and Dodge Lancer, Ford's Lincoln-Mercury Division import Merkur XR4Ti from their West German subsidiary, and GM's Pontiac Grand Am, Oldsmobile Calais, and Buick Somerset Regal. While consumer goods marketers often tailor

their promotion and distribution to specific age segments, the huge size of the baby boom generation makes it worthwhile to cater to that group with the development of entirely new products and prices.

The Affluent Maturity Market

For every ten baby boomers there are about nine consumers aged 50 and over. What's more, this group is extremely affluent, with about half the discretionary buying power of the nation and over three quarters of the personal financial assets. So you would think that consumer marketers would have descended on this greying group with a vengeance—but in fact, they've often been ignored in favor of everybody's fascination, the baby boom generation. Actually there are a couple of legitimate reasons why marketers don't approach the 50 and over consumer market boldly and directly: First, they're a pretty diverse group, and second, it's difficult to address them by age without offending them.

There's a fairly sharp distinction between those from 50 to 65 and those who are 65 to about 75, because of the frequency of retirement and the fixed incomes and additional leisure time for the older group. What's more, there's a trend toward earlier retirement, casting many younger consumers into the retiree category. There's also a break between those from 65 to 75 and those over 75 years of age, when energy and mobility often recede.

> To address mature buyers without offending them, Clairol promotes their hair coloring with the slogan "You're not getting older. You're getting better."

> As interested in the mature as in youth, McDonald's uses elderly actor John Houseman as a spokesman.

> Campbell's introduced their Soup-For-One to fit the appetites and the prevalence of singles among the aging.

> Recognizing that seniors often need reading glasses to see small numbers, Bulova helped them (and themselves) by introducing watches with larger numerals.

A special shampoo and conditioner for older consumers was introduced by Pfizer to handle their particular needs.

Marketers now have selective media to reach mature consumer markets with such magazines as *Modern Maturity, Prime Time,* and *50 Plus.*

THE CONSUMER GENDER GAP

Masculine and feminine consumers' choices in the marketplace differ for the same three reasons as they do for different age groups: Some are directly related to the sex of the consumer, some are influenced by preferences or sex roles prescriptions, and some are due to differential income and spending power between men and women.

The *primary* sexual characteristics of men and women create demand for products and services directly associated with sex. In the past, there were many taboos regarding promotion and distribution of such products. For instance, marketers of tampons or sanitary pads were restricted largely to media and sometimes even retail outlets devoted strictly to women, while condoms, purchased almost exclusively by men, were behind-the-counter or perhaps under-the-counter items. Today sexual attitudes are more liberal and relaxed, and marketers have begun promoting and distributing such goods through media and outlets common to both sexes. Yet open display of goods related to primary sexual characteristics may still create some negative attitudes and some resistance among older, more conservative consumers. Some controversy still remains.

Analysts estimate that about four out of ten condom buyers today are women. During the 1980s, sales have been growing at a rate of 10 to 15 percent per year, reaching about $200 million by the middle of the decade. Part of the feminine market consists of women who abandon oral contraceptives, largely for health reasons. But sales also escalated rapidly in recent years with the increased threat of incurable sexually transmitted diseases—first the Herpes virus, and later the lethal AIDS.

To encourage sales to women, Youngs Drug Products began picturing a young couple on the package for their Trojan brand.
Slower to respond, Schmid only more recently began picturing a
couple on their Sheik condom packages. But changes aren't confined only to packaging and promotion. Sheik and others have
also modified the product by including a spermicidal lubricating
agent, an ingredient familiar to many women who have used
contraceptive foam.

Consumer products related to *secondary* sexual characteristics, such as hair, skin, and body type, have begun to find their
way across the barrier to the opposite gender as sexual distinctions continue to blur in modern society. But breaking the barrier hasn't been quick or easy.

Skin care products are an excellent example. The entire product
category was once the exclusive domain of women. By the mid-
1980s, the masculine market was worth about $30 million, a six-
fold increase over what it was at the beginning of the decade but
still only a small fraction of the feminine market for skin care
products.

The Clinique brand led the way, beginning in Northeastern cities during the Christmas season of 1976. The strategy was to
emphasize fitness and health, rather than cosmetic value, as the
brand name implies. Not only the name itself, but also the product characteristics were carefully designed to win masculine acceptance.

Smooth surfaces and rounded edges and corners have feminine
connotations, and women's soap cakes are rounded and sized to
fit the feminine hand. By contrast, men grasp soap with their
entire hand, not just with their fingers, and they're accustomed to
sharp edges and square corners. So men's Clinique soap is
formed in a distinctly masculine brick-shaped bar. Nor do men
like scented products as women do, so Clinique provided un-
scented formulas.

Silver and grey colors, product names, wrapping, label composition—everything about the packaging was created to appeal to
male buyers. Clinique magazine ads show an open, obviously
masculine bathroom *medicine cabinet* containing shaving para-

phernalia and men's grooming aids, together with an array of "cosmetics-that-aren't cosmetics," each carrying the distinctive Clinique name.

Today Clinique products are sold exclusively in department stores throughout the country, but not in the men's department, as you might expect. Instead, they're sold at the women's counter, where trained skin care consultants can provide the kind of personal selling and service the products require to match them properly to individual skin type and coloration.

While *products* can sometimes cross over from one sex to another, individual *brands* usually can't. Though sex roles aren't as rigid as in the past, many consumers still adhere closely to them. While women accept masculine brands readily, men, and especially the elderly, downscale, macho types, reject feminine brands entirely. So marketers of products formerly associated with one sex who want to market it to both usually find it necessary to segment the market by gender and offer "his and hers" brands, or even different product names for the same basic goods.

The Gillette Company, long-time promoter of razors and shaving cream to male sports audiences, also markets razors for women, but with feminine brands: "Daisy" and "Lady Gillette." While women might accept the masculine brand, many men would reject it if they had to share it with the distaff market. Similarly, Faberge cosmetics have a distinctly feminine image, not likely to be acceptable to male consumers. So their masculine brand is Brut, a name welcome to even the most macho male. They also associate what is actually just a moisturizing cream with one of the last bastions of masculinity—the shaving ritual. You see, *real* men don't use perfume or moisturizer, but they do use after-shave lotion and "soother," of course.

THE CONSUMER'S FAMILY STATUS

The marital and family status of consumers has a dramatic effect on their purchase and consumption patterns, as noted in Chapters 9 and 12. There are several far-reaching effects that result from changes in marriage and family formation within the society. Perhaps the most significant during the 1970s, continuing throughout the 1980s, is the increased proportion of women in the nation's work force. But changes in family size and composition also have and will continue to have important effects on purchase patterns.

The Working Woman

By the mid-1980s, about 42 percent of American families were two-earner, 14 percent had three or more, and only 29 percent had one wage-earner. Over half of married mothers with pre-school children are working outside the home, and about two-thirds of them join the labor force when their children are all in school. Multiple-earner families have markedly more income and spending power than their single-earner counterparts. In 1979, the median income of two-earner families was 45 percent greater than those with just one wage-earner. In just five years, their advantage had grown to 56 percent, reaching about $31,700 for two-earner families in 1984.

> **Changing roles and greater economic independence for women result in markedly different family purchase patterns than only a few decades ago. For instance, in 1980, women purchased nearly four out of ten new cars, while about two-thirds of them intended to use the car to drive to work. Car makers can no longer appeal exclusively to the male buyers. Nor can marketers of household goods assume the vast majority of their market consists of housewives.**

When both heads of household are in the work force, this has a dramatic effect on the role structures within the family. Where once there was a great deal of specialization, with the husband the breadwinner and the wife almost exclusively responsible for homemaking, there's markedly less today. A study by Benton & Bowles advertising agency, reported in *Marketing News* on October 3, 1981, indicated some surprising facts about the self-reported roles and responsibilities accepted at least in part by husbands with working wives:

Nearly a third shopped for the family's food
Nearly half reported cooking for the family
Over half said they washed the family dishes
Nearly four out of ten vacuumed the house
Eight out of ten took care of young children

> In *Parents Magazine* and others Procter & Gamble advertises the benefits of Ivory Snow for laundering infants' clothes with color illustrations of a young, blue-collar father holding the baby, rather than mom in a prim housedress. More and more marketers of children's goods are appealing jointly to fathers and mothers, rather than to the mothers alone.

Later Marriages, Smaller Families

The traditional age for a woman to marry in this society has been from 20 to 24. But throughout the 1970s, the proportion of women in that age group who had never married rose by over 14 percent, reaching fully half the women by 1980. The trend continues in the 1980s, at an accelerated pace. It climbed another 8.5 percent in the first half of the decade, alone. Even though it seems remarkable today that nearly six out of ten women of that age have never married, the proportion is roughly the same as it was a hundred years earlier. Population demography fluctuates, but it often does so in a very cyclical way. The exception is the unprecedented separation and divorce rates: About 15 percent of women in their thirties are separated or divorced today.

Not only are people postponing marriage longer, they're also having fewer children and having them later in the life cycle. From 1970 to 1984, the porportion of American families with no children increased by about a third, while the proportion with only one or two children increased by about 18 percent. During the same period, families with three or more children decreased by a whopping 44 percent. Corresponding with these trends, the tendency of women to delay first conception beyond age 30 has been growing rapidly, though only slightly more than one out of ten firstborn children today have mothers over 30. Among women aged 30 to 34, the rate of first births has more than tripled in fifteen years, from 1970 to the mid-1980s.

These more mature mothers are different from their younger counterparts: They're usually white, better educated by far, and likely to be in professional occupations with relatively high incomes. Nor are their family buying preferences and patterns the same as others. They put more value on bold, contemporary designs in baby clothes and furniture than in the more traditional, sentimental, frilly, pastel styles. They also value versatility and portability in the things they buy for their children. They're more mobile and health conscious, and they value childcare services where they shop, play, or exercise. They're more susceptible to scientific or technical promotional appeals than to fear or sentimentality.

> **Johnson & Johnson's Child Development Toys are promoted with the appeal "Play, discovery, learning . . . they all happen together." They also provide a series of Play and Learning Guides, explaining what skills each toy encourages at each stage of the baby's growth. Such appeals are especially potent with mature, sophisticated parents.**

> **"Beech-Nut Stages—The right nutrition at the right stage." Referring to pediatricians and nutritionists, Beech-Nut Stages brand of baby foods is promoted in colorful magazine ads to young and not-so-young parents. This "scientific" approach ranges, in four stages, from single-ingredient, strained beginner foods to multi-ingredient, fortified foods to those with minibites to the "Table Time" line for those who have outgrown baby food. Beech-Nut even lists a toll-free hotline number for information about infant care and nutrition.**

Table 16. Percentage of Adults Completing College

Age	1980			1985		
	Men	Women	Both	Men	Women	Both
25–	20.9%	13.6%	17.0%	23.1%	16.0%	19.4%
25–34	27.5	20.9	24.1	25.2	22.5	23.8
35–44	25.1	16.6	20.8	31.2	21.3	26.2
45–54	20.5	11.0	15.6	23.3	14.2	18.6
55–64	14.7	8.6	11.5	19.4	9.9	14.3
65+	10.3	7.4	8.6	11.5	8.0	9.4

Source: American Demographics, January 1986, p. 29.

THE (ALMOST) EVER-BETTER EDUCATED CONSUMERS

As you might suspect, the overall trend in the United States is toward *more* formal education, though it's still an open question whether Americans are *better* educated. The percentage of the population with a college education is a fair index of educational trends across the board. In 1985, some 19.4 percent of people 25 years of age and over had graduated from college— up ten percentage points from the 9.4 percent in 1965, some twenty years earlier and up two percentage points from five years earlier, in 1980.

In general, the younger the adult consumer, the better-educated the person is likely to be. But for men, that doesn't always hold true, as Table 16 shows. Reading up the columns, from the older to the younger groups, the percentage of college graduates increases by age bracket for men, women, and for both in 1980, but only for women in 1985. A large proportion of the 35- to 44-year-old men, who were of military service age during the Vietnam War, have college educations. But only a much smaller proportion of their younger brothers, aged 25 to 34, have completed college.

Another visible trend is the fact that women are progressively closing the educational gender gap. With less and less disparity between the educational levels of the male and female head of household, joint decision making and greater sharing of responsibilities and roles can be expected as specialization based on sex decreases among both parents and their children.

Younger, better-educated consumers can easily be patronized by mass media ads focusing on the lowest common denominator of literacy and sophistication. But this market is also very responsive to technical–scientific appeals for consumer goods promoted both to them and to their children. Level of education is the main discriminator regarding acceptance or rejection of personal microcomputer systems for the home and family. Very small, limited, and inexpensive "home" computers have universally failed in the marketplace. By contrast, more expensive and sophisticated hardware and software with multiple functions for adults and children have survived and even thrived among better-educated, more affluent consumer segments.

> Marketers of personal computers, software, supplies, and accessories to parents of the computer generation have a very specialized and selective medium in *Family Computing*, the first magazine designed exclusively for this audience. With only about 400,000 subscribers, the magazine reaches a very select group: Over seven out of ten are between 25 and 44 years of age, have attended or graduated from college, and have incomes in excess of $25,000.

> Full-page ads in *Family Computing* magazine promote Woodbury's Playwrite word processing program for adolescent children. Designed for the relatively capable IBM, Commodore 64, and Apple Computers, the software package includes hardcover book jackets and inserts so the children can create their own books. With appeal to only the most literate parents and precocious children, the illustration in the ad shows a boy and girl at the computer. The dreams and aspirations of this pair are shown in mirage images above them: he in a professional baseball uniform at the stadium, she in a space suit on the surface of the moon. This sophisticated audience isn't likely to adhere closely to sex norms or expect it of their children.

Table 17. Projected Employment Percentages by Sector, 1982 to 1995

	1982	1995	Change
Goods-producing industries	28.8%	27.8%	−1.0
Agriculture	3.4	2.5	−0.9
Mining	1.2	1.0	−0.2
Construction	4.2	4.9	+0.7
Manufacturing	20.0	19.4	−0.6
Service-producing industries	71.2	72.2	+1.0
Transportation, communications, utilities	6.1	5.8	−0.3
Wholesale and retail trade	22.0	22.5	+0.5
Finance, insurance, and real estate	5.8	6.0	+0.2
Others (health, education, legal, business)	29.3	31.2	+1.9
Government	8.0	6.7	−1.3
Total employment	100.0	100.0	

Source: American Demographics, April 1985, p. 50.

THE CONSUMER'S OCCUPATIONAL STATUS

Occupations often influence or correspond to the social roles, social class membership, or lifestyle patterns of consumers. In Chapters 7, 10, and 13 we cited many examples of marketing to consumers in specific roles, social classes, and lifestyles. So at this point, we should examine some of the main occupational conditions and trends, to gain a sense of the occupational picture in the United States and where it's likely to go in the foreseeable future.

Some of the projected trends in employment by economic sector can be seen in Table 17. Service-producing industries, already dominant, will gain even more in the years to come. Of the goods-producing sectors of the economy, only construction is expected to occupy a larger part of the total work force. Construction jobs are more difficult to automate with computer

Table 18. Percentage of Workers by Occupational Status

	1960[a]	1970[a]	1982[b]
White-collar	41.9%	47.5%	53.8%
Professional and technical	11.0	14.5	17.0
Managerial and administrative	8.9	8.1	11.5
Sales	7.4	7.1	6.6
Clerical	14.6	17.8	18.5
Blue-collar	39.5	36.6	29.7
Crafts and trades	14.7	13.9	12.3
Operatives	19.0	18.0	12.9
Labor (nonfarm)	5.8	4.7	4.5
Service	12.2	12.8	13.8
Farm	6.4	3.1	2.7
Total	100.0	100.0	100.0

[a] *Historical Statistics, Colonial Times to 1970*, pp. 602–617.
[b] *Statistical Abstract of the United States*, 1984, p. 417.

technology than are those in other goods-producing sectors. Among service-producing sectors, health care, education, and legal and business services will most increase their role in the United States economy as a whole. The government sector and the transportation, communications, and utilities sector will occupy a smaller part of the work force. While employment will increase overall, occupations in some sectors will gain far more than in others.

Some of the major trends in employment by occupation in the past quarter-century are evident in Table 18. White-collar occupations gained rapidly while blue-collar jobs decreased in number. Employment in the farm sector shrank dramatically while jobs in service areas gained in number. It's also interesting to note that there's been an upscale shift within the white-collar categories. The proportion of blue-collar operative workers also diminished markedly, probably due in part to increased computer automation.

**Table 19. Projected Percentage Distributions of Family Income
           (In constant 1982 dollars)**

	1980	1985	1990	1995
Under $10,000	15.5%	14.6%	13.0%	11.6%
$10,000 to $19,999	24.8	23.8	21.5	18.9
$20,000 to $29,999	23.3	22.4	21.2	19.5
$30,000 to $39,999	16.6	16.5	16.9	16.8
$40,000 to $49,999	9.4	10.2	11.4	12.4
$50,000 and over	10.4	12.5	16.0	20.8
All families	100.0	100.0	100.0	100.0

Source: American Demographics, May 1984, p. 50.

CONSUMER INCOME AND SPENDING POWER

For prospective buyers to become actual customers, they need
two things: the *willingness* to buy and the *ability* to buy. The
level of demand for any given consumer product or service
depends in large measure on the income and purchasing power
of those in the market. So pricing decisions, as well as product
planning, promotional appeal strategy, and distribution policy
all depend to some degree on consumer income. Some marketers might choose a *skimming* price policy for very high-quality
goods, appealing only to the carriage trade while using exclusive retail outlets. Others may decide on *penetration* pricing for
goods of standard quality, appealing to the bulk of the market
while using intensive distribution though every available outlet. Both are segmenting and targeting primarily on the consumers' income level.

The Growth in Affluence

Average family income in the United States has been growing
in real terms (adjusted for inflation) over the past decade or so,
and it's expected to continue to do so. Table 19 shows the pro-

Table 20. Percentage of Full-Time Homemaker Women

Age Group	Percentage
16 to 24	12%
25 to 44	25
45 to 64	40
65 and over	64

Source: *American Demographics*, July 1985, p. 4.

jected percentage of families in each of six income brackets for fifteen years, from 1980 to 1995. The proportion of families in the three lower brackets, under $30,000 in 1982 dollars, is diminishing. The proportion in the upper two brackets, over $40,000 in 1982 dollars, shows a corresponding increase. Only the percentage of families in the mid-range, with $30,000 to $40,000 incomes in 1982 dollars, remains fairly constant over the entire time span. To the degree that these projections hold true, marketers can look forward to an increasingly affluent American consumer population.

Economic growth plays an important role in the increased affluence of Americans, but multiearner families are one of the main reasons for the growth in family affluence, as more and more women pursue careers outside the home. In fact, the exclusively homemaker lifestyle is typical only of women 65 years of age and over, as the breakdown in Table 20 shows. In 1982, about three out of four families with incomes of $30,000 or more had more than one wage-earner. By contrast, less than one-third of households with incomes under $30,000 had more than one wage-earner.

Travelers on the High Road

The marketers of consumer goods have a choice: They can chase buyers or they can chase dollars, but those two objectives

Table 21. American Family Financial Picture, 1985

Household Income Bracket	Percentage of All American Households	Percentage of All Household Income	Percentage of All Household Net Worth	Percentage of All Income From Capital
Under $30,000	70%	38%	36%	29%
$30,000–$49,999	20	29	24	27
$50,000 and over	10	33	40	44
All families	100	100	100	100

Source: American Demographics, July 1985, p. 4.

aren't the same. As Table 21 indicates, the majority of consumer spending power and the vast majority of strictly discretionary spending power is in the hands of only a minority of the most affluent American families. During the 1970s, the number of households grew by only about 1 percent while disposable income increased at three times that rate. The number of families with incomes of $30,000 or more grew at almost three times the rate of all household formation, as well. And the trend will not only continue during the 1980s, but it's expected to accelerate.

As family income increases, *discretionary* income (what remains after taxes and spending for basic necessities) soars even more rapidly. For instance, a 10 percent increase in family income might double or triple purely discretionary spending power. That's because every individual or family has many basic, fixed costs of living. As income begins to exceed those costs, only slightly more is spent on the basics, and the majority of the "extra" income goes for the purchase of discretionary consumer goods. While part is usually saved or invested and part is spent on very practical consumer products and services—investment in a business wardrobe or tuition for the children's private school—a substantial part is also devoted to luxury goods, the toys and indulgences of American life. So those who sell such goods find their markets growing by leaps and bounds as a result of only modest increases in total spending power.

Mention a mail-order catalog and people over 50 are likely to think of such traditional catalogers as Wards or Sears, providing general merchandise to farm families and working class townspeople. But that image is completely obsolete today. Catalog merchandisers segment and target their markets on the basis of income and they cover the entire spectrum, with the emphasis on the high side.

High-line catalog companies such as Jos. A. Banks Clothiers, The Talbots, or Horchow appeal to families with incomes of around $40,000. A step down, L.L. Bean, Eddie Bauer, or Land's End customers are likely to be in the $30,000+ family income bracket. Brookstone, Lillian Vernon, and, lately, Spiegel buyers are nearly as affluent.

Sears and J.C. Penney, along with such names as Harriet Carter and Lee Wards, appeal to families with incomes in the lower $20,000 range. Haband or Herrschners customers are a bit below that income level. Lane Bryant customer incomes are about $15,000, while Fingerhut catalog buyers have even lower family incomes. Catalog buying today isn't confined to a single income level, but each cataloger targets a specific family income segment.

The Coming Apart of the Middle Class

As the population and the number of families grows, the upper and lower classes are growing at more rapid rates than the middle class. Table 22 shows the percentage distributions of families across five income levels based on constant 1982 dollars, for 1969 and for 1983. The number of families in the upper category, the fastest growing group, swelled by 100 percentage points more than the middle category, the slowest growing group of families. The *proportion* in the upper category increased by 36 percent while the proportion in the lower category grew by 6 percent. Meanwhile, the proportions in the other three, middle categories diminished, although the upper-middle income group was nearly a constant proportion over the span of fourteen years.

Table 22. Growth in Number of Families by Income Category

	Real Income (1982 dollars)	Percentage 1969	Percentage 1983	Percentage Growth in Number	Percentage Change in Proportion
Upper	Over $41,456	8.2%	12.8%	+119%	+36%
Upper-middle	$29,840–$41,456	14.4	14.2	+40	−01
Middle	$18,426–$29,840	27.4	23.1	+19	−19
Lower-middle	$11,055–$18,426	20.6	18.6	+28	−11
Lower	Under $11,055	29.4	31.3	+51	+06

Source: American Demographics, January 1985, p. 21.

As the middle class shrinks, disappearing into the ranks of either the upper-middle or lower-middle class, many marketers must elect to follow one path or the other. Those who traditionally served the great bulk of the middle class market and attempt to continue targeting these masses will find themselves straddling an ever-widening span; a difficult feat, indeed.

With a history that spans almost the entire twentieth century, J.C. Penney undertook a $1.5 billion, five-year rejuvenation in the early 1980s. The goal: to win a substantial share of the lucrative consumer apparel, cosmetics, and home furnishings markets from high-line department stores and specialty shops. The target is the young, affluent working woman—a free-spender on fashion goods. In effect, Penney's is following hard on the heels of consumers riding the affluence trend. It shows! The new merchandising policy would surprise, if not shock a shopper today, walking through a Penney's store for the first time in the past few years. The question that remains is whether or not Penney's can successfully win the patronage of the new target market and do it quickly enough to compensate for the losses among their former lower-middle income market segment.

As it enters its centennial year, the nation's largest retailer, Sears, Roebuck is also remaking its image, including everything from fundamentals such as merchandising policy to cosmetic factors such as a new logo. In over 800 stores in all fifty states, some 40 million American families will find manifestations of the new vitality. Well over a hundred Sears "stores of the future" are leading the way in a $1.7 billion capital improvement program initiated in the early 1980s.

Sears is intent on leveraging on their gigantic customer base that includes over 125 million shoppers a year—about three out of four adults in the nation. Since there's not much room for expansion in the number of customers, the goal is to get more store visits and sell more merchandise (of every description, from athletic socks to corporate stocks) to the existing customer base. Yet Sears knows full well where the dollars are: They've set their sights on the upwardly mobile while trying to retain the middle ranks.

The Irresistible Urge to Splurge

As if the bifurcation of the traditional middle class isn't enough to give marketers a *splitting* headache . . . . But recently, consumers who don't seem to "know their place" on the income spectrum have added insult to injury. Certainly a nominee for "consumer craze of the decade," *splurging* has perhaps become the main contender as it sweeps across the entire income spectrum in more ways than one. There was a time when poor people bought old used "klunkers," middle class people drove middle class cars, and only the relatively wealthy indulged in luxury cars: Oh sweet nostalgia! Today's young baby-boomer family might well nurse their aging appliances or "early marriage" furniture along for yet a few more years while at the same time splurging on a new BMW or Volvo. Not always—it could almost as easily go the other way around—brand new home and furniture with the antiquated lead sled in the garage.

Historically, American consumers have kept their spending pretty well within their income limits. There's a strong tendency of late for consumers to hold the lid even more tightly on mundane purchases, punctuating their spending occasionally with a high-line splurge that puts a sharp spike in the dispersion of their buying pattern. Splurges come in two varieties: public and private. They're not all socially visible—some are purely personal self-indulgences, but others are showy indeed. Several factors underlie the tendency to deviate from "normal" income level expenditure patterns.

Growing affluence and far more discretionary spending power are part of it, but not the whole story. Baby boomers, now with young families of their own, were raised in affluence. Yet many find it hard to keep the economic pace—their "great expectations" are often disconfirmed. What better way to salve their disappointment than with a "compensatory" splurge? If one can't have it all, one can at least take a sample taste of "the good life." Then, too, the cultural prohibitions against pleasure and self-indulgence have relaxed among young and middle adults. Splurge spending on sources of personal pleasure is a way to cope with the pressures of life in the fast lane.

> New retail phenomena, warehouse membership club stores, have recently sprung up throughout the country. Large chains such as Price Club (21 stores), Costco Wholesale Club (18 stores), and Sam's Wholesale Club (17 stores), as well as many smaller chains and individual warehouse stores, offer prices on a wide array of merchandise well below anything obtainable at a conventional discount outlet. But their shelves aren't filled entirely with bottom-of-the-line merchandise, as you might think. Instead, you'll find labels such as Stouffers, Perrier, Chivas Regal, Zenith, Braun, Michelin, and Christian Dior among more modest offerings. And the parking lots correspond to the merchandising—the usual few-year-old economy mix, with plenty of Audis, BMWs, Volvos and Saabs, and the occasional Mercedes or Jaguar. This is a way for yuppies and would-bes to splurge economically—to indulge, with reason.

> If single stores can make it on this basis, why not whole malls? Sorry, but it's been done—probably over 350 times by the end of 1986: the newest-of-the-new retail concept—factory outlet *malls!* These modern but off-the-beaten-path malls are bargain-

hunter bonanzas: merchandise up to 50 percent off regular retail price. Offshoots of traditional factory outlet stores, they're clustered in a single neat but no-frills mall. Shoppers can indulge in a reverie of splurging on famous national brands and still open their Visa or MasterCard statement without popping Valium.

TAKING THEM THE WAY THEY ARE

Like everyone else, marketers are sometimes captivated by clever terms that conceal oversimplification. It's just easier to view markets in simple terms.

YUPPIES, BLESS THEM ONE AND ALL

Only about one out of five baby boomers is a young, upward-mobile professional with a $30,000 plus income, compared to about $21,500 for boomers as a whole. These are fairly confident strivers, often with liberal social views but conservative economic opinions. They're a fairly orderly, happy crowd who often see spending on socially visible consumer goods as an *investment* rather than just an expenditure.

NEXT COME "MUPPIES," BELIEVE IT OR NOT!

Faith Popcorn, president of Brain-Reserve, a New York marketing and advertising firm, likes the higher level of disposable income and lower sensitivity to fads typical of middle-aged (35 to 48 year old) upward-mobile professionals with incomes over $45,000. They're freer and buy with less guilt than their parents, and they're more idealistic, more content, and less driven than yuppies.

NOW MAKE ROOM FOR THE WOOPIES

These well-off consumers over 50 have incomes over 20 percent above the national average and spend more than four out of every ten consumer dollars. With fewer fixed expenses, they also have the lion's share of purely discretionary spending power. Most feel about ten years younger than they are, they're more likely to be "on top of it" than "out of it," and they buy the entire range of consumer goods.

Careful demographic analysis shows that fascination with yuppies is only partly deserved. There's a real benefit to getting back to basics: to the demographic data that are the bedrock for market segmentation, target marketing, and management of the marketing mix.

15

CHOICE
Picking at the Material Landscape

There's a chance I could lose my money on this.

Maybe it won't work or do what it's supposed to.

It looks a little dangerous and I could get hurt.

I wonder what my friends will think if I buy this.

Later I might feel really bad about buying this.

Purchase decisions would be very easy for consumers if it weren't for these five forms of perceived risk!

Consumer choice would be simple if the outcomes were perfectly predictable. But in fact, they almost never are. Sometimes things turn out better than buyers expect, sometimes
worse. So the purchase of just about any kind of consumer product or service involves some *risk* for the buyer. Small purchases
contain little risks and large purchases have big ones. But it's
not the *actual* risk inherent in a purchase that interests us at this
point, it's the risk that buyers *perceive*, real or not, that affects a
buying decision.

THE RISKS THAT CONSUMERS TAKE

When buyers make purchase decisions they experience two
different kinds of risk: objective and subjective. But there's
more to it than that. Perceived risk also takes on one or more of
five different forms. By recognizing the nature of their buyers'
perceived risk, marketers can provide the kinds of things that
will alleviate the risk and markedly reduce purchase resistance.

Objective and Subjective Risks

The *objective* risks of buying something are things that can be
measured—things that can be judged by some external standard or that other buyers would experience as well. Suppose a
consumer buys some colorful item of clothing that's labeled as
washable and promoted as colorfast. One risk the buyer might
perceive is the chance that the colors will fade quickly or,
worse yet, that they'll bleed into everything else that's washed
with it. We call this an objective risk because anyone would
experience about the same thing, and the negative outcomes
could be measured both in regard to the unsightly appearance
of the garments involved and in the dollars and cents it would
cost to replace them.

Marketers can help to reduce the objective risks buyers experience in several ways. Guarantees against defects in material

or workmanship are one way to reduce such risks. But aside from that, buyers exposed to objective risks are especially sensitive to highly *credible* information from people they recognize as *experts*. The acquisition of direct or vicarious *experience* also alleviates such objective risks for buyers. Finally, the *reputation* of the seller or brand provides additional assurance.

The five-year/50,000 mile warranty by auto makers is an example of one means of reducing the perceived objective risk for prospective buyers. When American Motors Company tested buyer interest in such a warranty, they found that twice as many women as men found it attractive. Women car buyers are likely to feel less competent to judge the mechanical reliability, and consequently they experience greater perceived risk regarding such a purchase.

The *subjective* risk prospective buyers experience is based on their uncertainty about what their own individual reactions will be, rather than on uncertainty about measurable, objective outcomes. For instance, faced with a choice about which motion picture to see, from among several popular alternatives, theatergoers try to anticipate their own reactions to different kinds of films—"Would I like this one better than that one?" There's little objective risk associated with this kind of decision. Whatever movie title is scheduled will be shown, it's not likely to be interrupted, the quality of the print is about the same for all current movies, the actors listed will appear, and so on. But different members of the audience are likely to respond differently to any one film, some with enthusiasm, some with disdain, and some with indifference. Reactions are almost completely subjective.

Warranties against defects in materials and workmanship do nothing to alleviate purely subjective perceived risk. The only warranty that does reduce subjective risk is a guarantee of "complete satisfaction or your money back." Consumers faced with subjective risk don't need or want information from *experts*. An expert authority probably won't have the same individual, personal likes and dislikes as the ordinary consumer. Instead, marketers should use endorsements by people who are closely similar to the typical buyer. The buying public knows full well that similar people have reactions similar to their own. In the previous example, a favorable review by a movie critic wouldn't tell teenaged student moviegoers much about whether or not they'll enjoy the picture. Endorsements of the film by other teenaged students would be more effective to reduce their perceived subjective risk.

> **Starting around the turn of the century, Sears, Roebuck guaranteed buyers complete satisfaction with the merchandise in their mail-order catalog. The buyer didn't need a specific reason for returning the goods for a refund; it was a "no questions asked" guarantee. Since that time, the vast majority of direct marketers, including catalogers and direct response advertisers, have offered a money-back guarantee of satisfaction. Without the opportunity to handle and inspect the goods, telephone and mail-order buyers experience high levels of subjective perceived risk. Guarantees of satisfaction are effective because the prospective buyer has little or nothing to lose by ordering the product.**
>
> **Such blanket return privileges remove or reduce a substantial part (though not all) of both objective and subjective risk. When return privileges are limited to a short period of time after purchase, they alleviate subjective risk but may do little to reduce objective risk regarding performance over time.**

FIVE FORMS OF PERCEIVED RISK

Mention purchase risk and most people think only of *monetary* risks: uncertainty about the value of the purchase or the chance that the buyers might lose the money they've spent on the product. That's just one of five different forms of risk with which buyers are concerned. The others are *functional* risk, *physical* risk, *social* risk, and *psychological* risk. The nature of the purchase and the characteristics of the buyer jointly determine what form(s) of perceived risk will be experienced.

Perceived Monetary Risk

The easiest to understand, monetary perceived risk is merely the chance that the purchase won't prove to be worth the price the buyer paid. The more conventional or traditional the product or service and the longer it's been on the market, the less monetary risk buyers will perceive. The "one-price" policy to which many stores and marketers adhere helps to reduce monetary risk. When prices are individually negotiated, the buyers have more fear that they'll be cheated or that they'll end up paying too much. Many department and specialty stores also offer *retroactive* sale prices to alleviate perceived monetary risk. If the goods go on sale within a certain period after a purchase, the buyer can return with proof of purchase and obtain the difference between what was paid and the special sale price.

The *amount* of monetary risk depends both on the degree of certainty or uncertainty about the value of the goods and on the size of the purchase. Small-ticket items don't involve much monetary risk for adult consumers because even if they lose, they won't lose much. But for large consumer durables—houses, cars, appliances, furniture, equipment, and the like—and for large-ticket services—air travel, vacation resorts, cosmetic surgery, school tuition—the monetary risk prospective buyers perceive will be commensurately greater than for low-cost purchases.

The characteristics of the buyer also influence the amount of perceived monetary risk. Those with larger amounts of monetary *risk capital* (monies they could afford to squander without suffering dire consequences) will perceive less monetary risk than those with little risk capital. In short, the more wealthy buyers can afford to take more chances and make more mistakes without suffering much from a loss. By contrast, those with little spending power are more concerned because they have less they can afford to lose. For instance, an adult would perceive little monetary risk in trying a new type of candy bar. If it's no good, they can drop it into the trash can and forget it; they won't miss the 25¢ or 50¢ they paid for it. But we've all been amused to see very small children standing at the candy counter, pondering with great intensity the relative value of the many options displayed before them. Those quarters don't come easy and there aren't that many jingling in their pockets: little risk capital—much perceived risk!

Perceived Functional Risk

Whether or not the product or service is *effective* or functions properly is an entirely different question from whether or not it's monetarily worth it's price. Functional failure can cost far more than the price of the goods, and in more ways than just monetary loss. A surgeon who promises to refund the medical fees if the patient dies on the operating table won't do much to alleviate the risk the patient perceives because it's *functional,* not monetary risk that's critical. Similarly, when you take an analgesic tablet, you're more concerned with whether or not your headache will disappear than you are about what the pill has cost you if it doesn't work. Consequently, sales volume of painkillers are often insensitive to price reductions and they sometimes have a positive demand curve, so buyer acceptance grows as the price increases. Effective function is all-important and monetary considerations don't count for much, if anything, when it comes to alleviating pain.

The degree of perceived functional risk depends in part on the nature of the product or service and also partly on the amount of *functional risk capital* the prospective buyer possesses. In the case of functional risk, the risk capital is defined in terms of the degree of need and the availability of substitute goods. For example, vacation travelers have more flexibility regarding their schedule than do business travelers. They can more readily *afford* (in a functional sense) to be late, so they have more functional risk capital. If the airline on which they have reservations has overbooked and they find they don't have a seat on the flight, it may be an inconvenience to take a later one, but it's not tragic. If the airline refunds their ticket price and allows them to travel free to compensate for the delay, the monetary saving is likely to be more than worth the trouble. They might even be delighted that it happened. Business travelers who must attend a conference or meet with an important client at a specific time have less functional risk capital—they can ill afford to be late. Nor are they likely to feel compensated by a free trip at a later time. After all, the delay has personal consequences, but it's all their employers' money and there's no personal compensation for the functional failure.

> **The United States Postal Service guarantees next-day delivery of letters and parcels sent by Express Mail. Senders can obtain a full refund if the parcel doesn't arrive on time. But private, competitive firms still thrive, such as UPS with Next Day Air service or Federal Express with Priority One overnight service. Their rates are substantially higher than the Express Mail rates, but they provide senders with more assurance that their parcels will arrive on time. *Functional* risk is usually far more important to the sender than monetary risk, and the money-back guarantee of the Postal Service does little to compensate for their poor reputation for prompt delivery.**

Perceived Physical Risk

Aside from the legal liability associated with it, the physical risk buyers perceive is of concern to marketers because it directly affects consumer acceptance of the goods. The products and services that are likely to have the highest perceived physical risk include those directly associated with health and safety, as well as electrical and mechanical products that could conceivably inure the user—drugs and medical or dental care and treatment, therapeutic devices, electrical or mechanical appliances, motor vehicles and especially motorcycles, some sports and recreational products and services, and the like.

The degree of physical risk capital consumers possess depends on how strong and robust or how frail and fragile they are. For instance, young people in normal good health perceive little physical risk on the ski slopes. They can be fairly confident that if they do have an accident and break a bone, tear a ligament, or dislocate a joint, they may have to wear a cast but they're likely to heal completely in a relatively short time. By contrast, elderly people see the sport as physically risky because the consequences of such an accident are more severe; they heal more slowly and sometimes incur permanent disability from injury to their limbs.

> Watkins Manufacturing Company stresses heavily in their promotion that their Hot Spring Spa has the UL Seal of Approval from the Insurance Underwriters' Laboratory. Prospective buyers of a stand-alone, above-ground, or indoor spa are often apprehensive because it's an electric appliance that contains water in which they're to immerse themselves. The many competitive spas that aren't UL approved sell for substantially less, but prospective buyers might well be apprehensive because of perceived physical risk. Approval by an independent safety expert agency markedly reduces such perceived risk and disposes consumers to select the more expensive Hot Spring brand.

Perceived Social Risk

Any consumer product or service that's socially visible is prone to perceived social risk. Specifically, social risk is the chance that buyers will lose social affiliation or status as the result of the purchase. In other words, they might become less attractive to or less respected by others in their social world. On the negative side, living in the "wrong" neighborhood, driving the "wrong" car, or wearing the "wrong" clothes or jewelry can be costly. On the positive side, living in the "right" neighborhood, going to the "right" school, or wearing "in" clothes will enhance the person's attractiveness and/or status in the eyes of others.

The amount of social risk capital consumers possess depends on the degree of status they have obtained and the quantity and quality of their affiliations. Those with prestigious positions and those who are very popular among the individuals and groups they value have more social capital they can afford to risk by innovative buying. If their image slips a little or if someone rejects them, they're still in a favorable social position. By contrast, those who are of humble status within their own social community, those who are only *marginal* members of the groups to which they belong, and those who enjoy little if any popularity among their peers can ill afford to take chances regarding the social acceptibility of the goods they buy.

Promotional appeals to affiliation or to status inherently reduce the perceived social risk of prospective buyers. Endorsements by *prestigious* figures alleviate perceived risk of loss of respect or status. Endorsements by *similar* others address perceived risks to social acceptance. It's important not to confuse the two. You'll recall that in the first chapter we distinguished carefully between affiliation and prestige needs; they're not the same and they're sometimes in opposition to one another.

We should also note that both prestige and attractiveness are *relative* to the social setting of the consumer. The relatively unsophisticated daylaborer or little-educated housewife denominates his or her status and attractiveness in terms of other laborers and housewives; neighbors, friends, and family. Regardless of their *global* social standing, they're variously popular and respected or unpopular and disrespected by others in the same social constellation. It's the same on the high end of the social ladder. A physician might be respected and admired by those in the local community, but his or her own perceptions of social risk capital are defined in terms of other physicians and professionals, and not so much by the regard of lay people.

> To convey status and prestige, one would expect a wristwatch to look like an extremely elegant piece of jewelry that only incidentally tells time. By contrast, a device that looks more like a scien-

tific instrument or an item of technical equipment might well be regarded by the buying public as highly functional but with little if any status value. A Rolex watch definitely falls into the latter category. Based only on it's appearance, one might expect to see it on the wrist of Jacques Cousteau, wearing a wet suit, but surely not gracing the arm of tuxedo-clad opera star Placido Domingo.

With ads in prestigious magazines such as *Town & Country*, Rolex uses endorsements by superstars such as Domingo to provide the status value for their brand name. About two-thirds of the copy is devoted to highlighting the prestige of the endorser in glowing terms. Only after documenting his brilliant career does the copy mention that his choice is Rolex. By such careful image management, Rolex took a design once appropriate to only a sports watch and transformed it into a unique social symbol.

Perceived Psychological Risk

When prospective buyers recognize there's a chance that the purchase might jeopardize their self-image or threaten their self-esteem, they perceive *psychological* risk. This form of risk is distinct from social risk because with psychological perceived risk, there's no consideration of what others might think or do. It's a personal, not a social thing, and other people may not even know of the purchase or consumption of the goods. There are strong cultural taboos against sensuality, self-indulgence, extravagance, laziness, and the like. We not only learn about these dictates and taboos, but we *internalize* them, so they're part of our conscience (or superego, if you prefer the Freudian approach). When consumers buy something that violates their taboos or goes against their own standards of behavior, they lose self-respect and may indulge in self-recrimination. Feelings of guilt, shame, regret, neglect, or irresponsibility are unpleasant emotions that momentarily disturb the person's psychological well-being. When prospective buyers suspect that a purchase might result in such feelings, the perceived psychological risk is likely to inhibit their buying.

The more positive the individual's self-image and the stronger the consumer's sense of self-esteem and self-respect, the more psychological risk capital the buyer has. Those with a weak self-image and little self-esteem are more likely to be devastated by remorse or regret. Those with more confidence and assurance, under the same circumstances, can more easily afford to shake their head, laugh at themselves, vow not to do it again, and let it go at that. So one's degree of psychological risk capital is a very personal thing, a function of individual personality. If there's one single factor that typifies innovators—buyers and users of innovative consumer goods—it's the personality trait of *venturesomeness*. Just beneath that trait there's almost invariably a strong sense of self-worth and self-esteem.

The more durable, luxurious, and expensive the goods, the more likely the buyers will experience psychological risk. Clothing, jewelry, and home furnishings are especially prone to this form of perceived risk because they're ever-present in the buyer's environment, sometimes for many years. Almost everyone has had the experience of buying such an item on an impulse or whim, only to live to regret it again and again, every time they encounter or notice it. That's likely to make the buyer exceptionally sensitive to psychological risk for subsequent purchases of that kind.

The Lane Company promotes their Shaker reproduction line of furniture in *Architectural Digest* as "museum authenticated." The copy stipulates, "Every America Collection piece is a potential heirloom . . . start collecting your heirlooms now." Lenox China and Crystal is promoted in the same periodical with the simple slogan: "Because art is never an extravagance." Marbro, advertising luxurious, elegant lamps and lighting in the same magazine, touts its designs as ". . . a wise investment in illuminated art." M. I. Hummel, the West German maker of elegant figurines, uses the slogan "Bringing quality of life since 1871."

As noted in Chapter 14, consumers in the baby boom generation readily accept luxury items, providing that they can view such purchases as "investments" rather than "expenditures," or that they can relate the goods to self-caring and quality of life, rather than to extravagance or sensuality. The promotional appeals cited here assuage any feeling of self-indulgence or extravagance and reduce potential perceptions of psychological risk.

Marketers are sometimes tempted to take an oversimplified perspective of the purchase decision task of consumers, viewing it only in the transactional terms of price and value, compared to competitive goods. Certainly the typical consumer couldn't articulate the types and forms of risk perceived during a purchase decision. But their lack of cognizance doesn't imply that they don't experience such risks. Many marketers could benefit substantially by asking themselves two questions about perceived risk:

> What kinds of perceived risk will buyers of our goods experience?
>
> What can we do or say to help them reduce or alleviate these risks?

Buyers are often willing to pay higher prices for consumer goods they see as less risky. Reduction of perceived risk can provide a competitive advantage.

THE PURCHASE DECISION PROCESS

Very few buying decisions happen instantaneously. They ordinarily take some time, ranging anywhere from less than a minute to weeks or months. So we commonly refer to the decision *process,* implying that there is a series of steps or phases the decisionmaker goes through. The time it takes to reach a decision and commit to the purchase varies from one consumer to the next, of course. But the duration and form of the buying decision process depends most heavily on the type of purchase the consumer is making. We'll examine five different kinds of decision processes in this section: *extended* decisions, *deliberate* choices, *policy* formation, *routine* purchases, and *impulse* buying.

The Extended Decision Process

Large ticket, infrequently purchased consumer goods usually warrant careful consideration by prospective buyers. Such purchases are ordinarily preceded by an extended decision process. But extended decisions aren't necessarily confined to only such products and services. Sometimes consumers engage in an extended decision process for relatively small items, especially if they're unfamiliar with the product class, if the product or service is a new, innovative one, or if the consequences are very important.

The things that distinguish extended decisions from other kinds of purchases are the importance of information and degree of comparison and evaluation of alternatives. The extended decision process typically begins with *need recognition*. Occasionally some form of market-related stimuli will lead to an extended purchase decision—an advertisement, discovery of an unfamiliar product or service, or the introduction of a new variety of the goods. But that's not the most common mode of initiation for an extended decision. More often changing circumstances in the life of the consumer will spark recognition of a need that can be satisfied with a purchase. For instance, one of the family cars or major appliances may break down and require expensive repairs, suggesting that it might be a good time to trade for a new model. Or the family might move to a new home and then realize that some new furniture would better fit the new surroundings. Once the need is recognized, the extended decision process begins.

Extended decisions are based on fairly extensive information. There are two kinds of information to be brought to bear on the decision: internal and external. Some information will have been acquired over time and retained in memory, in the form of existing attitudes and images. But usually it isn't completely adequate and the prospective buyers need more, or they may be unsure of whether their grasp of the alternatives is timely. At that point, they set about finding external information.

Marketers of infrequently purchased goods often pursue two promotional objectives simultaneously. On the one hand, they have to keep their brand or company name in the consumer's mind during the relatively long periods when there's no real need for their goods. But they also have to be ready with external information when prospective buyers begin their information search. These two objectives are very different. One is largely a *maintenance* objective—the object is to maintain awareness and a positive attitude and image, while actually waiting in the wings for the action to start. The other objective is to win a sale promptly by furnishing information about how the goods are superior to other alternatives.

Maintenance promotion is ordinarily done through advertising, using media to which the prospective buyers are regularly exposed. The ads highlight the brand or firm name and logo, and the copy is designed more to enhance and maintain an image and position in the consumers' minds than to spark some kind of specific action. *Purchase* promotion is of a very different sort. Often personal selling is required, and salespeople have to be trained to offer favorable *comparative* information. During the evaluation process, prospective buyers often visit more than one outlet and examine several alternatives with this type of decision. If the retail outlets handle competitive products or brands, their sales staffs may require some special incentives to promote the marketer's own product or brand.

> **In-store product brochures are one of the most potent promotional tools for buyers engaged in an extended decision process. And yet they're also one of the most ignored, overlooked, or neglected promotional devices. If you doubt it, visit the major appliance department of a local store and see how many brochures are available for the many products and brands offered. Or drop by an auto showroom while your car's being serviced, and check the display rack containing product brochures. Some firms invest millions in media advertising (and justifiably so) and**

yet do a completely inadequate job on their product brochures. Others have elegant and effective brochures composed by very capable adveritising agencies, only to undersupply their retail outlets or fail to maintain an orderly stock of brochures within the retail stores or outlets.

It costs a small fortune to get prospective buyers to visit a retail outlet and seek information. It's a real pity to fall down at that point, and there's a genuine competitive advantage to those routinely ready at the point of inquiry to furnish the prospect with a handsome, information-laden brochure explaining the major attributes and selling points of the product.

Sales brochures can also be provided in another effective way to consumers engaged in a search for information. Maintenance advertising, especially through print media, should capitalize on the fact that some of those exposed to the ads will be entering an extended decision process. One objective of the ad should be to win inquiry! The audience should be invited to make a toll-free call or to send a coupon for a complete product brochure or even a catalog of the company's entire line. If the cost is prohibitive, a small service charge might be required, with credit for it to be applied to a subsequent purchase.

The Deliberate Choice Process

Buyers often make a *deliberate* choice for smaller-ticket goods they don't purchase regularly. For instance, deliberate choices often precede the purchase of small counter-top appliances, incidental household goods, small items of furniture and home accessories, and the like. Clothing and inexpensive jewelry are also most commonly purchased with some deliberation. The main factor distinguishing deliberate choice from the extended decision process is that most or all of the deliberation and comparison takes place at the point of sale or on a single shopping excursion. That means that prospective buyers can and should be partially presold, prior to encountering the goods at the outlet. With this kind of purchase, comparison and evaluation take place at the point of sale, based on inspection, but shoppers should first be aware of the product, brand, or service as an alternative, in advance.

THE CONSUMER'S EVOKED SET

Things purchased with a deliberate choice are based on need recognition, often because of a change in circumstances or some occurrence that makes the goods necessary. For instance, clothing wears out, appliances give out, and supplies run out. Eventually consumers realize that they'll need to buy something to replace what's no longer usable or to meet some infrequently encountered need—new clothes for a special social event, for instance. Once they recognize the need, the realization leads directly to the question "What can I buy to take care of this need?" The products, brands, services, and stores that spring to mind as viable alternatives constitute the *evoked set* of goods for solving the problem or satisfying the need. These are the ones from which most buyers will eventually choose, following some deliberation and comparison among them.

It's possible that shoppers will encounter purchase alternatives within the store or at the point of purchase which weren't in their evoked set of alternative goods—possible, but not terribly probable. Even if they do, many will ignore them or elect to buy something with which they're more familiar. So those brands, products, or services that are already in the evoked set of alternatives when the need arises and it's recognized have a running start, so to speak. The promotional objectives for goods usually purchased after deliberation are devoted both to creating and maintaining awareness and to partially *preselling* the goods. It means that the advertising messages should relate the goods to specific needs and purposes. Actual comparison and evaluation will probably take place at the point of purchase or on one shopping excursion, so the marketers advertising messages needn't be directly comparative, though they can be. They should certainly generate continued awareness and maintain a favorable image.

The Policy Formation Process

One form of purchase decision, often ignored by marketers, is the formation of buying policies that will either lead directly to a specific choice or dictate how alternative goods will be evaluated. Policy formation ranges from very abstract assumptions and axioms—always buy a name brand, pick the cheapest one, you get what you pay for, never buy from a door-to-door salesperson—to very specific strategies and tactics: I'll get a credit card and always buy brand X gasoline. Consumer buying policies are important to marketers because once formed, they're likely to govern the outcomes of an entire series of purchases over an extended period of time, perhaps even for many years. What's more, buying policies implicitly affect a much larger and wider range of consumer purchases than most marketers think!

It's usually a mistake to think that a given consumer will apply the same basic buying policy to the purchase of many different kinds of consumer goods. For instance, one consumer may buy generic brands of breakfast food cereal, simply because it's the least expensive alternative. At the same time, the same person may make it a policy to buy only expensive, "top-shelf" brands of liquor, based on the assumption that there's a vast difference among the various brands and prices of distilled beverages.

It's often worthwhile for consumer goods marketers to study and assess the buying policies of their customers, and especially the "heavy" users of their goods. In many cases there's substantial consistency in the buying policies of consumer segments who prefer each of several competitive brands. If these buying policies can be discovered, they may explain in large measure why some buy and why others don't. The preferred goods tend to conform to the specific type of buying policy.

When marketing research indicates that consumer buying policies are an important aspect of the purchase decision, marketers

have a couple of promising options: They can gear the product, distribution, pricing, and promotion to conform to the dominant buying policy patterns, or they can maintain the marketing mix and work to modify the buying policies to enhance consumer acceptance.

Suppose, for example, that the preponderance of consumers in the market have a policy of buying the product from the nearest vendor or outlet. The marketer of a relatively high-quality, high-priced brand sold through exclusive distribution has two options: switch or hold. The maker could trade down on the brand name or introduce a less expensive sister brand, using extensive distribution and mass advertising for the popular-priced goods. Alternatively the maker could retain the present marketing mix and either focus on the market segment that doesn't use the dominant buying policy or use promotion to persuade the majority of the market that a buying policy more congenial to the brand would be more effective for this product.

The Routine Purchase Process

Consumers typically use a *routine* buying process for frequently purchased, small-ticket consumable goods—food, beverages, toiletries, household supplies, and the like. Individuals or families often maintain an inventory that meets everyday needs, and when the supply runs short or runs out, they repurchase the same or a substitute product to replenish the supply. The typical routine purchase process consists of two phases: a continuous string of purchases of the same product and/or brand, followed by one or more purchases that deviate from the pattern. After that, there's usually another string of consistent purchases.

Product, brand, store, or service loyalty is often defined in terms of the length of the purchase strings of the same goods. There are several things that can disrupt a consistent purchase string, and we'll identify the major ones. Postpurchase or postconsumption evaluation plays a major role. If the buyers are satisfied with the outcomes of purchase and use, they're likely to continue. If something changes regarding the goods, such as a slip in quality or a marked change in the goods, they may be prompted to switch to another alternative. But it's a mistake to think that consumers will continue so long as there isn't anything wrong with the particular goods they're routinely buying. In Chapter 1, we mentioned that people have a need for novelty and diversity. After several routine purchases of the same goods, some consumers will tire of it and they'll try something different. That happens even when their level of satisfaction with the goods they've routinely been buying is otherwise still very high.

Changes in the life circumstances of buyers will also disrupt a consistent purchase string. For instance, a family may move to a new home and abandon the supermarket chain that's been their favorite simply because a store of another chain is closer to their new home. Or new car buyers may decide to switch brands of gasoline because they feel some other brand would be better suited to the new models. Even relatively minor changes in the daily tasks or routine can cause changes in routine purchase strings.

There are some important market- or purchase-related factors that will also disrupt loyalty patterns for routine purchases. A change in the product or service, packaging, pricing, promotion, or distribution may disrupt loyalty. Since the goods have changed in some respect, some may feel they should extend the change by trying something entirely different. Even a stock-out situation may trigger the termination of a consistent purchase string. Some buyers may wait until the goods again appear at the usual outlet and others may seek out the same goods at another outlet. But many are likely to merely choose another product or brand from the shelf. They may return to their former favorite on the next purchase occasion, stay with the new alternative, or go into an exploratory mode and try several other options before settling back into a consistent string of purchases.

During a consistent string of routine purchases, buyers are ordinarily just following the routine and there's really no purchase decision involved regarding *which* alternative to choose. The only real decision during that time is *when* and *how much* to buy. It's during the more dynamic, unstable periods that product, service, brand, or store *choice* takes place. During a consistent string of purchases, the best predictor of what the consumers will buy is merely what they bought on the last occasion. But if they go into an *exploratory* mode, they're likely to try several options, and there's only a *small* probability that they'll purchase the same thing they did on the previous purchase.

Marketers of routinely purchased consumer goods engage in a more or less perpetual product, price, promotion, and distribution struggle with one another. The objective of the game is to hold onto one's own customers and at the same time, to spring some buyers free from their purchase strings of competitive brands, stores, or goods. Product modifications to provide "new, improved" goods are frequent, and packaging may also be modified regularly. Base prices may not often change, but there are many "special" sales, "cents-off" promotions, coupons, premiums, and the like, to tempt new buyers to the brand or store.

Within the supermarket or drug store, there's a constant battle for shelf space allocations and for placement of special displays. In-store samples may be offered at high-traffic outlets, and point-of-sale materials are placed and replaced. Meanwhile, media advertising constantly seeks to lure new buyers, sometimes with directly comparative ads. In the struggle for brand or market share for routinely purchased goods, marketers can afford to spend more to win a new customer than they'll obtain from a single purchase, because once they've bought, many are likely to stay with the brand, store, or goods.

In such markets, it's necessary to monitor one's own brand loyalty, as well as keeping a close eye on competitors' moves. It means constantly looking for vulnerabilities among competing goods that might provide an opportunity, and at the same time, protecting one's own share of the market with whatever counter-moves are required.

The Impulse Buying Process

Some consumer purchases involve little if any planning, deliberation, or evaluation; the goods are purchased strictly on the impulse of the moment. While a few consumers have been known to buy such large-ticket goods as a car, appliance, or piece of furniture on impulse, this form of purchase decision is most common by far for small-ticket consumable goods—candy, snacks, chewing gum, beverages, cut flowers, novelties, small gifts, and the like. There's little risk of any kind with such consumer goods, and often they provide a small reward, pleasing or amusing the buyer momentarily. Since the whole purchase decision process for impulse goods takes place at the point of sale and may take only a few seconds' time, marketers put great emphasis on packaging and point-of-purchase promotional displays.

> While giants such as Hershey and Mars (together, 70 percent of the candy market) battle it out for space on the shelf, or better yet, on the checkout counter, a host of smaller candy companies struggle to grab a hand to grab their brand. The struggle for prominent shelf space is extremely intense, since over two thirds of all candy is purchased purely on impulse. Candy makers first provide retailers with a wide variety of ever-changing point-of-sale racks and displays, then strive to protect their displays from intruding "squatter" brands.
>
> Rarely do candy buyers pick up the same candy bar twice in a row, so product innovation is rampant. Large candy producers create their newest treats in a web of secrecy and protect their trade secrets with security systems only slightly more sophisticated than those at the Pentagon. All this for a domestic market that's a mere $8 billion per year! And that's only a small fraction of the total market for impulse goods.

THE INNOVATION ADOPTION PROCESS

The consumer marketplace is very dynamic—things come and go at lightning speed. Most of the goods that are the lifeblood

of consumer marketers today didn't even exist a decade ago. So
let's conclude by looking at the five steps consumers typically
take in the process of adopting an innovation.

Awareness.   Consumers learn the brand name and product
attributes.

Interest.   Consumers relate the product benefits to their
own needs.

Evaluation.   Consumers compare the goods with existing
alternatives.

Trial.   Consumers obtain direct or vicarious product
experience.

Adoption.   Consumers choose the innovation as a permanent solution.

The more radical the innovation, the more expensive or important the goods to consumers, and the greater the risk aver-
sion of the prospective buyer, the longer the adoption process
will take. Marketers can monitor the market for their innovation
and adjust the marketing program to those steps where the majority of consumers reside at the moment.

During the initial *awareness* phase, wide distribution is important and saturation advertising is effective, with brief, frequently repeated messages highlighting the brand name, logo,
package, and basic identification factors. At the *interest* stage
the goods are positioned in the market and in the minds of
consumers by promotion to relate the product benefits to specific needs and types of buyers. During the *evaluation* phase
the product or service should be compared to alternatives. At
the *trial* phase samples may be distributed, in-store samples
provided, or promotion can be used to furnish vicarious trial
and endorsement by similar others. At the *adoption* stage the
results (acceptance or rejection) depend heavily on posttrial
evaluation. Absolute and relative prices are also important to
consumers here.

Marketers who understand and appreciate their consumers' problem-solving and decision-making tasks and the choice processes they typically use can materially help their buyers to make favorable choices. Both information and persuasion are required, but often the former is underemphasized and the latter overworked. When making a choice, consumers are trying to do two things: (1) decide which alternative has the greatest *expected value*, and (2) gauge the chances the actual value will *vary from what's expected*. In short, they want what's best for them, but not too risky. Marketing tactics that magnify expected value and simultaneously reduce risk are most effective.

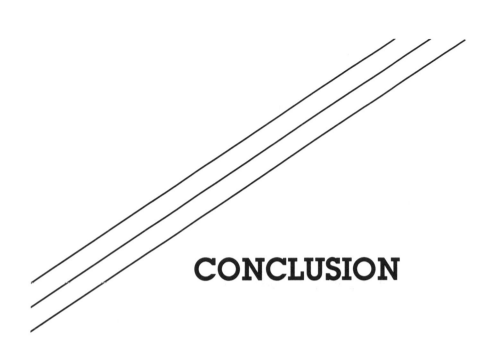

CONCLUSION

Characteristics of the marketplace
Identifying the market segments
Selecting specific target markets

Elements of the marketing program
Product or service characteristics
Pricing policy and administration
Distribution channels and outlets
Promotional programs and appeals

There's more to know about consumers and why they buy than one could learn in a lifetime! And by the time it was all assimilated, it would probably be obsolete anyhow. But we could say that about any complex, dynamic subject that's more art than science. Fortunately, none of us really needs a *complete* grasp of the details—we need only a *basic* understanding to have a good, firm foothold: a foundation on which to build effective, profitable marketing strategies and tactics.

ASKING THE RIGHT QUESTIONS

Often the right questions are at least as important as the right answers! What must we know about American consumers to understand *why they buy?* Here's a brief sketch of the most important issues and questions arising from the topics we've discussed throughout:

Needs. Where on the hierarchy of needs are those our goods will best fulfill? Which of the collateral need categories are our goods best able to satisfy?

Motives. To what conscious rational and subconscious psychological motives can we appeal? What are the buying motives, what incentives will work?

Personality. What value orientations most favor our goods? What interpersonal styles, interaction styles, and special personality factors are typical in the market?

Perception. Do our communications fit the consumer perceptual process? How should we appeal to the consumers' senses and overcome the barriers to perception?

Learning. What associations can we make for consumers between our goods and their needs? Can we improve conditioning by reward?

Attitudes. What's the nature of each component of the attitude toward our goods? What are the main functions our product attitudes serve for consumers?

Social Roles. For what social roles do our goods make good "props"? Where do our goods best fit in the consumers' role adoption process?

Affiliations. To what groups do our consumers belong and how are they influenced? What reference groups are important to our consumers?

Family. Is the individual or the family the relevant buying unit for our goods? What family structure and family purchase roles are most typical?

Social Class. Where on the social class ladder are our goods pitched? What are the mentality and main concerns of those in the social classes we target?

Culture. How do our goods fit with core cultural values? What cultural trends and changes are likely to affect buying and consumption of our goods?

Life Stages. At what phase in the individual and family life cycle are our main consumers? What are their dominant needs, values, and circumstances?

Psychographics. What value and lifestyle category typically buys and uses our goods? How do our goods fit into specific lifestyle patterns?

Demographics. Who are our actual and target customers in terms of their characteristics? What demographic segments are our best targets?

Choice. What type of choice process do our buyers most often use? What are the types and forms of perceived risk that affect sale of our goods?

These are the main topics for a quick check of consumer acceptability. Answers to these questions furnish a broad outline for further inquiry.

THE MARKETER'S JOB IN A NUTSHELL

We like to think of the marketing program as a bridge between what the firm can produce and market, on the near shore, and the needs, preferences, and desires of consumers, at the far shore. All the marketer has to know is *where* to build the bridge and *how* to build it. Sure, it sounds deceptively simple, but actually those are the two most elementary marketing decisions.

Dissecting the Consumer Market

Those who would try to be everything to everyone are likely to end up meaning nothing to nobody. If there ever was such a thing as a "mass" market—one, great, homogeneous mass of consumers—that day has surely long-since passed. Effective market segmentation means identifying market segments that are distinctively different from one another yet internally consistent in one or more important ways. But the question is, precisely what are those ways? That depends on what's being marketed, but many of the topics we've discussed here are good candidates for segmentation. Social classes, life stages, lifestyles, and demographic categories are especially popular, though the options aren't limited to those. Taking a good, long look at why consumers need the goods and how they use them should suggest which are viable segmentation criteria and which are less meaningful.

Once the market can be viewed as a series of distinct segments, rather than as a single, undifferentiated picture, the task becomes one of selecting those segments with the most potential—those with the greatest affinity for what the firm can make and/or market. Both experience and research clearly indicate that it's better to be the king in one or a few segments of the market than to be one of the pawns in the vast arena of the entire marketplace. Target market selection is a matter of deciding which segment(s) to approach—in effect, *where* to build the marketing bridge. The topics we've discussed here should help to define the shoreline on the market side. They furnish some landmarks indicating safe ground and maybe an occasional lighthouse or foghorn to warn away the unwary.

Managing the Marketing Mix

The more closely the marketing program—product, price, promotion, and distribution—fits the consumers in the target market, the more effective and profitable it will be. Many of the topics covered here indicate which product or service attributes or characteristics are likely to be greeted hospitably by those in the target market and which are likely to be unwelcome. They suggest how people in a given market segment will view the price and the value of the goods, and whether or not they're both able and willing to pay it. Some of the issues we've discussed bear directly on how consumers in different market segments view distribution strategies and retail outlets: why they shop differently and frequent different stores. These subjects also suggest a host of strategies and tactics for reaching the target segment with effective advertising and promotion.

Marketers only rarely have the opportunity to segment a new market, choose the initial targets, and create an entirely new marketing program. Even in such situations they don't have an entirely free hand. But regardless of the marketing program's stage of maturity, there are opportunities to make significant changes at many levels of operation. Effective marketing management requires systematically walking the marketing mix toward greater and greater consumer acceptance while maintaining its internal consistency and overall integrity. It's often effective to adopt an "ideal system" approach, identifying the optimum marketing program, based on relevant information about consumers. We've got to know where we're going before we can pick an appropriate route and head down the road. Documenting both what the program is now and what it should ideally be will furnish the guidelines for action and direct the thrust of the effort whenever an opportunity to fine-tune the marketing program presents itself.

The value inherent in an understanding of consumers isn't in having it, but in *using* it! As every experienced marketer knows, there are plenty of pitfalls out there in the marketplace—the yellow brick road to profitability has more than its share of potholes and it certainly isn't well-marked. We couldn't possibly give you a detailed roadmap of the best course through the consumer marketplace. The landscape shifts too rapidly and the scene is too complex for that. But perhaps some of the dominant landmarks that weren't very familiar before will now be a little more recognizable. Maybe seeing how some other marketers have steered their course through the consumer marketplace will identify a clear path or suggest effective ways you might go.

The absolutely perfect marketing program, the one that maximizes every advantage, minimizes every shortcoming, and optimizes on every opportunity, has yet to be created. But if we've accomplished our objectives, then at least the open trenches and dead-end roads should be more identifiable and avoidable. More important, the truly promising, the really lucrative opportunities should be more visible and open than they might have been.

NAME INDEX

345